S0-AUZ-447

Botanica's

500 POPULAR

VEGETABLES
HERBS, FRUIT
& NUTS

FOR AUSTRALIAN GARDENERS

RANDOM HOUSE AUSTRALIA

Publisher	Gordon Cheers
Consultants	Geoff Bryant
	Tony Rodd
Introduction	Tom Walker
Managing editor	Anna Cheifetz
Editors	Clare Double
	James Young
Designed by	Joy Eckermann
Production manager	Linda Watchorn
Picture research	Anna Cheifetz

Published in Australia by
Random House Australia Pty Ltd
20 Alfred Street
Milsons Point NSW 2061
Ph (02) 9954 9966   Fax (02) 9954 9008
http://www.randomhouse.com.au

First published 1999, reprinted 2001

© text Random House Australia Pty Ltd 1999
© photos Random House Australia Pty Ltd 1999

All rights reserved. No part of this book may be reproduced,
stored in a retrieval system or transmitted in any form or
by any means, electronic, mechanical, photocopying,
recording or otherwise, without the prior written
permission of the Publisher.

National Library of Australia
Cataloguing-in-Publication Data

500 popular vegetables, herbs, fruit & nuts for Australian gardeners.

ISBN 0 091 83600 X.

1. Gardening – Australia.
635

Film Separation PICA Color Separation Overseas Pte Ltd
Printed in Hong Kong by Sing Cheong Printing Co. Ltd

CONTENTS

Botanica

- A must for all gardeners
- An invaluable and enduring reference
- Over 10,000 plants
- Fully illustrated in color throughout

Botanica is the world's most authoritative, comprehensive and up-to-date single volume guide to plants for all gardeners and garden lovers that's lavishly illustrated throughout. Unrivalled in scope, **Botanica** features over 10,000 plants for you to choose from in its easy A to Z format that's fully illustrated in color throughout—from annuals, perennials, bulbs and roses, to trees and shrubs, ferns and palms, fruit and nut trees, orchids, cacti and succulents, lawns and ground covers, vegetables and herbs. Plus all the really practical information you need on care and cultivation from planting and propagating, to pest and diseases is at your fingertips. **Botanica** has been written in a fresh, easy-to-read style by a team of specialist plant experts and gardening writers.

1008 pages • 300 mm x 230 mm

A TO Z OF GARDEN PLANTS

PLANT HEADINGS
To make it easy to find the plant you are looking for, page headings on each spread indicate the first genus described on the left-hand page and the last genus on the right-hand page.

PHOTOGRAPHS
Photographs in **Botanica** *illustrate colour, growth habits and other ornamental features of the plants.*

CAPTIONS
Each photograph is captioned identifying the plant with its full botanical name.

MARGIN MARKERS
For ready reference, **Botanica** *has been printed with colored alphabet tabs in the margin that move down the page to help you find the plant you are looking for.*

GENUS ENTRIES
In the A to Z section, plants are arranged in alphabetical order by genus. Entries include plant descriptions, geographical origin, cultivation, pests and diseases, height and spread and hardiness rating by zone.

Introduction

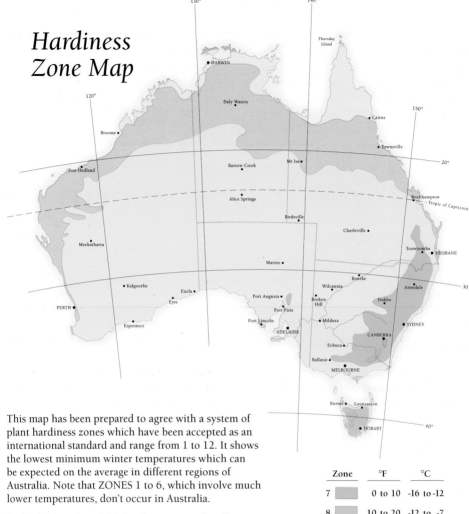

Hardiness Zone Map

This map has been prepared to agree with a system of plant hardiness zones which have been accepted as an international standard and range from 1 to 12. It shows the lowest minimum winter temperatures which can be expected on the average in different regions of Australia. Note that ZONES 1 to 6, which involve much lower temperatures, don't occur in Australia.

In the A–Z section of this book a zone number (for example, ZONE 8) is given at the end of each species entry. That number, which corresponds to a zone shown here, indicates the coldest areas in which the particular plant is likely to survive through an average winter. Note that these are not necessarily the areas in which it will grow best. Because the zone number refers to *minimum* temperatures, a plant given ZONE 7, for example, will obviously grow perfectly well in ZONE 8 but not in ZONE 6. In the lower zones, plants such as annuals and perennials can be started from seed in a covered area, then planted out when the likelihood of the last frost is over. Plants grown in a zone considerably higher than the zone with the minimum winter temperature in which they will survive might grow well but they are likely to behave differently. Note also that some readers may find the numbers a little conservative; we felt it best to err on the side of caution. The map does not attempt to indicate a plant's water requirements or drought hardiness; where significant, this information is given in the text.

Zone		°F	°C
7		0 to 10	-16 to -12
8		10 to 20	-12 to -7
9		20 to 30	-7 to -1
10		30 to 40	-1 to 4
11		40 to 50	4 to 10
12		50 to 60	10 to 16

Hardiness zones are based on the average annual minimum temperature for each zone.

Humans derive their food mainly from plants or animals that eat plants. This system means that plants produce and animals consume. For about 2 million years, during the hunter-gatherer period, berries, nuts, fruits, leaves, grains and tubers were all collected rather than grown. The earliest forms of agriculture only began to develop when humans formed more permanent settlements around 10,000 years ago, and we began to grow our own food, to sow and reap, to plant and harvest.

Over thousands of years, however, the move from subsistence agriculture to commercial production in many countries has meant that growing our own food is no longer necessary for survival and gardens have evolved into mainly ornamental landscapes. Most of us now buy rather than grow our own food, but there are still good reasons for growing edible plants in the garden. Growing your own can save money, ensure a continual and regular supply of fresh food, and provide exceptionally tasty produce that can be harvested at the peak of perfection. It can also be a good way to grow unusual or expensive vegetables and fruit and to grow organic food free from chemical additives (at least if pesticides are used you will know which ones).

Eating fresh fruit and vegetables is also vital for our health—we need to eat plants for healthy growth and to fuel our bodies. With the aid of the sun's energy, carbon dioxide from the air, water and certain inorganic nutrients obtained mainly from the soil, plants produce sugars, starches, cellulose, fiber, proteins, waxes, oils, vitamins and other compounds, such as organic acids, that are needed by our bodies.

We now know that in addition to carbon, hydrogen, and oxygen, plants require at least 13 different elements to grow. These include nitrogen, phosphorus, sulfur, calcium, magnesium and potassium—so-called major elements or macronutrients. Smaller amounts of iron, manganese, copper, zinc, boron, molybdenum and chlorine—micronutrients—are also needed. Plants also take up elements and nutrients such as iodine, selenium, and cobalt from the soil, elements which are also important for human health.

Home-grown fruit and vegetables taste great and can be chemical free.

Try unusual varieties such as this yellow Swiss chard in your home garden.

PLANNING A PRODUCTIVE GARDEN

There are a number of factors to consider when establishing a productive garden. These include how much space you have available for planting in the garden, aspect, the soil (including its texture, structure, depth and drainage), shelter, water supply and of course the climate in your area.

Space

Edible plants can be grown on even the smallest window ledge or balcony—some, like herbs, even enjoy being restricted in small pots, and tomatoes, capsicums and small fruiting trees can also be grown in containers. Self-sufficiency is not a realistic option unless you have a large garden or piece of land at your disposal. Most people, however, just want to supplement their diet with some home-grown produce and there are a number of ways of using even a limited space creatively. Ornamental trees can

be replaced by fruiting varieties, for example, and vegetables such as lettuces, spinach and kales, many of which have attractively colored or textured leaves, can be planted in flower borders as part of a decorative display. It is important to plan for easy access and maintenance when organizing a vegetable garden. Plants that need continual care, or are used on a daily basis (like herbs) are best grown near to the house; large beds of seasonal crops, like potatoes or carrots, can be sited further away.

Aspect

Most vegetables, fruit and herbs need an open, sunny site for maximum productivity. A site that slopes gently toward the sun is ideal as this will ensure that plants receive good drainage and plenty of sunlight, providing the longest possible growing season. On steep slopes there is the danger of erosion, although this can be minimized by

Even a small corner of the garden can be used to grow vegetables or herbs.

Grow tall crops where they will not throw shade onto lower-growing ones.

Healthy soil contains all the essential nutrients plants need to grow.

At home, as at this organic vegetable farm, well-prepared soil is the key to a good harvest.

growing crops across the slope or making some terracing. On flat sites, arrange taller crops such as tomatoes, beans, peas and sweet corn at the back of plantings or in north- to south-facing rows to minimize shading. Summer annuals, like eggplants and tomatoes, need large amounts of sun. In shady gardens grow such plants in containers and move into the sun to give them enough heat and light to ripen the fruit.

SOIL

Texture and structure

Good soil is the key to a successful crop. The quality of your soil will depend on its nutrient content (influenced by the parent material from which it is formed), the slope of the land, the climate, the organisms (the plants and animals that have used the soil) it contains and its age. It is vital to assess the quality and content of your soil before deciding which plants to grow.

Soils vary in their physical and chemical properties and may contain large stones, gravel, sand, silt and clay. Silt and clay soils comprise tiny, smooth-textured particles that stick together and can impede drainage. While this means nutrients are not easily washed out of silt and clay soils, they are prone to water-logging which can rot roots and make cultivation difficult. Sandy soils are gritty, drier and drain readily; they are easy to cultivate, but hold little water and nutrients. The best garden soil is loam, which contains similar amounts of sand, silt and clay. Once you have determined which type of soil you have, you can improve the texture by adding sand to soils rich in clay and silt, or clay and silt to sandy soils.

The structure of the soil—how much organic matter (decomposing plant and animal matter) it contains—is also an important part of soil health. While the rock particles in soil contain minerals and essential nutrients, it is organic matter that provides nitrogen (essential for plant health) and encourages soil microbes and earthworms. These microbes and organisms help to break down organic matter in the soil and increase the level of nitrates in the soil. This allows soil particles to bond together like crumbs, forming large and small pores in the soil through which roots and water can readily move. Adding organic matter to heavy soils, rich in silt and clay, improves drainage, will make seed beds easier to cultivate and the soil more workable after heavy rain. Organic matter also enables soils to warm more quickly and retain more water and nutrients (particularly useful for sandy soils). Intensive cropping can quickly deplete soils of organic matter so feeding your soil regularly is important.

Drainage

Poor drainage can seriously affect plant health, leading to growth problems and diseases. Deep, well-drained soil is ideal for growing edible plants. Hardpans (compacted soil) can restrict root penetration. The compact layers can also restrict drainage, trapping water around plant roots. Shallow soils over stones retain little water and few nutrients. Digging a hole about 3 ft (1 m) deep to expose the soil profile is a good way of assessing the drainage in your garden and of determining your soil type as well as variations in texture and structure.

Compact layers can cause drainage problems and force roots to grow horizontally along the top of the layer rather than downwards, until sometimes the roots find a crack that they will penetrate to explore below. Where drainage is occasionally restricted, for example during wet winters, rusty mottling may occur in the soil; greenish blue stains imply more prolonged periods of poor drainage while pale gray and blue layers show permanent accumulations of water. If the water table is high and the hole has water in the bottom peat may have accumulated. Fill the hole with water and wait for it to drain away; if the peat is deep enough, correct drainage and management may be very effective.

Where compacted layers are near enough to the surface and underlain by more open material, deep cultivation will break them up and improvement can be dramatic. For less serious drainage problems, incorporating plenty of organic matter in the soil will improve air movement and structure. Animal manure and compost and sand will improve the texture and structure of poorly drained soil. Adding materials like gypsum to clay soil can improve drainage. Where drainage is very poor, you may need to ask for professional advice. Installing a drainage system using underground pipes to drain excess water to a sump or making raised beds can be effective ways of solving the problem.

Raised beds are easy to maintain and reduce the risk of compacted soil.

Raised beds consist of squares or rectangles of boards, at least 6 in (15 cm) deep, filled with topsoil and separated by paths. It may be necessary to bring in more soil from outside to fill the beds. The paths between the beds can be covered with straw, composted sawdust or similar material, which can then be used later as an organic mulch. Raised beds are particularly useful for gardeners who do not like digging. The beds should be narrow enough to allow raking, weeding and hoeing from the paths to minimize the amount of walking over the bed, which may compact the soil, especially when wet.

Aim for a soil pH of 6.5 if you want to grow a wide range of edible plants.

pH levels

The pH value of a soil describes how acid or alkaline it is. Acid soil has a pH of less than 7 (any soil below pH 4.5 is extremely acid); alkaline soil has a pH above 7. Pure distilled water is completely neutral with a pH of 7. The pH of your soil will affect which nutrients are available and therefore which plants are best suited to your conditions — different plants like different conditions. Soil testing laboratories can give advice on soil pH and available levels of elements such as potassium, phosphorus, calcium, magnesium and sulfur, or you can question successful gardeners in your neighborhood to discover their practices.

Most plants grow well at a pH of about 6.5, so this is the pH to aim for if you want to grow a wide range. Some, however, prefer acid soils. Potatoes, sweet potatoes (kumara), yams (oca), rhubarb and watermelons will grow well down to a pH of about 5, whereas beets, carrots, celery, cauliflowers, leeks, garlic, onions, and lettuces prefer a pH of 6.5 to 7. Most fruits grow well on moderately acid soil, and blueberries prefer an acid soil.

Acid soil can be improved by adding lime. The amount of lime needed to raise the pH will vary with the soil type. Sandy soils, low in clay and humus, need less lime than clay or peaty soils. A coarse sandy soil needs about ½ lb (250 g), a loam about 1 lb (500 g), and organic and clay soils 2.2 lb (1 kg) of limestone per square yard (square meter) to raise the pH by one unit (for example, from 5.5 to 6.5). Sometimes the subsoil can be very acid, so you may need to add lime to this as well as to the topsoil.

Once you have raised the pH of your soil to 6.5, the aim is to keep it there. One way of doing this is to rotate your crops — a 4-year rotation of vegetables, with the most acid-sensitive crops grown immediately after liming in the first year, finishing in the fourth year of the rotation by growing potatoes and other acid-tolerant plants. A pH check will then show whether more lime is needed for the first year crops. It is important when adding lime not to add too much. Over-liming can make your soil too alkaline and can also lead to deficiencies of trace elements such as iron, manganese, zinc and boron.

Naturally occurring alkaline soils are often found on limestone, in saline conditions, or in areas where there is very low rainfall. Adding organic matter to the soil can help correct mildly alkaline conditions, but it may be necessary to add sulfur, peat moss and pine needles, or even mineral supplements where alkalinity is a real problem.

FERTILIZERS AND MANURES

The soil provides plants with the nutrients they need for good growth. All plants need nitrogen (N), phosphorus (P) and potassium (K) in varying amounts, as well as smaller quantities of calcium, magnesium, sulfur and other micronutrients. Most herbs grow well in any soil as long as it is well drained, and do not need high levels of nutrients. However, leafy vegetables, such as spinach and lettuce, need large amounts of nitrogen for good foliage growth, as do plants producing large fruit like melons and pumpkins. Citrus need a good supply of iron and also boron and zinc for good fruiting. Citrus trees should be fed in both spring and autumn. In late winter or early spring, when most fruits start to produce new growth, an application of general fertilizer is advisable. All fruits will respond to generous mulching with compost or similar material. This will not only help to smother weeds but avoid deep cultivation and damage to fine surface roots, especially of citrus.

Natural soils vary greatly in the amounts of nutrients they contain so feeding the soil by applying fertilizers and manure is the best way to maintain a high state of fertility and good physical condition. This improves soil structure and will provide plants with all the essential nutrients they need. The nutrients removed by crops or lost in drainage water can be restored by adding bulky organic manure, and organic and inorganic fertilizers to the soil. There is much debate as to the relative benefits of organic over inorganic fertilizers, but in general they perform different functions.

Inorganic fertilizers

Intensive cropping can remove large amounts of nutrients. There are few soils capable of sustained production without the need to bring nutrients in from outside in the form of fertilizers. Soil

Leafy plants like these brassicas need nitrogen for foliage growth.

Applying fertilizer in granule form.

tests, leaf analysis or visual symptoms on plants are all ways of assessing whether your soil is lacking specific nutrients or needs lime.

Inorganic fertilizers may be applied as liquid, granules or powder and are a good way of correcting specific problems and releasing nutrients quickly into the soil. This can be an important consideration when planting fast-growing vegetable crops. Many gardeners use compound or general fertilizers that contain a mixture of nitrogen, phosphorus, sulfur, calcium and potassium and more rarely magnesium and trace elements. Most fertilizers are labeled to show the percentage of each of the three major nutrients they contain (the N:P:K ratio) and it is important to match the fertilizer to your soil type to avoid overloading the soil with unnecessary ingredients.

Although it is now possible to use inorganic fertilizers to supply all the nutrients needed by plants (hydroponically grown vegetables, for example, are grown using just water and synthetic fertilizers), these products do not improve the structure and texture of the soil and can quickly leach away with heavy watering or rainfall. Continuous cropping without any attempt to maintain soil organic matter leads to deterioration in the physical condition of the soil. When this happens, soils with high levels of silt and clay become sticky and more difficult to cultivate. Rain or spray water can easily compact the soil, forming a skin that hinders growth or prevents the emergence of seedlings, and the soil may also erode more readily.

Organic fertilizers

Bulky organic fertilizers, such as compost and manure, supply valuable plant nutrients just like inorganic

Organic fertilizers: cow manure (left), blood and bone (center), and compost (right).

fertilizers, but have the added advantage of containing high levels of organic matter. This ensures that the soil stays both nourished and in good physical condition, and helps it to retain moisture. As well as supplying at least some or all of the essential nutrients, they encourage earthworms and other soil organisms and microbes, which improve soil structure by breaking down the organic matter, thus increasing the amount of nutrients available to plants. The disadvantage of organic fertilizers is that they can vary greatly in their nutrient levels, composition and water content, and animal manure may contain weed seeds and pathogenic organisms. Organic fertilizers also release nutrients more slowly than artificial fertilizers. This can be an advantage, as nutrients are less likely to be leached from the soil, but means they must be applied further in advance of planting.

One of the biggest variables in the content of organic fertilizers is the amount of nitrogen they contain. Leaf litter, for example, contains high levels of nitrogen while straw and sawdust have much lower levels. Plants such as cabbages, which need lots of nitrogen, may suffer from nitrogen deficiency and remain stunted, pale green and yellowish if nitrogen levels fall below a certain level. Legumes such as peas and beans, however, which do not take up their nitrogen from the soil, will grow well as long as they have adequate supplies of all other essential nutrients. One way of avoiding nitrogen deficiencies if you are using an organic fertilizer with a high straw content is to grow legumes like peas and beans immediately afterwards. Materials such as sawdust, with very low nitrogen levels, are best composted before use.

Compost

Compost can be made from any organic material including straw, kitchen waste, leaf litter, crop residues, garden cuttings, or grass clippings. Microorganisms, bacteria and larger organisms such as earthworms and insects all work on this waste, decomposing the organic matter to provide a nutrient-rich soil additive. For the best compost, a mixture of

A compost bin in your garden provides free plant food.

coarse and finer organic waste should be layered in a heap or a bin. Water and air are needed for decomposition, so it helps to turn the mixture regularly and ensure that it remains moist. Materials like straw and sawdust can take a long time to decompose but adding nitrogen-rich blood and bone, poultry manure or urea can speed up the process. As with other organic fertilizers, the amount of nitrogen released into the soil will depend on the ingredients used in the compost. Because the microorganisms that help decomposition also need nitrogen to multiply, compost containing materials with a low nitrogen content (like kitchen waste or sawdust) will not immediately release their nitrogen into the soil. This type of compost may therefore cause a temporary nitrogen shortage when first dug in, and until it is fully broken down; to avoid any problems, wait a few weeks before planting or sowing.

Many commercial composts are also available and include city compost made from garden waste, bark compost, spent mushroom compost, and pig slurry that has been composted with sawdust. Spent mushroom compost is excellent for the kitchen garden and can be forked or hoed in lightly like other fine compost; it contains some lime and gypsum and its regular use may prevent the need to add lime to the soil.

Animal manures

Animal manures are also excellent soil builders but vary greatly in composition and N:P:K values depending on the animal, the food eaten, the proportion of additional matter (like straw and sawdust) which might have been used as bedding, and whether the manure includes urine as well as dung. Dung contains organic nitrogen, sulfur and phosphorus as well as calcium phosphate, magnesium and trace elements but very little potassium. Gardeners using animal manure should look out for potassium deficiency in their crops, which shows up in cabbage as a brown marginal scorch on the older leaves. Poultry manure is excellent for vegetable gardens as it is richer in nitrogen, sulfur and potassium than other animal manures. Battery-hen manure is best composted with sawdust, bark or straw before use.

Because of the wide variation in composition of bulky manures it is difficult to recommend actual weights to use per square yard (square meter); this may vary from 5½ to 22 lb (2.5 to 10 kg). The heavy use of rich material, for example, may make it unnecessary to supplement the soil with fertilizers, which is the aim of organic growers.

Organic fertilizers such as blood and bone, dried blood and fishmeal provide more concentrated sources of nitrogen, phosphorus and sulfur than organic manures, so less is needed. However, they leave no significant residual organic matter after their decomposition so their main value is as a source of slow-release nutrients; they are used at rates of 2 to 6 oz per square yard (50 to 150 g per square meter). Although such fertilizers meet the needs of those who object to synthetic fertilizers, they contain little potassium and are no substitute for bulky manures or inorganic fertilizers that contain potassium.

Check crops for potassium deficiency if you use animal manure.

IMPROVING THE SITE
Weeding
Most soils need some improvement before planting begins. Weeds should be dug out before any food crops are planted, and removing annual weeds before they flower and set seed will reduce time spent on weeding in the future. Weeds with deep roots can be dug out. If there is a really serious problem with perennial weeds, such as twitch grasses and thistles, you may need to use a herbicide. Choose carefully, however, as many are not suitable for use on soil that will be used for food crops. Ground dug for the first time may contain weed seeds which can persist for several years. Extra vigilance may be needed for a few years to prevent them seeding. They should be hoed, preferably early on a hot day. During long wet periods it may be necessary to remove weeds by hand. Use the hoe regularly between widely spaced crops such as brassicas and keep down weeds among potatoes and sweet corn until they completely shade the ground. Peas and onions may need hand-weeding.

In some cases, you may need to remove turf to establish a vegetable garden. Lawns are rich in organic matter and should be incorporated into the soil rather than skimmed off. Turn the turf over and dig it into the soil, adding a layer of manure when the turf is broken up. Most soils will also benefit from 'bastard trenching,' especially where compact layers exist naturally or have been formed by the passage of heavy traffic during house-building. First mark out the plot into horizontal strips. On the first strip, remove the topsoil to a spade's depth and move it to the far end of the plot. Next, fork over the exposed subsoil and add any crop residues, kitchen waste, skimmed-off turf from the next strip or bulky organic manure to the trench. Cover with topsoil dug from the next strip. Repeat the whole process until you reach the last strip, where the topsoil from the first strip can be used to cover the final trench.

Layers of straw, newspaper or other organic material can also be used to smother turf and turn the site into a productive garden. In winter, cover the turf with a thick layer of paper, then a layer of straw or a thick mulch to keep it in place. Tuberous crops such as potatoes can be grown in holes dug through

Prepare your vegetable garden site then mulch to cover new soil over winter and protect your growing plants.

the layers and will help to break up the soil and turf, allowing other plants to be grown in the next year.

Water
There are few areas where a shortage of water will not restrict plant growth. Vegetables and fruit are particularly vulnerable, as crops will be damaged or may droop if plants have insufficient water. Plants extract water from the soil through their roots and release it into the atmosphere through small pores in their leaves called stomata. This is called loss by transpiration. Water is also lost directly from the soil by evaporation. The combined loss from plants and soil is called evapotranspiration and is affected by temperature, humidity, wind speed, sunshine hours, sunlight intensity and the length of day (stomata close at night). Evapotranspiration, defined as the maximum requirements of a crop if it is never short of water, can be roughly estimated and is much higher in summer than in winter.

A potato crop may transpire about $\frac{1}{5}$ in (5 mm) of water a day in summer or 6 in (150 mm) a month, whereas a crop of cauliflowers during winter may transpire only $\frac{1}{2}$ in (15 mm) in a whole month. If monthly rainfall in summer were only 2 in (50 mm), growth would be affected unless the soil could supply 4 in (100 mm) of water; 2 in (50 mm) of rainfall in winter, however, would exceed requirements by $1\frac{1}{2}$ in (35 mm), and would restore soil moisture. If the soil were saturated already the excess water would drain through the soil.

If we know how much plant-available water the soil holds, the rainfall and evapotranspiration rate, we can calculate weekly or monthly water requirements. Sandy soils hold about $1\frac{1}{2}$ in (30 mm) of available water to a depth of 20 in

Water generously to encourage root growth.

These hedges provide shelter for low-growing plants.

(50 cm), loams about 3 to 4 in (75 to 100 mm) and peats about 5 in (125 mm). If roots are able to penetrate deeply, they can tap more water and deep-rooting crops like asparagus and fruit trees are much less likely to suffer from a shortage of water as soils dry out than, for example, celery or strawberries.

It is better to water generously and deeply than to apply frequent sprinkling, which encourages shallow rooting. Moisture can also be conserved by applying bulky organic materials, such as straw and compost, and by ensuring that high levels of organic matter are maintained in the soil. Using an efficient drip or sprinkler system will also ensure that plants receive adequate water at the right time of day—watering early in the morning, for example, will minimize evaporation and allows foliage to dry before evening.

Shelter
Wind can be a serious problem in many gardens. Leaves may be damaged, stalks broken, tall plants like Brussels sprouts blown over, and others loosened so their roots are exposed. Rows of crops like peas and beans may also be flattened unless held up with stout supports. Cold winds can also delay maturity by checking growth. Walls and fences provide effective permanent shelter and can also be used to grow crops such as grape vines, passionfruit, blackberries, peaches and other fruits—especially useful in small gardens where space is at a premium. Hedges are another good means of filtering strong winds and sheltering lower-growing crops. Windcloth can be used as a temporary measure while hedges are established and many productive crops can be used for hedging, including hazelnuts, closely planted fruit trees (apples, pears, plums, feijoas) and bushes of blackcurrants, gooseberries, redcurrants and Cape gooseberries. Tall-growing Jerusalem artichokes, a relative of the sunflower, make excellent windbreaks.

It is a mistake to use tall-growing trees to provide shelter around a vegetable and fruit garden. The roots from poplars, pines and eucalypts travel long distances, robbing soils of water and nutrients, and poor crop growth can often be traced to invading tree roots.

Harvest cherries promptly before they fall and spoil or are stolen by birds.

Hoe in fertilizer and compost when planting row crops such as these.

SOWING AND PLANTING

What you choose to plant will depend not only on your garden conditions but on your tastes and how much time you have at your disposal. Some crops need a lot of continuous care, including regular watering, pruning, and spraying; others require little attention after planting, but may need time for harvesting. While many vegetables, once mature, can be left in the ground for a few weeks or picked when needed, fruits like peaches, apricots and most berries quickly spoil or may be stolen by birds if they are not harvested as soon as they are ripe.

When sowing row crops such as onions, carrots, parsnips, beets, spinach, silver beets, sweet corn, turnips, and swedes, a handful of fertilizer should be sprinkled along 1 to 2 yards (1 to 2 meters) of the row, thoroughly hoed in so as not to contact seeds when sown, followed by about 17½ pints (10 liters) of compost, also hoed in. When the seed bed has been prepared, draw your finger or a stick along the line to the appropriate depth for the type of seed (small

seeds like those of carrots need only a shallow row, for example), cover them over, firm them in with a rake and keep the soil moist, preferably with a gentle soak hose, until the seeds germinate.

When planting, experiment with between one-third to one-half a handful or even more of fertilizer at each site, forking in thoroughly, followed by the forking in of 4½ pints (2.5 liters) of compost. Firming in the plant by hand leaves a hollow which under dry conditions can be filled with water and topped up again until the plants are established. It may sometimes be necessary to add extra soil later with more fertilizer or more compost if growth is not good. Potatoes and other tubers can be planted after similar preparation. If trees or shrubs, such as berry fruits, are to be planted with balls of soil attached to the roots, larger holes will be necessary and fertilizer and compost should be thoroughly worked in before planting.

When planting lettuces, leeks, celery and herbs close to each other, fertilizer and compost can be hoed in as for row crops. In the case of leeks and celery, it may be easier to make double rows of shallow trenches and to fork in fertilizer and compost before planting. This makes it easier to water celery, which needs a great deal of moisture, while the molding up of soil around leeks will increase the length of white stem.

The land is often ridged at least slightly for some crops such as strawberries and asparagus. Strawberries may be grown for 3 years or so while asparagus may last for 20 years on suitable soil. Rhubarb, like strawberries, may occupy the same ground for a few years before needing to be divided and replanted; such crops are best kept in areas separate from the rotation of vegetables.

SUCCESSIVE CROPPING

Given a sufficient area it is possible to extend the sowing and planting time of some crops to prolong harvesting for months. In wetter, cooler climates, soils may not be suitable for planting until early spring. It will be earlier in warmer climates but may even be mid-spring in the coldest areas.

Among the first crops to sow are long-keeping onions, carrots, beets, parsnips, radishes, peas and broad beans. These days, most gardeners buy troughs of lettuce plants, cabbages, cauliflowers, broccoli and herbs, but seeds can also be sown if your preferred cultivars are unavailable. Radishes and some lettuce

With careful planning you can ensure a constant supply of seasonal produce.

varieties are suitable for growing between other crops, such as peas, which are usually sown in double rows fairly wide apart.

If you can sow only one row of peas, try mixing early, medium and late varieties to extend the picking, otherwise sow a row of early peas and when these are 2 in (5 cm) high, sow a row of medium, followed by later cultivars. In this way harvesting can extend over 3 months.

Broad beans can be sown in autumn and will be ready by late spring, and the season extended until mid-summer from spring-sown beans. More carrots, beets and parsnips can be sown until at least mid-summer in most areas for harvesting over winter and early spring. Japanese (short day) onions can be sown from late summer to early autumn to mature in late spring or early summer and thinnings used as spring onions from mid-winter; these large sweet onions keep until late autumn, after which the

By planting several varieties you can enjoy alliums (here, red onion) all year round.

long-keepers sown in spring can be used until late spring and early summer. Other members of the onion tribe include leeks, garlic, shallots and spring onions. Shallots and garlic are often planted in mid-winter but can give better results if planted in late winter. Leeks are usually planted in summer to crop over winter.

If your garden is too small to grow all the potatoes you need, planting a few early potatoes every several weeks will provide a regular supply of new pota-toes. Unless protection is provided frost will restrict the length of the growing season. There are cultivars that reach digging size in 80 days, others that take 3 or 4 months, and main crops that may take up to 5 months to mature. There are so many cultivars available that the best advice is to follow individual choice or local preferences. The main consider-ation is to buy certified seed to avoid the disappointment of poor crops caused by virus diseases. In humid areas, it is also important to control blight although some resistance to blight is being bred into modern cultivars. Repeated crop-ping of potatoes may lead to problems from eelworms, but again new cultivars have varying degrees of resistance.

Other members of the solanum family include tomatoes, capsicums and eggplants: in this order they become more demanding of warmer conditions than potatoes. While potatoes may be grown outside almost anywhere for a few months, there are areas where all tomatoes need to be grown under cover, while capsicums are risky in some areas, and eggplants need a long warm period to crop well. Protection with frost cloth until early summer or for protection in autumn will enable many subtropical species to be grown. Melons, zucchinis and cucumbers also come into this category. Lettuces can be planted every few weeks throughout the year and are another crop to benefit from frost protection over winter when growing suitable cultivars such as 'Winter Imperial' or 'Triumph'. Frost cloth may also allow sweet corn seed to be sown earlier in some districts, early spring being common. Sowing further crops (until mid-summer) when the previous sowing is 4 to 6 in (10 to 15 cm) high will extend the harvest throughout autumn.

The many different kinds of beans are important foods. Broad beans are normally sown from autumn to spring, being frost-tolerant. Other beans are frost-tender and are usually sown from early spring to mid-summer. While fertilizers may be needed in early stages of garden development, eventually excess nitrogen will encourage the dense growth of bean and pea foliage to the detriment of yield. Try compost, as legumes should be able to fix most of their own nitrogen. Dwarf beans like peas may need some support, but the climbing beans will need support up to 3 yards (3 meters), either in rows or wigwams. The large fleshy roots of scarlet runners will survive over winter where the soil does not freeze to any depth and can be grown for several years in a permanent position.

Different cultivars of cabbages, cauliflowers, broccoli and oriental cabbages can be grown year round in most areas. Brussels sprouts are best planted from late spring to mid-summer for harvesting over winter. Good garden shops will vary the cultivars available in troughs, so you can buy varieties suitable for planting in any season.

FRUIT

A wide range of fruit can be grown in your own garden, although a small garden is not the place for tree fruits unless they are grown on dwarf stocks or as espaliers. Stonefruits include apricots, cherries, nectarines, peaches and plums. Pipfruits include apples and pears. Citrus are numerous, including grapefruit, lemons, limes, mandarins, tangelos, and oranges. They often need some protection during cold winters. Canefruits include blackberries, boysenberries, loganberries and raspberries. Bush fruits include grapes and Cape gooseberries, commonly grown in home gardens; blackcurrants, blueberries, gooseberries and redcurrants which do best in cooler areas; and guavas, which will grow where citrus do well. Guavas also make attractive hedges which trim well. Other fruits which will need warmer conditions include feijoas, figs, kiwifruit, melons, passionfruit and tamarillos.

Citrus limon ripening on the tree.

Replant strawberries at regular intervals depending on your local climate.

Planting fruit

The climate in your garden will dictate to a great extent which fruits can be grown there, as the levels of sunlight available will govern the development of fruit. Subtropical fruits, such as figs and passionfruit, and citrus are not usually planted until late spring or early summer when all risk of frost is over. Other mainly deciduous fruits are best planted from autumn to winter. Strawberries produce best results in warmer areas if replanted every year in mid-autumn, and every 2 to 3 years in cooler areas.

CULINARY HERBS

No home garden is complete without some herbs. Mint, parsley, thyme, chives and sage are perhaps the most popular but basil, marjoram, coriander (cilantro), rosemary, dill and fennel provide other interesting flavors. Mid-winter is a suitable time to plan a herb garden; even a small herb garden will amply reward

the space allotted to it. Most nurseries supply both annual and perennial herbs. Perennials make useful edging plants, while some of the annuals are best sown in small rows. Herbs are particularly suitable for containers, especially the least fussy varieties which can tolerate dry conditions and poor soil, and need little attention. They include basil, cilantro, dill, marjoram, rosemary, sage and savory.

Some popular herbs

Basil is an annual, best planted out after late frosts or sown during summer. Both the leaves and flower stems are used. Cut flower stems as they appear or tie them up in bundles for winter use.

Chives are perennials, propagated by division. They need a good, fertile soil and should be cut down to ground level several times a season to encourage good growth of spring onion-like stems.

Coriander (cilantro) is an annual, planted or sown in spring and thinned to 16 in (40 cm) apart. Use the young leaves in soups or stews.

There are several species of marjoram. Sweet marjoram (*Origanum majorana*) is treated as an annual, grown 8 in (20 cm) apart, while pot marjoram (*O. vulgare*) is grown as a perennial 10 in (25 cm) apart and trimmed back occasionally. The aromatic leaves are used both fresh and dried.

Mint is a perennial usually propagated by rooted cuttings of young shoots. The many different types including spearmint (*Mentha spicata*) require a rich moist soil. Because of its capacity to spread, mint needs a confined space such as a section of steel drum sunk into the ground.

Parsley is a biennial and should be planted or sown twice a year in spring and late summer. It needs a rich soil and is good for edging. The most popular

You can create a varied herb garden in a small space.

type is probably curly-leaved parsley.
Watch out for aphids.

Rosemary is a perennial usually
propagated by cuttings. It needs a sunny
position and can be trained over a wall
or even raised as a standard.

Sage is a perennial usually propagated
from tip cuttings but is easily grown
from seed in spring. Large-leaved strains
that flower little are best and should be
trimmed back after flowering to keep
plants compact and stop them from
becoming 'leggy.'

Savory is a strongly-flavored herb
used in seasoning. Summer savory
(*Satureja hortensis*) is a tender annual and
can be sown in rows during spring and
thinned to 12 in (30 cm) apart. Winter
savory (*S. montana*) is a perennial,
needing good drainage. It can be raised

by cuttings taken in spring or by
dividing old plants.

PESTS AND DISEASES

These can cause severe losses unless
control measures are taken. Most people
will want to take advantage of plants
bred to resist certain pests and diseases.
Organic growers will only want to use
natural products or methods such as
companion planting, biological controls,
integrated pest management and the like
and should join local groups of organic
growers to obtain the best advice.
Others will want to use the latest
insecticides and fungicides approved for
use by the home gardener.

As these are expensive, most people
prefer to wait before spraying until they
see pests, in particular aphids and

Brassicas are particularly vulnerable to caterpillars.

caterpillars on brassica crops. Fungal diseases such as blight on tomatoes and potatoes or septoria leaf spot on celery are usually difficult to control once they take hold, but their spread can be delayed if caught in time. Take the best local advice on suitable pesticides.

ROTATING CROPS

Many soil-borne pests and diseases can be controlled by practicing suitable rotations. It helps to avoid growing the same crop or members of the same family year after year on the same plot. Such families include the onion tribe (garlic, leeks, onions, shallots); brassicas (sprouts, cabbages, broccoli, cauliflowers, Chinese cabbages, kohl rabi, swedes, turnips, radishes); legumes (peas, broad beans, dwarf beans, scarlet runners); solanums (potatoes, tomatoes, capsicums, eggplants); and cucurbits (marrows, zucchinis, pumpkins, squashes, cucumbers, melons). Beets, silverbeets and spinach belong to the same family as do lettuces, endives, chicory and salsify; carrots, parsnips, celery and celeriac belong to another family and, for example, are all susceptible to damage from carrot fly.

A 4-year rotation

Divide area into 4 equal parts A, B, C, and D and begin in late winter.

Plot A: Finish harvesting leeks. Plant garlic and shallots in early spring followed by long-keeping onions. Sow beets and spinach during spring and summer. Plant brassicas from spring onwards. Harvest Japanese onions, garlic and shallots from early to mid-summer and long-keeping onions from late summer to mid-autumn. Sow or plant lettuces, endives, and chicory for winter and spring harvest after harvesting members of the onion family.

Plot B: Sow or plant lettuces in spring and summer on a different area from the previous year. Plant succession of brassicas on a different area from the previous year. Sow carrots and parsnips and plant celery from spring to summer. Sow major area with sweet corn from early spring to early summer. After digging in first 2 rows of sweet corn in early autumn, sow broad beans in mid-autumn.

Plot C: Dig in sweet corn residues as soon as harvested and sow peas from late winter to mid-spring and dwarf and runner beans from early spring to mid-summer. Plant cucurbits after the risk of late frost is over in an area not previously used for sweet corn. Dig in pea and bean residue immediately after harvest and plant autumn, winter and spring brassicas.

Divide your vegetable garden into areas and rotate crops to control pests and diseases.

Plot D: Dig in crop residues as harvests are completed and plant early potatoes in late winter (earlier in the warmest areas and later in colder areas) followed by the second early crop and a main crop from early to mid-spring (later still in warmest areas). Plant tomatoes, capsicums, eggplants, yams, and sweet potatoes when risk of frost is over. Plant leeks from early summer after harvesting early potatoes and sow Japanese onions in early autumn. Harvest main crop potatoes from early to late autumn and other crops as needed on maturity. Lime, if a soil test shows it is needed, after harvesting potatoes and other crops and before planting leeks and onions.

The following year, in plot D follow procedure on plot A. On plot A follow procedure on plot B. On plot B follow procedure on plot C and on plot C grow plot D crops. Keep rotating in future years. If preferred, crop residues can be composted rather than dug in. Asparagus (moderate to high pH), rhubarb (low pH), globe artichokes and scarlet runners (moderate pH) can be allocated a 'permanent' area for some years. Herbs can be used to edge paths but mint needs a confined space. A note on weeding: peas and onions may need hand-weeding but in the above rotation, peas follow sweet corn and onions follow potatoes, both of which are good for weed control.

Vegetables

ABELMOSCHUS

This genus of around 15 species is from tropical Africa and Asia. It includes the vegetable okra or gumbo *(Abelmoschus esculentus)*, grown for its edible young pods, and several other species grown as attractive ornamentals. In older books all the species were included in the larger genus *Hibiscus*. They are annuals, biennials or short-lived perennials with tough bark (sometimes used for fiber) and maple-like leaves. Some species die back to a large tuber in the tropical dry season. The hibiscus-like flowers occur in shades of yellow, pink, orange or red.

Cultivation

Grow *Abelmoschus* species in fertile, well-drained soil and in a sheltered position in full sun. They are tropical plants requiring long, hot summers for successful growth. Soak seed for 24 hours before sowing in spring. Harvest the young pods in summer or autumn before they reach 3 in (8 cm) long. Rust disease can be a problem: spray with a fungicide.

Abelmoschus esculentus
syn. *Hibiscus esculentus*
Okra, gumbo, lady's fingers

Long cultivated in parts of Africa and Asia (where it originated), this 6 ft (1.8 m) tall species was taken to the Americas with slaves from West Africa where it has remained a traditional ingredient of many dishes in the USA's Deep South. It has attractive red-eyed yellow flowers. Both flower buds and the long starchy immature pods are edible. *Zones 9–11.*

Abelmoschus esculentus cultivar

AGARICUS
Mushroom

Mushrooms are among the few fungi actively cultivated. They are, of course, grown for their edible fruiting bodies, not their beauty. Mushrooms are all similar in general appearance but vary considerably in size: the white or pale pink to beige caps, with pink to brown undersides, range from ½ in (12 mm) to over 6 in (15 cm) in diameter. As many fungi are highly toxic, **take great care** to accurately identify any collected in the wild before eating them—edible and inedible species are very similar in appearance.

Cultivation

Cultivating mushrooms is quite unlike growing any other garden crop. Generally grown in the dark, they require warm, moist conditions and a suitable growing medium; special care is needed with the compost mix to get the pH right. Once established, they are largely self-sustaining, but it can take considerable trial and error to get the first crop. Insects and rodents can be a problem, so it is important to keep the growing area clean.

Agaricus campestris
syn. *Psalliota campestris*
Mushroom, button mushroom

This common fungus can be grown indoors or outdoors, under houses or in sheds, as long as the conditions are fairly dark, humid and the temperature is constant, ideally 50–55°F (10–13°C). Special compost is needed, and most home gardeners are best buying a mushroom kit from their nursery and following detailed instructions. Mushrooms are usually ready to harvest within 5 weeks—they can be harvested at the button, cap or flat stage of growth. Pick them by twisting out, not pulling. *Zones 5–11.*

ALLIUM

This large genus consists of more than 700 species of bulbous perennials and biennials that occur in temperate regions of the northern hemisphere and range in height from 4 in to 5 ft (10 cm–1.5 m). A number of ornamental species, with beautiful brightly colored flowers, come from west and central Asia. Common to the genus is the pungent oniony smell emitted when the leaves are bruised or cut. All species have umbels of flowers borne on narrow, erect stalks; each flower is sheathed in bud by membranous bracts. The bulbs vary from very fat to quite slender and new bulbils are usually produced at the base, sometimes also in the flower stalks. Some alliums with edible leaves and bulbs, such as onions, are used as vegetables; those used for flavoring, like garlic and chives, are listed under herbs.

Cultivation

Alliums prefer a sunny, open position in fertile, well-drained, weed-free soil. *Allium cepa* may need the protection of a cloche if the soil is cold. Watch for onion fly, stem eelworm, rust and onion white rot. Propagate from seed or bulbils.

Agaricus campestris

Allium ampeloprasum
Wild leek, kurrat

Ideal for rocky, coastal sites, this allium has a tall, robust habit with cylindrical stems reaching a height of up to 4 ft (1.2 m). Papery bracts enclose the globe-shaped umbels, dropping off as the hundreds of tiny dull pink flowers open. Leaves are grayish green, up to 18 in (45 cm) long with a waxy texture and rough margins. One of the larger, leafier alliums, its bulb has a garlic-like flavor—some strains are cultivated as vegetables in the Middle East. Sow seed or bulbils in spring or summer, and harvest young leaves from late winter to early summer. *Zones 6–10.*

Allium cepa
Onion, spring onion, scallion, shallot

Onions were popular with the Greeks and Romans but never eaten by the Egyptians who regarded them as sacred.

The spring onion is an immature onion which has not yet made a bulb. This species has given rise to a vast number of cultivars, varying in size, shape, color and flavor. Bunching onions or shallots or scallions belong to the **Aggregatum Group**; plants in this group have a cluster of small bulbs with a more delicate taste than spring onions and can be used instead of chives. The standard onion belongs to the **Cepa Group**. The tree onion belongs to the **Proliferum Group** which bears small bulbs at the top of the flower stalks. Sow seeds or immature onions in mid-spring, in holes ½ in (1 cm) deep and 12 in (30 cm) apart. Water moderately. Harvest in late summer when the leaves begin to yellow. Sow shallots in early spring. Sow spring onions in autumn for an early spring crop, or in spring for a summer crop. In warm climates, seeds can be sown at any time of year. *Zones 4–11.*

Allium ampeloprasum cultivar

Allium cepa cultivar

Allium cepa, Proliferum Group cultivar

Allium cepa, Proliferum Group cultivar

Allium cepa, Aggregatum Group cultivar

Allium porrum

Allium fistulosum cultivar

Allium porrum 'Giant Winter Wila'

Allium fistulosum
Welsh onion, Japanese bunching onion

Unknown in the wild and with obscure origins, this species grows to around 24 in (60 cm) tall. It is distinctive for its hollow, chive-like leaves and flowering stems which each carry a dense umbel of numerous green flowers in summer. The leaves of Welsh onion are used as a green vegetable for salads and stir-fried dishes. Sow seed as for *Allium cepa* in autumn for a spring crop or in spring for a summer crop. Harvest leaves when young and tender. *Zones 6–9.*

Allium porrum
syn. *Allium ampeloprasum* var. *porrum*
Leek

Of uncertain origin but now widely distributed in cooler parts of the northern hemisphere, the leek has

Allium porrum 'Mammoth Blanche'

broad concave leaves, the sheathing bases of which form a tight cylinder — the edible part. The flowering stem can be 3 ft (1 m) or more tall, with a large, spherical head of tiny gray-green to dull reddish flowers. Leeks are easier to grow than onions and more suited to cold climates. Sow seed in spring or summer, or plant seedlings 8 in (20 cm) apart with 12 in (30 cm) between rows, filling each hole gently with water. Harvest as needed once the base of the leek is at least 1 in (2.5 cm) thick. Leek cultivars vary in the size of their stems, color of their leaves and cold tolerance. **'Giant Winter Wila'** is one of the blue-leafed cultivars that mature through winter. **'Mammoth Blanche'** is typical of the very fat leeks, with bases up to 2½ in (6 cm) in diameter, grown for their particularly thick and fleshy stems. **'Musselburgh'** is another popular variety with heavy, thick stems and large, broad leaves. *Zones 5–10.*

APIUM
Celery, celeriac

Over 20 species of biennials and perennials make up this genus in the carrot family, found throughout Europe, temperate Asia and cooler parts of the southern hemisphere. The wild *Apium* species have leaves in basal tufts, or spread along creeping stems; these are divided to varying degrees into fleshy segments. Tiny white flowers are borne in umbels. One species is cultivated world-wide as an annual vegetable. The most common form, celery, is grown for its stalks, or petioles, which can be eaten raw or cooked.

Cultivation

Celery needs plenty of moisture and has fairly shallow roots, so apply moisture-retentive humus to the soil and provide regular water and fertilizer for tender,

succulent stalks. Self-blanching varieties are now widely available; unlike older varieties, they do not need to be grown in a trench to blanch their stalks. Sow seeds in a starter bed or tray in late spring or early summer and transplant seedlings to permanent beds trying not to disturb the roots. Grow self-blanching plants close together to help keep light off stalks; the green or non-blanching types can be more widely spaced.

Apium graveolens
Celery

The wild celery of Europe is a strong-smelling biennial growing up to 3 ft (1 m) and found in marshy locations along the coast. It has finely divided

Apium graveolens cultivar

Apium graveolens var. *dulce* cultivar

leaves and bears loose compound umbels of late summer flowers. Domesticated for over 2000 years, selection and breeding has resulted in numerous cultivars which can be divided into 3 groups: *Apium graveolens* var. *dulce* is the common celery, characterized by its long, succulent, leaf stalks with leafy green tops. Sow seed from mid-spring to mid-summer and cut the stalks before flowering—it has quite a short growing season in many areas and the timing of flowering will vary according to the temperature. *A. g.* var. *rapaceum* is celeriac and has a swollen, edible rootstock like a turnip and slender leaf stalks that are usually discarded. It requires similar growing conditions to celery but needs a long growing season to make a large root. The leafy tops of leaf celery or *A. g.* var. *secalinum* are used like a herb for soups and stews. In China a similar type of celery is grown for its stalks and leaves. *Zones 5–10.*

Apium graveolens var. *rapaceum* cultivar

ASPARAGUS

This large genus not only includes the edible asparagus, *Asparagus officinalis*, but also up to 60 other perennial species. Many are commonly called ferns, but in fact they belong to the lily family in its broadest sense (botanists have recently recognized many smaller families in place of one large one with very diverse elements). As interpreted here, the genus *Asparagus* includes only cool-temperate, herbaceous species, mainly from Europe and Asia. The shrubby and climbing species from Africa are de-scribed under the genera *Protasparagus* and *Myrsiphyllum*.

Cultivation

To grow edible asparagus, it is critical to select the correct garden bed as the crowns can grow undisturbed for over 20 years. The chosen bed, in full sun, should be well dug over, manured and have good drainage. Grow asparagus from seed in early spring or, if available, from crowns which will produce an earlier crop. Space plants 12 in (30 cm) apart and do not harvest the young shoots or spears until the third spring to allow the crowns to mature; always allow a few shoots to elongate to build up the plant's food reserves. For white spears, cut the shoots well below the soil surface just as spears become visible.

Asparagus officinalis
Asparagus

A frost-hardy perennial thought to originate from the Mediterranean region and western Asia, this vegetable seems to have been cultivated since at least Greek times for medicine or food. If allowed to grow uncut, the emerging asparagus spear will develop into a branched, ferny, erect stem with many tiny, linear leaves. Female plants produce numerous red berries which should be removed before self-seeding occurs. **'Mary Washington'** is a variety well liked for its long, thick spears, but the newer F1 hybrids often provide higher yields. *Zones 4–9.*

ATRIPLEX
Saltbush

This is a genus of around 100 species of annuals, perennials, subshrubs and

Asparagus officinalis cultivar

Asparagus officinalis 'Mary Washington'

Atriplex hortensis var. *rubra* cultivar

shrubs found throughout temperate and subtropical zones. Most of the ornamental or useful shrubby species come either from the western and central USA or from inland Australia. Some have edible leaves, similar to spinach and are nutritious fodder plants, valued for their ability to thrive in saline soils. They are also fire resistant, can withstand varied conditions, and are often useful in erosion control. Most have a grayish white appearance due to a fine coating of scales or bladder-like surface cells. The leaves are variable and may be small and rounded or toothed and sometimes arrowhead shaped. There are separate male and female flowers, both of which are usually small and insignificant; some species also have conspicuous spongy fruit.

Cultivation

Species from coastal habitats will thrive with exposure to salt spray. Others from arid environments prefer a dry atmosphere. They are easily grown in any soil, in full sun. Frost hardiness varies with the species, though most will tolerate moderate frosts. Propagate from seed or cuttings.

Atriplex hortensis
Mountain spinach, orache

An annual of uncertain, probably central Asian origin, the edible leaves of this species are popular in many central European countries for salads or boiling. It grows to 8 ft (2.5 m) tall and produces heads of small yellow-green flowers from mid-summer. The lower leaves, similar to those of spinach *(Spinacia)*, grow to 4 in (10 cm) long and are roughly triangular with shallow lobes. Sow seed in early spring, or in autumn in warm climates and harvest the leaves in summer. *Atriplex hortensis* var. *rubra* (syn. *A. h.* var. *atrosanguinea*) is a purple-foliaged, red-stemmed variety. *Zones 6–10.*

BARBAREA

Occurring throughout northern temperate regions, the dozen or so biennial and perennial species in this genus are sometimes called land cress as they are similar in appearance and use to watercress. They are most often found in damp soil along streamsides and in hollows. The smooth green leaves, initially in a basal rosette, are usually deeply lobed along the lower edges, with a large, rounded segment at the ends. Strongly flavored, the foliage can be used in salads or boiled as a vegetable. The rosettes elongate into erect, leafy flowering stems branching into dense heads or spikes of small bright yellow flowers.

Cultivation

Easily grown in damp soil in sun or part-shade, they may be invasive where conditions favor them. Sow seed in late summer and gather the leaves in autumn and winter. Remove the flowerheads to encourage more luxuriant foliage.

Barbarea vulgaris
Water cress, winter cress, yellow rocket

Native to Europe and North Africa, this species has naturalized widely in other cool-temperate regions. It is a biennial or short-lived perennial making rosettes of glossy deep green leaves. The branching flower stems, up to 3 ft (1 m) tall, bear bright yellow blooms from late spring. *Zones 6–10.*

BETA
Beet

This genus of 6 species of broad-leafed annuals, biennials and perennials, native to Europe, west Asia and North Africa, has produced several important garden

Barbarea vulgaris cultivar

Beta vulgaris subsp. *vulgaris* cultivar

Beta vulgaris subsp. *vulgaris* cultivar

and commercial vegetables—all cultivated races of one species, *Beta vulgaris*.
The genus belongs to the saltbush
family, as do spinach *(Spinacia)* and
orache *(Atriplex)*, and its species often
grow in the wild in saline coastal
habitats. Beets have a well-developed
tap root and large basal leaves.
Flowering stems rise from the foliage
bearing numerous inconspicuous
greenish flowers followed by small,
slightly prickly dry fruits, normally
thought of as the 'seeds'.

Cultivation

All beets are relatively easy to grow in
loose soil enriched with compost. Water
well to encourage steady growth. Sow
seeds in spring in cooler climates, or at
any time of year in warmer ones.
Beetroot seeds are sown about 8 in
(20 cm) apart; when the first leaves
appear, weed out the weaker seedlings.
Keep the soil moist. In warm climates,
the beetroot can be harvested almost all
year round; in cold climates the roots are
picked and stored over winter. Swiss
chard (silver beet) is fast growing, so
plant at a wider spacing in an open
position in deep, fertile soil that has been

Beta vulgaris subsp. *vulgaris* cultivar

previously cultivated. Water frequently
—any check in growth or sudden
change of conditions can lead to bolting
(premature flowering).

Beta vulgaris
Beetroot, chard, silver beet

The original wild form of this well-
known species, now classified as **Beta
vulgaris subsp. maritima**, is an erect or
sprawling perennial from the west
European and Mediterranean seashores
with succulent, salt-resistant foliage that
can be gathered as a vegetable. Domestication has led to a number of cultivated
races of food plants, most of which
behave as biennials or annuals. Botanists
now group them all under the botanical
name **B. v. subsp. vulgaris**, though they
are rather diverse in growth form and
part of plant used. The leaf vegetables
are Swiss chard (including silver beet

Beta vulgaris subsp. *vulgaris* cultivar

Beta vulgaris subsp. *vulgaris* 'Pablo'

Beta vulgaris subsp. *vulgaris* 'Bolthardy'

Beta vulgaris subsp. *vulgaris* cultivar

and ruby chard) with large, puckered leaves, popular as a spinach substitute in warm climates or grown partly for ornament if a red leaf-stalked form; and spinach chard with smaller, flatter leaves that can be harvested over a long period. Cultivars may have white or colored leaf-stalks and veins: ruby chard has very dark leaves with bright red stems and veins. The root vegetables include the familiar beetroot with its swollen red roots and its many cultivars like **'Bolthardy'**, which is resistant to sudden temperature changes and will not run to seed, and **'Pablo'**; sugar beet, similar but with pale roots, like the yellow **'Golden'**, which are sweet-tasting and contain extremely high sugar levels; and mangel-wurzel, used mainly for livestock fodder. *Zones 5–10.*

BRASSICA

This genus has produced a diverse range of important vegetables. It includes about 30 wild species of annuals, biennials and subshrubs from all over the Mediterranean region and temperate Asia. Thousands of years ago, botanists believe spontaneous hybrids occurred between several of the wild species and from one such hybrid arose the major group of vegetables now classified as *Brassica oleracea*. Another large assortment are included under the name *Brassica rapa*. Other species include the mustards and rape, grown for the oils in their seeds. The genus *Brassica* in its more primitive form is characterized by its usually lobed leaves, 4-petaled yellow to white flowers and small, spindle-shaped fruiting capsules containing rows of tiny seeds. Most parts of the plants contain some hot-tasting mustard oils, which give the characteristic 'bite' to raw cabbage as well as the much more intense flavor to mustard.

Cultivation
Most brassicas love lime-rich, moist, well-drained soil. Seedlings should be raised in seed beds and then carefully planted out 6 to 8 weeks later in a sheltered, sunny spot in soil that has been previously used for a different crop. They are particularly prone to pests and diseases, and the use of insecticides can be hard to avoid. Ensure soil is kept weed-free and not too wet. Club root is a common disease in these vegetables, and crop rotation should be practised.

Brassica juncea
Indian mustard, mustard greens

This species, now thought to have originated as a hybrid between *B. rapa* and *B. nigra*, is cultivated for its pungent seeds used to flavor many dishes and for its seed oil, used in Asia for cooking. An annual growing to 3 ft (1 m), it has bright yellow flowers that mature to 1½ in (35 mm) long pods containing smooth brown seeds. The species has also given rise to a diverse range of leaf vegetables, little known in Europe but popular in east Asia, including the various Chinese mustard greens and the Japanese mizuna of which **'Red Giant'** is a cultivar. Sow seed in summer in cool areas for harvest in late summer to autumn, or in autumn in warmer regions for winter harvest. *Zones 6–11.*

Brassica juncea 'Red Giant'

Brassica oleracea, Acephala Group, 'Moss Curled'

Brassica napus
Rape

This annual or biennial species in its
more typical form includes the major
oilseeds rape and canola, the latter being
the product of recent breeding. In
winter-rainfall temperate regions these
crops are seen as a patchwork of brilliant
yellow fields covering the countryside in
spring. The **Napobrassica Group**
consists of the root vegetable swede
(Swedish turnips, rutabaga), mostly
grown as an annual winter crop. Similar
to turnips but larger and sweeter, swedes
are frost-hardy and prefer a light, fertile
soil. Sow seed in late spring and thin
seedlings to 12 in (30 cm) apart; harvest
from autumn to winter. *Zones 5–9.*

Brassica nigra
Black mustard

This annual, growing to 6 ft (1.8 m) or
more, is a native of Europe. Four-
petaled yellow flowers, borne in long
clusters in summer, are followed by
beaked pods each containing up to
12 brown to black seeds. Sow seed in
spring; harvest the edible young leaves
in summer and the seeds, a major source
of table mustard, in autumn. *Zones 7–10.*

Brassica oleracea

Thought to have originated as an ancient
hybrid between 2 or more of the wild
Mediterranean species, this is the most
important of the *Brassica* species and one
of the most versatile of all cultivated
food plants. In its various forms it yields
edible roots (kohlrabi), leaves (cabbage), shoots (Brussels sprouts) and
flower buds (cauliflower and broccoli),
as well as a few ornamentals, for
example the colored-leafed kales, and
curiosities such as some forms of giant
kale, the 'trunks' of which have been
used as walking sticks! The vegetable
brassicas associated with this species
include thousands of named cultivars,
which are most conveniently divided
into the following cultivar groups.

The **Acephala Group**, the kales and
ornamental kales—these are flat-leafed
or curly-leafed cabbages that do not
form a head, popular in northern Europe
because of their tolerance to cold. Some
forms can grow thick, knobby stems up
to 6 ft (1.8 m) or more tall. Sow seed in
spring or plant curly kales in summer
(flat-leafed kales do not tolerate trans-
planting). Harvest the leaves as needed
in autumn. In Scotland, the broth made
from their leaves is a traditional High-
land dish. **'Moss Curled'** is representa-
tive of the kales with tightly curled
leaves that look a bit like parsley; **'Tall**

Brassica oleracea, Acephala Group, Osaka Series cultivar

Brassica oleracea, Acephala Group, 'Chou Palmier'

Scotch' is another typical, curly cultivar. Ornamental kales, used for bedding and also sold in pots by florists, have leaves usually lobed or dissected and strikingly veined with purple, pink, yellow or white. **'Chou Palmier'** is an old variety with narrow, recurved, heavily textured, bluish leaves borne in a rosette on the top of the stems; the **Osaka Series** is a modern strain of mixed colors, the leaves undivided but with frilled edges.

Brassica oleracea, Botrytis Group cultivar

Brassica oleracea, Botrytis Group cultivar

The **Botrytis Group**, or ordinary white cauliflower, has been a popular vegetable since the Renaissance. The densely massed, tiny, abortive flower buds and the stalk that bears them are white and tender, with a mild flavor. It is a vegetable that is not easy to grow to perfection and the flower buds are easily bruised and damaged. It needs humus-rich soil for large, compact head production. For a summer crop, sow seed in a seed bed in autumn and plant out in spring, about 20 in (50 cm) apart; for autumn crops, sow in spring and plant out in summer. Apart from white, cultivars with pale green, pink and purple heads are known. **'Early Purplehead'** is purple-green, but the purple disappears on cooking. Typical white cultivars include **'Mini'**, early maturing with heads of 4 in (10 cm) or so across, and **'Snowball'**, which is late maturing with a large head.

The **Capitata Group** are the cabbages in all their diversity of form and coloring, possessing in common the tight, many-layered head of leaves. Innumerable cultivars vary in their time to maturity; **'Golden Acre'** and **'Green Coronet'**, for example, are typical early-maturing cultivars while **'Greengold'** is a large late-maturing hybrid. They also vary in their seasonal tolerance (**'Hardora'** and **'Hawke'**, for instance, are both very hardy). This ensures that cabbages can be grown worldwide in many different climatic zones. Their nutritional value is high. Among cultivars, the shape of the

Brassica oleracea, Capitata Group, 'Hardora'

Brassica oleracea, Capitata Group, 'Hawke'

heads of leaves varies greatly from rounded, like the compact **'Primax'**, to oval or conical, like the spring cabbage **'Sugarloaf'**. Red cabbage, with its purplish leaves, is a slow-maturing cabbage that needs a long growing season, but its solid, chewy flesh makes it the best type for pickling and frying; **'Mammoth Red Rock'** is one of the best red cultivars. The Savoy cabbages (**Sabauda Subgroup**) have wrinkled, strongly veined leaves: they are extremely frost-hardy and will thrive in very cold conditions. They tend to be larger and more strongly flavored than ordinary cabbages. **'Drumhead'** is a favorite Savoy cultivar, as are **'Karvoi'**, **'Ludessa'** and **'Ormskirk'**. A number of **Savoy Hybrids**, crosses between Savoy and white cabbages, have also been developed; they have denser heads of crinkled leaves than Savoys and are very hardy; **'Santana'** is a typical cultivar.

The **Cymosa Group** includes all the broccolis which, like cauliflower, are grown for their densely massed flower buds and fleshy stalks; the buds are further advanced and are not pure white but green, purplish or yellow-green.

Brassica oleracea, Capitata Group, Sabauda Subgroup, 'Karvoi'

Brassica oleracea, Capitata Group, Sabauda Subgroup, 'Ludessa'

Brassica oleracea, Capitata Group, Sabauda Subgroup, 'Ormskirk'

Brassica oleracea, Cymosa Group cultivar

Brassica oleracea, Cymosa Group, Romanesco cultivar

'Broccoli' is Italian, coming from *brocco*, 'sprout', and it was in Italy that nearly all the different types of this vegetable evolved. Seeds should be sown in rows in spring; place groups of 3 seeds 8 in (20 cm) apart, then thin the seedlings. **Calabrese** is the common type with broad, fleshy, green or purplish heads maturing in summer. **'De Cicco'** is a pale green, early-maturing cultivar; **'Green Duke'** is a popular commercial variety in the USA, with flat heads and an uneven shape, and **'Waltham 29'** is also popular. **Romanesco** broccolis are more cauliflower-like in both appearance and flavor with tight hemispherical heads forming many neat conical points; maturing later than Calabrese, they are usually pale yellow-green in color and very decorative. Sprouting broccoli produces many narrow-headed buds on long asparagus-like stalks among the

Brassica oleracea, Gemmifera Group, 'Troika'

Brassica oleracea, Gemmifera Group, 'Icarus'

Brassica oleracea, Gongylodes Group cultivar

leaves. Sow seed in a seed bed in spring and plant out in summer in rows 24 in (60 cm) apart—they develop over winter and can be picked over a long season in spring and early summer; **'Italian Green Sprouting'** is the best known variety. All broccoli is best picked and eaten when young because once the yellow flowers begin to open it becomes coarse in both texture and flavor. It is best grown in raised beds. Do not allow the plant to flower, as it will stop growing. Grubs and waterlogging are two major problems.

The **Gemmifera Group**, the Brussels sprouts, are grown as biennials for the miniature cabbage-like heads which grow on the elongating stems, one below each of the large leaves. Timing is crucial when planting Brussels sprouts since the heads need to mature in the coldest part of the year in order to form compact hearts. In warm climates sow in summer, in cold climates in mid-spring. In autumn, remove any yellowing leaves and make sure the soil stays firm around the stem of the plant. There are many cultivars suited to different soils and yielding smaller or larger sprouts. **'Icarus'**, **'Jade Beauty'** and **'Long Island'** are widely grown cultivars, **'Lunet Hybrid'** is a popular commercial variety with small sprouts late in the season; **'Troika'** is also popular; and **'Ruby Red'** has reddish sprouts.

The **Gongylodes Group** is the name that covers kohlrabi (a word of German

Brassica rapa, Chinensis Group cultivar

Brassica rapa, Pekinensis Group cultivar

origin). This root vegetable resembles beetroot in its growth form with a swollen, bulb-like stem base. With a slightly nutty flavor reminiscent of both turnip and cabbage, it can be eaten raw or cooked. Young leaves are edible and are white to pale green or purple, depending on the cultivar. Sow seed 10 in (25 cm) apart in spring in warm areas, in summer in cool areas; harvest in autumn and winter. Weed lightly as root disturbance will slow growth. **'Earliest Erfurt'** and **'Early Purple'** are fast-maturing cultivars, the latter with purple leaves; **'Purple Vienna'**, **'White Vienna'** are also popular and commonly grown. *Zones 6–11.*

Brassica rapa

After *Brassica oleracea*, this is the next most diverse of the brassica species in terms of the number of vegetables and crops it contains. Its wild form, referred to as **B. rapa** subsp. *sylvestris*, is a common weed found on road verges and among crops. In common with most of the cultivated varieties it has quite large flowers, about ½ in (12 mm) across, which are bright yellow. There are also some lesser known cultivar groups in *B. rapa*, which include additional leaf vegetables and oilseeds.

The **Chinensis Group** includes the Chinese vegetables known as pak-choi (bok-choi in Cantonese) — annual plants forming loose rosettes of bright green leaves with very broad white stalks, like silver beet. The crisp stalks form the main bulk of the vegetable. The plants run to seed quickly, so should be sown in small groups every 10 days from autumn to early spring in warm climates, or from spring to early summer in cool climates. Harvest the entire plant or take a few leaves as needed after 6–8 weeks. **'Joi Choi'** is a recent F1 hybrid with very white stalks.

The **Pekinensis Group** is the Chinese pe-tsai, also known as wom-bok or Chinese cabbage. The plants resemble lettuces (especially the cos lettuce) in growth form, but have strongly veined leaves. This fast-growing vegetable was introduced to Europe only in the nineteenth century and is easy to grow as long as it is kept moist. Sow seed in late spring and summer and harvest in autumn and winter. The leaves are commonly tied together around the developing heart, and the whole plant is harvested. **Michihili Group** cultivars like **'Jade Pagoda'** are early maturing; **'Hong Kong'** gives high yields. **Wong Bok Group** cultivars mature later in the growing season.

The **Rapifera Group**, the turnips, is the best known cultivar group in the West. A moderately frost-hardy biennial, the turnip is grown as an annual for its fleshy roots. It was a staple food of the northern European working classes until the potato upstaged it. It is best suited to cooler regions of the world. To produce a quick crop, sow seed in spring or autumn in fertile soil in rows and keep young plants moist throughout the growing period. The roots of cultivars are purple-topped, like the early maturing **'Purpletop White Globe'**; yellow as in **'Scots Yellow'**, an old cultivar of carrot-like form; or white like **'Tokyo Cross'**, a quick-maturing, heat-tolerant white turnip, and **'White Stone'**. **'Shogrin'** is unusual as it's grown primarily for its edible leaves. *Zones 7–11.*

Brassica rapa, Pekinensis Group cultivar

CAPSICUM
Pepper, chilli

This genus of about 10 species of annuals and shrubs from tropical America is renowned for the fiery hot taste of its fruits, used in many of the world's cuisines. Most eastern and southern Asian dishes would not be the same without them. The plants have soft but tough branches and smooth green leaves. The inconspicuous white flowers are borne singly or in small groups in the leaf axils, followed by fleshy hollow fruits that vary greatly in size, shape, color and flavor— generally, the smaller the fruit the hotter the taste. The innumerable cultivated races are usually divided among only 3 or 4 species. Some chillies are grown as ornamentals for their brightly colored fruits; they are easily confused with the similar-looking ornamental solanums whose fruits are poisonous.

Cultivation

The larger fruited chillies and sweet peppers, as well as the shorter-lived of the small chillies are grown as summer annuals and require a long, warm, humid season to ripen their fruit. The plants need rich, friable soil, as their roots are quite deep, and ample water for maximum growth. In warmer areas seed can be sown *in situ* in spring; in colder regions sow under glass and transplant when frost danger is past. The shrubby chillies require only a sheltered spot against a wall in a warm climate, and are easily propagated from cuttings. Harvest the fruits in summer and autumn.

Capsicum annuum
Capsicum, pepper

This one species encompasses most of the variation in fruit characteristics found in the genus as a whole—from the large sweet bell peppers used in salads to some of the smallest and hottest of the

Capsicum annuum, Conoides Group cultivar

Capsicum annuum, Conoides Group, 'Red Missile'

Capsicum annuum, Fasciculatum Group cultivar

Capsicum annuum, Fasciculatum Group cultivar

Capsicum annuum, Grossum Group cultivar

Capsicum annuum, Grossum Group cultivar

Capsicum annuum, Grossum Group cultivar

chillies. Despite the specific name, plants also vary from bushy annuals to quite long-lived shrubs up to 6 ft (1.8 m) tall. The species' main defining characteristic is that the flowers are mostly solitary with recurved stalks.

The many cultivars are divided into groups, depending on fruit size and shape; within each group cultivars also vary in fruit color, including shades of red, yellow, green and purple. The **Cerasiforme Group** (cherry peppers) have small, hot, globular to egg-shaped fruit; some of these are also used as ornamentals. **Conoides Group** cultivars have erect conical fruits, most small and hot, some grown as ornamentals with multi-colored fruits — **'Red Missile'** is a typical example. Its fruit start out creamy white and ripen purple through red. The **Fasciculatum Group,** known as red cone peppers, have clusters of erect elongated fruits. The well known **Grossum Group** includes the main salad peppers—pimento, bell, sweet and cubanelle peppers. The fruits are generally large and hollow, ripening from yellow to red; although some, like **'Golden Belle'**, have yellow fruit and a few, including **'Purple Belle'**, have purple peppers. Cubanelle cultivars like **'Gypsy'** are popular because they are much more prolific than the other peppers in the group. The **Longum Group** includes the cayenne peppers and paprika and banana peppers, with elongated and usually curved, moderately hot to very hot fruits. **'Long Sweet Yellow'** is a popular banana cultivar with long pale yellow fruit that ripen to red. *Zones 8–12.*

Capsicum frutescens
Tabasco pepper, chilli pepper

This species consists of short-lived perennials and longer-lived shrubs, the latter sometimes growing to 8 ft (2.5 m) tall and becoming quite woody. They are distinguished from *Capsicum annuum* by having two or more flowers in most leaf axils, their stalks recurved only at the top and generally smaller leaves. Grown as a perennial, *C. frutescens* has short stems, woody at the base, about 3 ft (1 m) high. Fruits vary considerably between the cultivars but all are small to very small and very hot; they are used mainly for pickling or in hot sauces. The **Tabasco** strain comes from the town of that name in southern Mexico, while **Thai Hot** is a strain renowned in Southeast Asia for its fierce taste. *Zones 9–12.*

CHENOPODIUM

Weedy annuals and perennials account for most of the 100 or so species in this worldwide genus, but it includes a few

Capsicum annuum, Longum Group cultivar

useful plants as well. These are mostly low-growing plants with leaves similar to spinach and terminal clusters of tiny greenish flowers. Some are used as green vegetables, some as medicinal herbs, while 2 species were grown as grain crops in the high Andes before being displaced by European cereals. The common weed fat hen (*Chenopodium album*) is valued as a poultry feed and its young leaves were once used as a vegetable. *Chenopodium bonus-henricus* is the most commonly cultivated as a perennial leaf vegetable.

Cultivation

Chenopodium bonus-henricus requires a moist temperate climate, a sheltered position and fertile, well-prepared soil with good drainage. Plant in early to mid-spring; harvest in summer. Propagate from seed or divide plants from the previous year.

Chenopodium bonus-henricus
Good King Henry, blite

This perennial makes a 12–15 in (30–40 cm) high and wide clump, the leaves broadly arrowhead-shaped. In late spring and summer it produces narrow panicles of tiny yellow-green flowers. The tender young leaves can be used like spinach, or the emerging roots can be blanched and eaten like asparagus. *Zones 4–9.*

Chenopodium bonus-henricus

CICHORIUM

This genus of 8 species of annuals and perennials from Europe, western Asia and northern Africa is closely related to the lettuce genus *Lactuca*. Two species are grown in temperate-climate gardens mainly as salad plants, sometimes blanched. The plants have basal tufts of large, crisp, tongue-shaped leaves, which exude pinhead drops of milky sap when broken. Their usually blue, dandelion-like flowerheads are borne on tall branched stems and open only for the morning.

Cultivation

Mostly frost-hardy, they need full sun. When growing as leaf vegetables plant in fertile, humus-rich, well-drained soil and keep moist, or the plants will run to seed early. Sow seeds 12–15 in (30–38 cm) apart in a shaded position in late summer. Apply a liquid fertilizer occasionally while the plants are growing. Harvest in autumn. Watch for attack by slugs and for rust-fungus and mildew. They can also be propagated from root division.

Cichorium endivia cultivar

Cichorium endivia 'Sally'

Cichorium endivia
Endive, escarole

This close relative of chicory is an
annual or biennial grown for its leaves,
which are usually eaten green as a bitter
salad; they resemble lettuce but are more
sharply flavored. The plant is loose
hearted, like a mignonette lettuce but all
green. The wild origins of endive are
uncertain, and it may be an old hybrid.
'Batavian' is a particularly broad-leafed
endive with a large head of edible
foliage. Other popular varieties, such as
'Green Curled' and 'Sally' have more
divided and crisped leaves. *Zones 4–10.*

Cichorium intybus
Chicory, witloof, radicchio

In some countries chicory is best known
as a coffee substitute, as the roots are
roasted and ground for this purpose. In
France, Belgium and Italy, however, this
species has produced a range of leaf
vegetables widely used for cooking—the
true 'endive' of the French belongs to
this species, not to *Cichorium endivia*. It
has the same geographical range as the
genus as a whole and is also widely
naturalized along roadsides in the
temperate regions of other continents,
conspicuous by its pale blue flowers in
summer and autumn. Chicories vary
greatly in leaf coloring and shape, some
having red or purple-shaded leaves, such
as 'Palo Rosa Bella', others having curly

Cichorium intybus cultivar

Cichorium intybus 'Palo Rosa Bella'

or deeply cut leaves. They can be grown
either like small lettuces for their leaves,
or forced indoors for their shoots. The
latter method is popular in cooler
regions where blanched shoots or
'chicons' are produced by forcing the
roots into growth in a dark cellar in
winter, or by tying the leaves around the
growing shoot. 'Witloof' is a popular
cultivar for forcing indoors, where it
produces enlarged roots and leaves, both
of which are edible. *Zones 4–10.*

COLOCASIA

This genus of the arum family from tropical Asia consists of 6 species of evergreen tuberous perennials. The large, prominently veined leaves are heart- or arrowhead-shaped and held on tall stalks that join the blade a little in from the edge. The flowering stems appear at any time of the year and are like small pale yellow or cream calla lilies, with a delicate fragrance. At least 2 *Colocasia* species are grown for their edible tubers and others are occasionally grown as ornamentals. Cooked young shoots are eaten like asparagus; the starchy tubers can be boiled or roasted like potatoes.

Cultivation

Frost-tender plants, they like a sheltered but sunny position and fertile, humus-rich soil. Keep the soil around the plant base firm to support the slender stem. Plant in spring, water abundantly in the summer growing season and harvest tubers 8 months after planting. Propagate by division.

Colocasia esculenta

syn. *Colocasia antiquorum*

Taro

Widely grown in many tropical and subtropical regions for their edible tubers, this species can stand 4–8 ft (1.2–2.4 m) tall, the long leaf-stalks supporting heart-shaped, mid- to dark green leaves up to 24 in (60 cm) long; the plants can spread by slender runners. *Colocasia esculenta* var. *antiquorum* (eddoe) has smaller but more numerous tubers. The ornamental cultivar **'Fontanesii'** has dark purple stalks and bronze-tinted leaves. The innumerable edible cultivars vary in the presence and amount of irritant crystals in the tubers, which may need removal by repeated boiling. *Zones 10–12.*

CUCUMIS

Cucumber, gourd, melon

Two genera of the cucurbit family— *Cucurbita* and *Cucumis*—have produced a range of very important food plants. *Cucumis*, in particular, has given us the cucumber and also most of the melons. It consists of 30 or more species and occurs wild in Africa, southern Asia and Australia. Annual or perennial tendril climbers or prostrate scrambling vines, they have thin, lobed or angled leaves and white or yellow flowers, of different sexes usually on the same plant. The cucumbers produce cylindrical to spherical, usually green-skinned fruits. Some are striped or have irregular rows of warty or prickly protuberances, others are completely smooth. They are mostly used as salad vegetables, for pickling, or can be lightly cooked.

Cultivation

Plant in humus-rich soil and water generously. A dry climate is preferable as humid conditions can affect the quality of the fruits and make the plants susceptible to the fungus anthracnose. Hand pollinate if growing melons on a small scale. Propagate from seed.

Cucumis sativus

Cucumber, gherkin

A native of India, the cucumber is an annual trailing plant that grows to 18 in (45 cm) high with a 6 ft (1.8 m) spread. It has leaves with shallow, pointed lobes and yellow funnel-shaped flowers. The usually green-skinned fruit have a crisp white flesh with numerous seeds that are eaten with the flesh when immature. Cucumbers come in many different shapes and sizes, representing different cultivated varieties, though the flavor varies only slightly. Some smaller types have been developed for pickling and

Cucumis sativus cultivar

are known as gherkins. In cool climates, cucumbers are normally grown in greenhouses, or the seedlings are raised under glass in winter or spring for summer planting. Train cucumber vines on a frame or trellis to keep the fruit away from the soil. They are quite vulnerable to downy mildew, though the long green kinds are more resistant than the short 'apple' cucumbers. All cucumbers are picked at an early stage of maturity, which encourages further fruit production as well as yielding tastier cucumbers. Plant in spring or early summer, harvest summer or autumn. *Zones 9–12.*

CUCURBITA
Marrow, pumpkin, squash

All 27 species of this important genus are native to the Americas, mostly from the warmer, drier regions. Archeological excavations have established that their history of domestication dates back to 7000 BC in Central America and 1000 BC in North America. Modern pumpkins and squashes come in a vast array of shapes, sizes and colors and it is often difficult to assign a particular cultivar to a species. Some recognized species are in fact believed to be ancient hybrids. The cultivated species are annuals, generally with trailing stems radiating from a central root, and large, rough-textured leaves that are lobed in varying degree. Different sexes of the large orange or yellow flowers are borne on the same plant; the fruits develop below the female flowers, which soon wither and drop off. Classification of cultivar groups is complicated by the great variation in common names used in different countries: the 'pumpkin' of North America is usually *Cucurbita pepo* or *C. moschata*, while elsewhere pumpkin may refer to *C. maxima*. Some pumpkin varieties have produced enormous fruits, sometimes exceeding 400 lb (180 kg).

Cultivation

Most species of this genus are easy to raise, needing just a warm, rich soil. In warm climates sow seed from early spring to late summer; in cold climates sow indoors in early summer, watering all seedlings well before planting. Plant seedlings 38 in (90 cm) apart for bush varieties, and 4 ft (1.2 m) apart for trailing varieties. They grow best planted on raised mounds of soil mixed with well-rotted compost and manure. Keep well irrigated as they are water hungry. Harvest in autumn. Check for slugs.

Cucurbita maxima
Pumpkin, autumn squash, winter pumpkin, winter squash

Originating in subtropical South America, this species has long-running stems and large, nearly circular leaves

Cucurbita maxima cultivar

Cucurbita maxima cultivar

that are hardly lobed. Its distinctive feature is the fruit stalk, which is large, not ridged, and a soft corky texture. It includes a large group of pumpkins with very hard blue-gray or orange skins, including the gigantic show pumpkins, some of the pumpkins used for livestock feed, and some of the winter squashes including a great variety of shapes, sizes and colors, often with ornamented skins. **'Crown Prince'** has very attractive, gray-blue fruit that keeps for a long time and is very good for cooking. **'Golden Nugget'** is a bush variety with small, late-maturing fruit that has deep orange, slightly sweet flesh. **'Laternenkürbis St Martin'** is a popular European cultivar. *Zones 9–11.*

Cucurbita maxima 'Laternenkürbis St Martin'

Cucurbita pepo cultivar

5-lobed. The fruits vary greatly but are often elongated or bottle-shaped and some are bent over at the top (crook-neck squashes); they include also the butternut and other pumpkins. Most cultivars of this species ripen their fruit in autumn or winter. One of the most popular cultivars, **'Butternut'** has golden yellow-orange bottle-shaped fruit with a straight neck. *Zones 8–11.*

Cucurbita pepo
Gourd, pumpkin, summer squash, vegetable marrow
Originating in Mexico and southern USA, and possibly an ancient hybrid, this species has given rise to a broader range of cultivars than any other. The plants can be either compact or have long trailing stems and the leaves usually have deep, overlapping lobes. The summer squashes vary from elongated to broad and flattened with scalloped rims and there are some crooknecked

Cucurbita moschata cultivar

Cucurbita moschata
Crookneck squash, pumpkin, winter squash
Originating somewhere in Central America, this species was probably the earliest to be domesticated. The stems are long running or may climb by tendrils, and the leaves are shallowly

Cucurbita pepo cultivar

Cucurbita pepo 'Atlantic Giant'

varieties; a number also have ornamented skins. Vegetable marrows have
long fruit with rather tender skins,
usually green or yellow; an important
development from these are the
zucchinis or courgettes, harvested when
very immature and treated like a green
vegetable. Vegetable spaghetti is a
variety of squash with rather dry,
shreddy flesh. A number of pumpkins
also belong to this species, some used
mainly for stock food; they do not keep
well and are normally eaten soon after
picking. **'Atlantic Giant'** has large
striped fruit. **'Rouge Vif d'Etampes'** has
rich vermilion fruit. *Zones 8–11.*

CYNARA

The 10 species of perennials, thistle
relatives from the Mediterranean of
statuesque proportions, are grown for
their large silvery gray, deeply divided
leaves and their thistle-like flowerheads.
The genus includes the globe artichoke,
with its edible immature flowerheads, and
the cardoon which has edible leaf stalks.

Cultivation

Grow in full sun and in a fertile well-
drained soil. To be seen to best
advantage they need plenty of space.
Propagate from seed by offsets that are
formed around the crown.

Cynara scolymus
Globe artichoke

Once considered to be an aphrodisiac,
the globe artichoke has delicate, gray-
green leaves and is easy to grow in most
soils and positions. Make sure it has
enough space (one or two plants are
enough in a small garden). A rich soil

Cucurbita pepo 'Rouge Vif d'Etampes'

will mean better production. Plant suckers rather than seeds about 3 ft (1 m) apart in early spring. Remove yellowing leaves and stems in autumn.

Cut the plump flower buds from the plants in spring and summer before the flowers begin to open. Watch for leaf spot disease. *Zones 6–10.*

Cynara scolymus cultivar

DAUCUS

This genus of about 25 species of annuals and biennials has a wide natural distribution in Europe, temperate Asia, Africa, Australia and New Zealand and in the case of the carrot, *Daucus carota*, an even wider distribution in cultivation. The carrot is the only form cultivated and is not a wild species as such but a form of one developed over centuries by cultivation. Cultivated carrots are generally biennials producing ferny, divided leaves and a fleshy, usually orange tap root in their first year, then a long flowerstalk with a large flattish umbel of tiny white flowers in the second year. Wild carrots generally have white roots (some purple) but cultivated varieties have been developed with orange, red or yellow roots.

Cultivation

Sow carrot seed *in situ* any time from early spring to early autumn, in a sunny site in fertile, well-drained, loam soil.

Sow in rows about 10 in (25 cm) apart, making sure the earth is firmly compacted around the seeds. Keep the ground moist and thin the rows out when the seedlings are about 1 in (2.5 cm) high. Carrots give high yields even in a small garden and can be stored in bins or boxes between layers of sand. Harvest carrots as soon as they are big enough in winter, as wet weather causes the root to split. Check for carrot-root fly, greenfly and aphids. Propagate from seed.

Daucus carota subsp. *sativus*
Carrot

This everyday root vegetable is thought to have originated in Afghanistan and was introduced to Europe 600 years ago. Many varieties are available including 'Nantes' and 'Touchon' which have a longish, cylindrical root with a distinct orange-yellow core and orange-red skin. *Zones 3–11.*

Daucus carota subsp. *sativus* cultivar

Daucus carota subsp. *sativus* cultivar

Daucus carota subsp. *sativus* cultivar

DIOSCOREA
Yam

Named after the Greek physician Dioscorides, this very large genus of about 600 species is found throughout the tropics as well as in some more temperate regions. Many produce poisonous tubers, but there are about 10 species that are regularly cultivated and are edible when cooked. Yams are slender climbing plants and the tubers can be formed both below and above ground. The alternate leaves are heart-shaped and the spikes of tiny flowers are either solitary or clustered. The fruits are capsules containing winged seeds.

Cultivation

These frost-tender plants require good drainage and a fertile soil high in organic matter, like well-rotted manure or compost dug in at planting time in spring. Each plant should be staked. The period of growth is from 7 to 12 months, varying with the species. If the tubers are not dug up they continue to grow for years. Propagate from seed, by division or by slicing small pieces, each with 2 or 3 dormant buds, from the upper part of an old tuber.

Dioscorea alata
Greater yam

Widely grown in the West Indies and in West Africa, this is by far the most important of the cultivated yams. It has pointed heart-shaped leaves and bulbils are sometimes borne on the stem. These can be used for propagation. Each plant may produce up to 3 large tubers which have a brown outer skin and white flesh; they are high in starch and contain about 70 per cent water. Different cultivars produce tubers of different shapes. The tubers store well. *Zones 10–12.*

Dioscorea elephantipes
syn. *Testudinaria elephantipes*
Elephant's foot, Hottentot bread

Although this species was once cooked and eaten by the indigenous people of southern Africa, it is now grown primarily by succulent plant enthusiasts. It is a twining plant with heart-shaped leaves, but its most striking feature is the enormous tuber, which sits on the ground; its thick corky bark is broken up into broad plates or ridges. It requires deep soil, good drainage and ideally, semi-arid conditions. It is also useful as a greenhouse plant. *Zones 10–11.*

ELEOCHARIS
Spike-rush

This genus contains about 150 species of rhizomatous sedges occurring in most parts of the world. They have erect, green cylindrical stems, each topped by a short spike of tiny flowers among flat, overlapping bracts. One species, *Eleocharis dulcis*, is cultivated in China and southern Asia for its edible tubers, which are eaten fresh or cooked.

Cultivation

Eleocharis dulcis needs rich soil and a hot summer. Traditionally the tubers are planted about 3 ft (1 m) apart in spring, and the soil flooded to a depth of about 4 in (10 cm). In autumn the field is drained and the tubers dug up. In warm areas plants can be raised in shallow water or ponds.

Eleocharis dulcis
Water chestnut, Chinese water chestnut

This is the species most commonly grown in Asia for its dark brown edible tubers, which have a nut-like texture and a sweet taste. Each tuber produces a tuft of long tubular leaves and numerous slender horizontal rhizomes. It grows to a height of 3 ft (1 m). *Zones 9–12.*

Dioscorea elephantipes

GLYCINE

This is a genus of 18 species of slender, twining or trailing perennial legumes, the majority native to Australia but some from eastern Asia and the Pacific islands. They have alternate compound leaves composed of 3 leaflets and pea-like flowers followed by narrow, oblong seed pods. The only cultivated species is *Glycine max*, the soya bean.

Cultivation

Frost-tender, the soya bean thrives in hot humid summer climates in fertile, well-drained soil. Water well in dry periods. Sow seed in spring and harvest pods in late summer or autumn.

Glycine max
Soya bean, soybean

The soya bean is an ancient Chinese crop and has been used for at least 5000 years as a food and medicine. The origins of the plant are obscure, but it is believed to have derived from *Glycine soja*

Glycine max cultivar

(syn. *G. ussuriensis*), a wild plant from eastern Asia. It is a branching, twining perennial with a varying height of up to 6 ft (1.8 m). The alternate, trifoliate leaves are softly pubescent. Small white or lilac pea-flowers borne in summer are immediately followed by hairy pods containing 2 to 4 seeds. Numerous cultivars of this important agricultural crop have been developed. *Zones 9–11.*

HELIANTHUS

This genus of the daisy family includes the Jerusalem artichoke, with edible tubers, some others used as ornamentals or for livestock fodder, in addition to its best known member the sunflower, one of the world's most important oilseed plants. Consisting of around 70 species of annuals and perennials, all native to the Americas, they have large daisy-like, usually golden yellow flowerheads, which make a long display from summer to autumn. The plants have hairy, often sticky leaves and tall, rough stems.

Cultivation

Jerusalem artichokes are easy to grow in most well-drained soil and may even become invasive. Plant the tubers in spring, 6 in (15 cm) deep and 18 in (45 cm) apart. Harvest in autumn after flowering.

Helianthus tuberosus
Jerusalem artichoke

This sunflower relative gained the common name 'artichoke' because its edible tubers were thought to taste like those of the true artichoke *(Cynara scolymus)*; 'Jerusalem' came from a mis-

hearing of the Italian for sunflower, *girasole*. Native to the USA and Canada, it is sometimes regarded as a weed; it spreads rapidly, making a forest of slender stems terminating in small yellow flowerheads. A popular vegetable in some parts of Europe, it is not always realized that the tubers contain the carbohydrate inulin, not used by the human digestive system, therefore having little food value. Native Americans fermented the tubers in pits, converting inulin to digestible sugars. *Zones 4–10.*

Helianthus tuberosus cultivar

Ipomoea batatas cultivar

IPOMOEA

syns *Calonyction, Mina, Pharbitis, Quamoclit*

Morning glory

This large genus of some 300 mostly climbing, evergreen shrubs, perennials and annuals is widespread throughout the tropics and warm-temperate regions of the world. It includes sweet potato and some of the loveliest tropical flowering vines. Most species have a twining habit and masses of funnel-shaped flowers, which in many species wither by midday. The flowers are usually short-lived, lasting only one day (or night), but bloom prolifically and in succession.

Cultivation

Sweet potatoes need a warm, ideally tropical, climate. They prefer moderately fertile, well-drained, sandy soil and a sunny position. In spring, plant pieces of sprouted tuber or cuttings in soil that has been fertilized and dug thoroughly; water well while the tubers grow. Harvest in late autumn when the leaves die back.

Ipomoea batatas

Sweet potato, kumara

From Central America and the Pacific islands, this perennial climber comes in both white-fleshed and orange-fleshed forms. It has entire, toothed or 3-lobed leaves and flowers with a lavender to pale purple tube that is darker on the inside. *Zones 9–12.*

LACTUCA

Lettuce

This widespread genus of around 100 species is best represented in temperate Eurasia. It includes a number of common weeds but is best known in the form of *Lactuca sativa* — the common lettuce — which appears to have been in cultivation for at least 5000 years and is thought to be derived from the weedy 'prickly lettuce', **L. serriola**, whose seeds also yield an edible oil. Species may be annual, biennial or perennial and range from 4 in (10 cm) to over 6 ft (1.8 m) high. If allowed to flower, this member of the daisy family has large sprays of small blooms, often mauve or yellow. The non-edible species contain very bitter compounds that have sedative properties and some have been used medicinally.

Cultivation

They are easily grown in any moist but well-drained, humus-rich soil in full sun or part-shade. In cool climates sow seed from early spring to late summer; in warm climates, from autumn to mid-spring, though some heat-tolerant varieties can be grown in summer. Thin the seedlings gradually until they are 12 in (30 cm) apart. For tender, succulent leaves ensure soil remains moist. Shade young plants in hot weather and feed at intervals with weak liquid manure.

Lactuca sativa
Common lettuce

This leafy annual, grown for its succulent crisp leaves, comes in a large number of shapes and flavors. Popular types include the common iceberg or crisphead with globular heads like pale green cabbages; cos or Romaine lettuce with tall upright growth and crisp well-flavored leaves; butterhead, a small variety with waxy light green outer

Lactuca sativa cultivar

Lactuca sativa 'Black Seeded Simpson'

Lactuca sativa 'Bubbles'

leaves and a firm heart; and the popular loose-leaf varieties with leaves that can be picked a few at a time as they mature. All come in an array of cultivars. **'Black Seeded Simpson'**, a loose-leaf variety with good vitamin C content, is popular in the USA. **'Bubbles'** is a compact semi-cos with blistered leaves, sweet and nutty. **'Buttercrunch'** is a loose-hearted cultivar with very crisp central leaves. **'Frisby'** has tight heads of bright green, crinkly leaves. **'Green Salad Bowl'**, a loose-leaf variety with bright green frilly leaves, is good for cutting all summer.

Lactuca sativa 'Frisby'

Lactuca sativa 'Green Salad Bowl'

Lactuca sativa 'New Red Fire'

Lactuca sativa 'Lakeland'

Lactuca sativa 'Lollo Rossa'

Lactuca sativa, Oak Leaf cultivar

'**Lakeland**' is an excellent, crisp-leafed iceberg variety that is similar to '**Great Lakes**'. '**Lolli Bionda**' is a loose-leaf, non-hearting variety with decorative frilly leaves that can make an ornamental edging plant. '**Lollo Rossa**' is another loose-leaf variety; its rich reddish purple curly leaves may be cut at any time of year. '**New Red Fire**' is an iceberg with a green heart and reddish bronze outer leaves. The **Oak Leaf** types are loose-leafed, the leaves divided into narrow, finger-like lobes: '**Red Oak Leaf**' has reddish brown leaves; '**Red Salad Bowl**' has reddish brown leaves with a hint of bitterness. Other red-leafed lettuces include the Batavian loose-leaf '**Red Sails**', with crinkled dark reddish bronze

Lactuca sativa 'Red Sails'

leaves,and the smooth-leafed **'Rouge d'Hiver'**, one of the hardier red lettuces for winter cutting. **'Saladini'** is sold as a seed mixture of many different types of loose-leaf lettuces and lettuce-like greens. **'Simpson Flute'** has bright green frilly leaves. **'Target'** is a tight-hearted, almost cabbage-like lettuce. Celtuce, *Lactuca sativa* **var.** *augustana* (syn. *L. s.* var. *asparagina*), has an edible stem, similar to celery stalk and edible bright green, curled leaves. *Zones 7–12.*

Lactuca sativa 'Rouge d'Hiver'

Lactuca sativa 'Target'

Lactuca sativa 'Simpson Flute'

LYCOPERSICON
Tomato

There are 7 species in this Central and South American genus of annuals and short-lived evergreen perennials, closely allied to the much larger genus *Solanum* which includes the potato and the eggplant. The tomato was cultivated at the time of the Spanish conquest by the Incas in Ecuador and Peru and the Aztecs in Mexico. For centuries it was regarded with suspicion by Europeans; it was only in the early nineteenth century that the tomato finally gained worldwide acceptance as a food plant. The genus name *Lycopersicon* is from the Greek meaning 'wolf peach' and applied originally to an unrelated Egyptian plant; Linnaeus somewhat arbitrarily named the tomato *Solanum lycopersicum* and the name stuck.

Cultivation

Tomatoes require a long, warm growing season. In cool climates the seedlings need to be started under glass in spring so fruit development can take place during the brief summer. Plant in fertile, well-drained soil that receives at least 6 hours of direct sunlight. Position stakes before planting and set plants about 24 in (60 cm) apart when all danger of frost is over; in cool climates use cloches to protect young seedlings. Keep soil moist but not too wet and feed regularly while fruit are developing. A variety of pests and diseases attack tomatoes, and disease resistance is one of the main aims of breeders.

Lycopersicon esculentum
syn. *Lycopersicon lycopersicum*
Tomato

This soft-stemmed, spreading plant up to 6 ft (1.8 m) high has strong-smelling, deeply lobed leaves and yellow flowers followed by soft succulent fruit. The fruit are generally red or yellow and vary considerably in size and shape among the numerous cultivars. Fruit allowed to

Lycopersicon esculentum cultivar

Right: *Lycopersicon esculentum* cultivar

Lycopersicon esculentum var. *cerasiforme* cultivar

ripen on the vine before harvesting have the most flavor. Among the most widely grown traditional red cultivars are **'Beefsteak'**, which is tall, with large rounded fruit, **'Grosse Lisse'**, with very sweet, large soft fruit, and **'Phyra'**, a popular cultivar in Europe. **'Tiny Tim'** is a bushy tomato, excellent for growing in containers and producing medium-sized fruit. Some cultivars have plum- or pear-shaped rather than rounded fruit: **'Red Pear'** has pear-shaped red fruit, while **'Yellow Pear'** yields big crops of golden yellow, pear-shaped fruit, 2 in (5 cm) long. The elongated Roma tomatoes, popular in Italy, include **'Plumito'** and **'Super Roma'**. An unusual group are the eastern European black tomatoes, like **'Black Russian'**. Cherry tomatoes, sometimes designated by the name *Lycopersicon esculentum* **var.** *cerasiforme*, bear long decorative strings of cherry-size, sweet red, orange or yellow fruit. *Zones 8–12.*

Lycopersicon esculentum cultivar

Lycopersicon esculentum 'Phyra'

Lycopersicon pimpinellifolium
Currant tomato
As its common name implies, this species from northern South America has fruit the size of currants, mostly under ½ in (12 mm) in diameter. The vigorous plant is very prolific, bearing fruit in 2 rows on long sprays. The tiny tomatoes are used mostly for pickling and sauces. The plants' vigor and disease resistance make them a useful rootstock for the production of grafted tomatoes, now available in nurseries. Currant tomatoes have also been used recently by plant breeders to introduce new genes to cherry tomatoes. *Zones 8–12.*

MANIHOT
There are about 100 species of trees and shrubs in this genus, all attractive foliage plants found in tropical and warm-temperate America. Several species have economic importance as food crops. The long-stalked leaves are 3- to 9-lobed, while the bell-shaped flowers appear in racemes or panicles.

Cultivation
These plants require a warm wet growing season followed by a dry period and good drainage. Propagate from cuttings of mature stem about 6 in (15 cm) long.

Manihot esculenta
Cassava, tapioca
A variable species, cassava is a shrubby perennial, 3–10 ft (1–3 m) high, with palmately lobed leaves of up to 9 lance-shaped leaflets. The roots, which radiate from the base of the plant, may grow up to 4 ft (1.2 m) long and contain about 30 per cent starch. Cassava meal, obtained from the tuberous roots is used in soups and puddings, to preserve meat and sauces and as a glue. A form of sugar, various alcoholic drinks and acetone are other end products. Cyanide is also obtained from the roots. *Zones 10–12.*

MARANTA

This is a genus of 32 species of ever-green rhizomatous perennials from the tropical forests of Central and South America. One species, *Maranta arundinacea*, is an important crop plant: it is better known to cooks as arrowroot. Apart from the beautifully marked and textured leaves, they are known for their habit of 'going to sleep' at night. The leaves spread by day and stand erect at night.

Cultivation

Arrowroot requires a tropical climate and thrives in sandy, low-lying areas but needs plentiful water in summer. Propagation is mainly by division of the rhizomes in early summer and the starchy roots are harvested after 6–12 months' growth. They are pounded and washed in water. The starch is collected after it settles from the strained water.

Maranta arundinacea
Arrowroot, Bermuda arrowroot

Native to the West Indies and northern South America, this species has been spread elsewhere in the tropics and subtropics as a crop plant. It grows to about 6 ft (1.8 m) with erect branching stems, lance-shaped leaves and white flowers. The rhizomes and roots yield a starch, regarded as one of the most palatable and digestible of all starches and hence suitable nourishment for people recovering from illnesses. It was said to have been used by the native West Indians as a poultice to absorb poison from arrow wounds, hence the common name. *Zones 11–12.*

MEDICAGO
Medic, medick

This genus of 50 to 60 species of annuals, perennials and small shrubs originates in Europe, Africa and Asia and includes lucerne, *Medicago sativa*, an important commercial crop. The species are variable in size and form, although trifoliate leaves with fine hairs are common throughout. The foliage color may be bright green to silver-gray. The pea-like flowers, which are generally yellow, are carried in racemes of up to 50 blooms. They are mainly borne in summer.

Cultivation

Lucerne *(Medicago sativa)* prefers deep, well-drained soil and a temperate climate with adequate winter rainfall. Sow seed in autumn in warm areas, spring in colder climates. Harvest the seeds in late summer or autumn. Sprouts can be germinated indoors at any time of year, either on wet paper towelling or by placing pre-soaked and drained seed in a closed container.

Medicago sativa
Alfalfa, lucerne

Native to Europe, this perennial clover-like plant of the pea family has a long tap root and short clusters of purplish flowers. From time immemorial it has been used as forage for cattle, but is now also eaten in the form of sprouting seeds. Delicious in salads and on sandwiches, the sprouted seeds produce very fine shoots with a delicate, pea-like flavor. *Zones 6–10.*

OXALIS
Wood-sorrel

This is a large genus of 500 or so species of bulbous, rhizomatous and fibrous-rooted perennials and a few small, weak shrubs. Though found around the world, the greatest number of species are native to South Africa and South America. *Oxalis tuberosa* is grown for its edible tubers, used like potatoes; other species are grown for their ornamental flowers. The leaves are always compound, divided into 3 or more heart-shaped or more deeply 2-lobed leaflets in a palmate arrangement (like clover). The funnel-shaped flowers are usually pink, white or yellow, and are carried in an umbel-like cluster on slender stalks.

Cultivation
Oxalis tuberosa is hardy to most frosts and prefers a position in sun or part-shade with mulched, well-drained soil. Plant the tubers in spring and provide moderate water; harvest in winter.

Oxalis tuberosa

Oxalis tuberosa
Oca

This species is second only to the potato in importance as a root vegetable in the cooler parts of South America. Its knobbly translucent tubers are up to about 2 in (5 cm) in diameter and may be round or elongated with color varying from white to yellow or pink, sometimes with darker streaks. Only the white-tubered form will flower. Above ground, it forms a tangle of weak stems with plain green 3-part leaves; the small flowers are yellow. *Zones 7–10.*

Pastinaca sativa cultivar

Pastinaca sativa cultivar (leaves only)

Phaseolus coccineus cultivar

PASTINACA

Only one species is cultivated in this genus of 14 species of biennials or perennials found throughout Eurasia. It is the parsnip, grown for its fleshy white root with a distinctive flavor. It has simple or pinnate leaves and yellow flowers.

Cultivation

Grow in full sun in well-drained, deep, friable, stone-free soil that has been well dug. Improve poor soil with plenty of compost, but do not use fresh manure as it may cause misshapen roots. Sow seed in spring in groups of 3, spacing the groups 5 in (12 cm) apart; thin out the seedlings once they emerge. Harvest the roots when the leaves start to yellow and harvest in winter. Watch for slugs, canker, celery fly or greenfly.

Pastinaca sativa

syn. *Peucedanum sativum*

Parsnip

A hardy root vegetable related to the carrot, the parsnip is nutritious, sweet and can be grown year round in warm climates and from mid-spring in cold climates. A strong-smelling biennial that reaches 3 ft (1 m) in height, it has pinnate leaves 4–12 in (10–30 cm) long and flowers in summer. *Zones 7–10.*

PHASEOLUS

Bean

This genus, native to warm-temperate to tropical regions of the Americas, contains 36 annual and perennial species, some familiar as garden crops. Twining climbers with thin, usually bright green, trifoliate leaves, they bear racemes of white, yellow, red or purple flowers, followed by long, flat or round seed pods. In some species the pods are eaten, in others it is the beans within.

Cultivation

Beans thrive with a long, warm growing season, plenty of sunlight and ample moisture. They prefer a humus-rich yet light and well-drained soil. Some are also suitable for planting in tubs or flower beds. Sow seed from mid-spring to early summer. Watch for slugs.

Phaseolus coccineus 'Achievement'

Phaseolus coccineus cultivar

Phaseolus coccineus cultivar

Phaseolus coccineus
Scarlet runner bean

This vigorous climber comes in different varieties and can grow up to 12 ft (4 m) high. It needs a sheltered position. Sow seed in late spring in double rows 2 in (5 cm) deep and 12 in (30 cm) apart.

Provide plants with support using canes or a fence or trellis. Pick pods in summer when they reach 6 in (15 cm) long. These perennials last for several years, though they bear most heavily in their first year. **'Achievement'** has larger leaves and the flower's keel is orange. *Zones 9–11.*

Phaseolus lunatus
Lima bean, oca

Originally from Central and South America, this twining perennial climber is now widely cultivated in tropical and subtropical countries for its swollen white seeds, which are eaten either fresh or dried. It is normally cultivated as an annual. Because of its tropical origin, the lima bean needs warmer growing conditions than the French bean, but has the same cultivation method. *Zones 10–12.*

Phaseolus vulgaris
French bean, kidney bean, string bean, haricot bean

The major bean species both for green and dried beans, *Phaseolus vulgaris* displays great variation in pod, seed and growth characteristics. Thought to be a cultivated derivative of a wild species *(P. aborigineus)* from the northern Andes, it was already widely planted in pre-Columbian times. An annual, it was originally a climber but many cultivated strains are 'dwarf beans' that are better adapted to mechanical harvesting. The beans can also be divided into those grown as pulses, including the borlotti, pinto, haricot and navy beans, and those grown as green beans (a few are dual-purpose); these go by many names, including French beans, snap beans, string beans and stringless beans. The pods vary in length, whether they are round or flat, and in color from cream to yellow, green, blue-green, red or purple;

Phaseolus vulgaris cultivar

seed color may vary almost as much. Popular green bean cultivars include **'Blue Lake'**, a climber with very plump, long, tender pods, slightly bluish green; **'Bountiful'** with pencil-slim, round-sectioned beans; **'Gourmet's Delight'**; **'Hawkesbury Wonder'**, an old Australian variety, once very popular as a commercial crop; and **'Kentucky Wonder Wax'**, a climber with large golden yellow pods. **'Majestic'** is a bushy plant with round-sectioned, small-seeded, stringless beans; **'Pioneer'** is an Australian cultivar, producing long fleshy stringless pods; and **'Purple King'**, a purple-podded climbing bean that turns green when cooked. **'Slenderette'** is another popular commercial variety with small stringless

Phaseolus vulgaris 'Gourmet's Delight'

pods about 4 in (10 cm) long. There are also a number of dwarf varieties, including **'Royal Burgundy'**, which has curved, deep purple pods and purplish foliage; and **'Tendercrop'**, a dwarf with straight, plump stringless green pods. Sow seeds in spring when soil temperatures rise above 59°F (15°C) with repeat sowings to mid-summer. Sow bush varieties 2 in (5 cm) deep and 3 in (7 cm) apart, in rows about 18 in (45 cm) apart. Sow the seed of climbers 6 in (15 cm) apart in double rows 24 in (60 cm) apart; support the stems with crossing canes. The beans should be ready to harvest in about 60 days. *Zones 7–11.*

PHYLLOSTACHYS

Made up of 80 species of medium- and large-growing bamboos from Asia, these evergreen plants have spreading rhizomes that may sprout some distance from the parent plant. They are ideally suited to grove planting, and are mainly grown for their decorative foliage and graceful habit. Several bamboos, however, are cultivated for their edible shoots which are especially used in Chinese cuisine. The woody stems have nodes at intervals, and the insignificant flowers take several years to appear; as with most bamboos, the plants then die.

Cultivation

Temperate-climate plants, bamboos thrive in a sheltered position that is not too dry. Propagate from seed in either spring or autumn, or by division in spring. If they must be confined to a specific area, they can be grown in large tubs.

Phyllostachys edulis
syn. *Phyllostachys pubescens*
Edible bamboo, moso-chiku
Native to China, this bamboo has also been grown for centuries in Japan for its edible shoots. Of the several bamboos grown for eating, this species accounts for most of the canned bamboo shoots traded round the world and used in Chinese cookery. A medium-sized bamboo, it can reach 18 ft (6 m) or more in height, with deep yellow stems up to 2 in (5 cm) in diameter and tending to arch outwards. The new shoots elongate at a remarkable rate, sometimes by as much as 20 in (50 cm) a day, and should be harvested as soon as they appear above ground in spring, before they become too woody. It is moderately frost tolerant. *Zones 8–11.*

PISUM
Pea

This genus originated in the eastern Mediterranean region and peas have been part of the human diet for at least 5000 years. Only 2 species are recognized in this genus, the wild pea and the garden pea, *Pisum sativum*, grown for its tender green peas. Garden peas come in two forms: dwarf, or bush and climbing. There are many varieties of each form including the sugar or snow peas which have tender, sweet, edible pods.

Cultivation

Peas are a cool-season crop that can be enjoyed both in spring and autumn. Peas need a sunny, well-drained, previously manured soil that contains some lime and dolomite. Sow seed in mild climates from autumn until spring. Young plants are not injured by frosts, but the blossoms and pods are. In cold winter areas, sowing can be timed to give maturity when frosts have passed. A support of stretched wire on short stakes helps keep the dwarf varieties off the ground and increases productivity. Watch for mildew, mites and blight.

Pisum sativum
Garden pea

This annual species grows to 6 ft (1.8 m) tall and has branched tendrils and leaflets in pairs of 1 to 4. The flowers, to 1¼ in (3 cm) wide, are white, sometimes with pale or dark purple markings. Plant seedlings 2 in (5 cm) apart in rows 4 in (10 cm) apart. When seedlings are 3 in (8 cm) high stake them with short twigs. Keep weeds down and water when dry. Pick the pods from the lower stems. Popular cultivars include **'Alderman'**; **'Melbourne Market'**, an early-maturing dwarf cultivar with wrinkled peas; **'Snow Flake'** and **'Sugar Bon'**; and **'Telephone'**, a climbing, long-podded cultivar, producing a good crop over a long season. *Pisum sativum* var. *macrocarpum*, the snow pea or

Pisum sativum var. *macrocarpum* cultivar

Pisum sativum cultivar

Pisum sativum var. *macrocarpum* cultivar

Pisum sativam var. macrocarpum cultivar

mange-tout pea, prefers a temperate climate and a moist sandy soil. Sow 2 in (5 cm) deep when the garden is frost free and use a trellis for climbing varieties. Pick the pods when they are still immature. Snow pea cultivars include **'Mammoth Sugar'**, a tall, heavy cropping pea with pods 4 in (10 cm) long and **'Oregon Sugar Pod'**, a bushy plant with flat pea pods. *Zones 3–10.*

RAPHANUS
Radish
Eaten by Egyptian slaves and the ancient Chinese, the well-traveled radish has been used for centuries as an important cooked vegetable (the winter variety) and in salads, pickles and garnishes (the summer variety). There are 3 species in the genus; many varieties are grown in different parts of the world and vary in form from globe-shaped, oblong to cylindrical or tapered. The outside of the root varies from white through pink, to red, purple and black; some are 2-toned.

Cultivation
Radishes prefer light, moisture-retentive, well-drained soil. Sow in rows 12 in (30 cm) apart; thin out the seedlings so that the roots are not competing. Summer varieties need a little shade and should be sown at 14-day intervals through summer for a continual crop. In hot weather, keep well watered. Harvest 4 weeks after sowing in warm climates. In cooler climates wait a further 3 weeks. Winter-maturing varieties may take up to 60 days to mature and are best sown later in summer or autumn. Do not leave in the ground too long as radishes turn woody. Keep birds away from the young leaves.

Raphanus sativus 'French Breakfast'

Raphanus sativus cultivar

Raphanus sativus
Radish

This Chinese annual grows to 3 ft (1 m) and spreads to 18 in (45 cm). It has an erect, hollow stem and rough, alternate leaves. White or lilac flowers with strongly marked veins and 4 petals are borne in branching clusters. **'French Breakfast'** has cylindrical, scarlet roots with a white tip and is fairly mild tasting; very popular cultivars with round, scarlet roots include **'Rex'**, **'Round Red'** and **'Tarzan'**. *Zones 6–10.*

RHEUM

This genus contains 50 species of rhizomatous perennials from eastern Europe and central Asia to the Himalayas and China. It includes the edible rhubarb and several ornamental plants grown for their striking appearance and for their large basal leaves, which are coarsely toothed and have prominent midribs and veins. The minute, star-shaped flowers appear in summer and are followed by winged fruits.

Cultivation

Edible rhubarb is frost-hardy, preferring cold winters but a site in full sun or part-shade. It is best grown from root divisions planted in spring in fertile, phosphorus-rich soil, or can be grown from spring-sown seed. Harvest the stalks in summer by gently pulling off some of the thickest stalks as needed. Watch out for slugs and crown rot.

Rheum × *cultorum* cultivar

Rheum × *cultorum* cultivar

Rheum × *cultorum*

syns *Rheum* × *hybridum*, *R. rhabarbarum*
Rhubarb

One of the few plants grown for its edible leaf stalks, rhubarb is a tough, vigorous perennial, now thought to be a hybrid of *Rheum rhaponticum*. In spring its large leaves quickly expand from the woody, winter-dormant rhizome. The stems, at first green, are ready to eat when they have reddened. Flowering stems, usually removed from cultivated plants, if left to develop will grow to 5 ft (1.5 m) tall and are topped with heads of small red-flushed cream flowers. Eat stalks only; leaves are poisonous. *Zones 3–9.*

SECHIUM
Choko, chayote

The 6 to 8 species in this genus are native to tropical America. They are strong-growing perennial vines with 10 in (25 cm) bright green heart-shaped leaves. They are frost-tender in temperate climates. Give them plenty of space to grow, as their tendrils will grip onto and climb almost anything. The large green fruits can be boiled, baked or stewed; do not overcook or they will be tasteless. Young shoots can be cooked like asparagus.

Cultivation

Grow only in warm regions in well-drained, loose soil enriched with plenty of compost. Water well when plant growth is under way. At least 12 hours daylight is required for flowering. Propagate in spring from seed, cuttings or plant the whole fruit — on its side with the narrow end slightly exposed. Harvest young shoots in spring and the fruit in summer.

Sechium edule
Chayote, choko, chow chow, christophine, vegetable pear

This high-climbing species has thick-ened, tuberous roots and 3- to 5-lobed leaves with minute teeth. Pale yellow

Sechium edule

Solanum melongena cultivar

male flowers appear in long racemes; female flowers have a green tinge. The fruit appear in summer and are usually pear-shaped, smooth or softly spiny. *Zones 10–12.*

SOLANUM

There are over 1400 species in this genus including trees, shrubs, annuals, biennials, perennials and climbers from a range of habitats worldwide. Some are evergreen, others semi-evergreen or deciduous. The genus includes important food plants like the potato and eggplant (aubergine), though many species are dangerously poisonous. Ornamental species are grown for their flowers and fruits. The leaves are arranged alternately, while the showy flowers are solitary or in clusters, star-shaped to bell-shaped, ranging in color from white and yellow to blue and purple. The fruits are berries that contain many seeds.

Cultivation

These warm-climate plants have a wide range of requirements; most prefer full sun and rich, well-drained soil. They are commonly grown from seed in spring or cuttings in summer. They are prone to attack by spider mite, white fly and aphids.

Solanum melongena
Aubergine, eggplant, mad apple

This tropical vegetable native to Asia bears small to large fruit, their color

Solanum melongena cultivar

ranging from white through dull pinkish tones to purple-black, depending on the variety. It is an annual with erect stems (that can be spiny), ovate leaves and pale blue or deep purple flowers. A relative of the potato and tomato, it needs warm conditions and low level humidity. Sow seed in containers in spring, transferring seedlings outdoors when any danger of frost has passed. Keep moist when in growth and harvest the fruit in summer; it is ripe if it gives slightly when squeezed. *Zones 9–12.*

Solanum tuberosum
Potato

Native to South America, this is one of the most widely eaten of all vegetables. A perennial plant, it grows to a height of 30 in (75 cm) with a spread of 18 in (45 cm). It has an erect, hairy, green stem and large—to 15 in (38 cm)— pinnate, dark green leaves with 3 or 5 pairs of heart-shaped leaflets. The flowers occur in pendent clusters of white or pale violet. Potato cultivars vary in the color, size and best uses of their tubers: **'Desiree'** is a spreading cultivar with purplish black stems, producing red potatoes with pale yellow flesh; **'King Edward'** is a popular British variety introduced in the early 1900s with red- and white-mottled, kidney-shaped potatoes. **'Kipfler'** produces a heavy crop of kidney-shaped potatoes with white skins and yellow flesh. **'Pink Fir Apple'** is mainly used as a salad potato; the tubers are long and cylindrical with pink skin and waxy flesh. **'Pontiac'** is a very popular commercial

Solanum tuberosum cultivar

Solanum tuberosum cultivar

Solanum tuberosum cultivar

Spinacia oleracea cultivar

delicate, rich green large leaves that are eaten when young in salads or cooked. Two kinds are traditionally grown: the smooth seeded or marginally frost-hardy summer spinach and the fully frost-hardy prickly seeded winter type which generally has more lobed leaves.

Cultivation
Spinach develops a long tap root so benefits from a deep, enriched soil with good drainage. It is a cool season, short-day crop and grows best during the cooler temperatures of spring and autumn. Sow seed in spring or autumn, thinning seedlings so that plants are 10 in (25 cm) apart. Keep the soil free of weeds and well watered so that the plants will not run to seed. Harvest the first leaves in 8 weeks. Watch for chewing insects and downy mildew.

variety in Australia and has white-fleshed tubers. Plant seed tubers in rows in spring, 4 in (10 cm) deep and spaced 16 in (40 cm) apart. They prefer sandy, humus-rich soil. Keep well watered while in growth; harvesting will depend on the variety of the potato—new potatoes are harvested in summer, other varieties in autumn. *Zones 6–11.*

SPINACIA
Spinach
The Chinese have the first record of the spinach plant in the seventh century; it was later introduced to Spain in the eleventh century and from there spread to the rest of Europe. The genus consists of 3 species of fast-growing annuals with

Spinacia oleracea
English spinach
Native to the Middle East and partial to cool climates, this species can be a challenge to grow well. It has flowering stems to 3 ft (1 m) tall and the entire or dentate leaves are bright green. The small flowers are unisexual. *Zones 5–10.*

Spinacia oleracea cultivar

Taraxacum officinale

TARAXACUM
Dandelion

Botanists disagree about the number of species in this genus of humble weeds and wildflowers—some place it as low as 60, others as high as several hundred, including many hybrids. Most dandelions are perennials with thick tap roots, though some are biennials. They have basal rosettes of crisp green leaves, usually with sharply toothed or lobed edges. Hollow, unbranched flowering stems each bear a solitary flowerhead consisting of numerous narrow ray florets and lacking a central disc. All parts of the plants exude fine droplets of white latex when broken or cut. Some species, notably *Taraxacum officinale*, have long been used medicinally or for food; their blanched leaves and sliced roots are added to salads and the roots are roasted and ground as a coffee substitute, in the same way as the related chicory.

Cultivation

Dandelions are easy to grow in a sunny position in moist, well-drained soil. If growing as a salad vegetable treat the young plants like lettuce—sow seed, or plant pieces of tap root in spring, feed and water well and harvest the leaves before flowering, when they are less bitter.

Taraxacum officinale
Common dandelion, pissenlit

Native to Europe but found naturalized through most of the world except the tropics, this familiar plant has leaves of very variable outline, from almost smooth edged to deeply and closely lobed. The flowering stems, up to about 12 in (30 cm) tall, bear bright golden flowerheads up to 1½ in (3.5 cm) across for much of the year in milder climates, though in cold climates the plant dies back in winter. The flowers are used to make tonics, beer and wine. The plant has diuretic properties, hence the French common name of *pissenlit* or wet-the-bed. *Zones 3–10.*

TETRAGONIA

This genus allied to the ice plants (*Mesembryanthemum*) contains about 50 species, all from the southern hemisphere. They are sprawling or scrambling annuals or perennials or small shrubs. Many species have flat, rather succulent edible leaves like miniature spinach leaves; green or yellow flowers are held in axillary clusters of between 1 and 5.

Tetragonia tetragonioides

Cultivation
Many are invasive plants that are only too easily grown. They thrive in humus-rich soil in sun or morning shade and prefer ample summer moisture. Soak the seeds overnight and sow them in spring. Water regularly and harvest the leaves as needed in summer.

Tetragonia tetragonioides
syn. *Tetragonia expansa*
New Zealand spinach
Sir Joseph Banks brought this perennial plant back to England from New Zealand in the eighteenth century, but it became more popular in the USA and Europe. It occurs widely in Australia as well. A weak, almost prostrate plant up to about 12 in (30 cm) tall, it spreads to 3 ft (1 m) or more. *Zones 8–10.*

TRAGOPOGON
Widely distributed over Europe and temperate Asia, this genus consists of over 100 species of annuals, biennials and perennials belonging to the daisy family. They have solitary or sparsely branched stems, grass-like leaves and terminal, star-shaped flowerheads that are followed by large heads of thistle down. One species, salsify *(Tragopogon porrifolius)* is cultivated for its edible taproots and for its young shoots which can be used like asparagus.

Cultivation
Tragopogon grow best in temperate climates and prefer a light soil, free from stones. Sow the large seeds in lots of 3 in spring. Keep 20 cm (8 in) between the groups and 12 in (30 cm) between the rows. Mulch with compost to keep weeds down and water to maintain moisture. Harvest the roots from autumn onwards; shoots can be harvested the following spring.

Tragopogon porrifolius
Salsify, oyster plant
This biennial has narrow, grassy leaves and hollow stems bearing pinkish mauve flowerheads. It is valued for its edible white tap roots which can be baked, roasted, boiled or made into soup. This species is fairly pest and disease free, and is often grown as a companion plant. *Zones 5–10.*

VALERIANELLA
Lamb's lettuce
This genus consists of 50 or so species of annuals and biennials which occur naturally in temperate regions of the northern hemisphere. The 2–5 in (5–12 cm), linear to lanceolate leaves are rather succulent and usually in a rosette; the flowers may be white, rose or blue, and are borne in terminal cymes. Some species occur as weeds on arable land, but improved selections are cultivated in western Europe where they provide a useful winter salad crop.

Cultivation
Most species are frost resistant, but will not tolerate continual dryness. They can be grown in any sunny position in well-drained soil. Grow from seed sown in autumn or spring.

Valerianella locusta
Corn salad, lamb's lettuce
A minor weed of crops in cool to cold climates and a hardy grower, this is a good substitute for lettuce in winter. Sow the seeds in late summer and early autumn in a sunny spot in the garden. Place seeds 10 in (25 cm) apart. Make sure the soil is lightly raked and forked. Ideally, it should be planted where another crop was previously grown. Keep the soil moist and harvest the leaves as they are needed. Watch for slugs. *Zones 4–9.*

VICIA
Vetch, tare

This legume genus of around 140 species of annuals and perennials is found mainly in temperate areas of the northern hemisphere. Closely related to the sweet-pea genus *Lathyrus*, most species have the same tendrils at the ends of their pinnate leaves; an exception is *Vicia faba*, the broad bean, which has an erect habit and lacks tendrils. This is also the only species cultivated for its pods. The small flowers, usually borne in short spikes or clusters from the leaf axils, are typical pea-flowers in form though not opening very wide, and are mostly white, pink, purple or pale yellow. The pods that follow are often hairy or downy.

Vicia faba cultivar

Cultivation

Broad beans are a winter to spring crop and need a temperate climate for successful cultivation. Sow seed in autumn in well-drained, limed and manured soil (mounded into ridges if necessary), preferably following a non-leguminous crop in the same plot; where frosts are severe, delay sowing until early spring. Young plants may need staking and should not be over-watered. Harvest the beans while still green and tender, usually 2 to 3 months after planting. Watch for aphids.

Vicia faba
Broad bean, fava bean

Believed to be one of the earliest domesticated crop plants, broad beans are not known in the wild but may have been derived in cultivation from *Vicia narbonense*. An annual, growing about 30 in (75 cm) tall, it has thick, erect stems and coarse, gray-green foliage. The white flowers (red in some cultivars) with a blackish central blotch are clustered in the upper leaf axils and are followed by large, downy green pods, which can be up to 24 in (60 cm) long in some cultivars but usually much less; the large seeds, tender when immature, are white, green or occasionally crimson. As well as the vegetable strains, some varieties of this species are cultivated for fodder, known as horse beans and tic beans. Broad bean cultivars can be divided into long-podded and short-podded varieties. Popular long-podded beans are '**Aqua-dulce Claudia**', an especially frost-hardy cultivar; '**Early Long Pod**'; '**Exhibition Longpod**', a heavy cropping plant with white beans; '**Leviathan Longpod**'; and '**Red Epicure**', which has unusual red beans in a green pod. Short-podded cultivars include '**Green Windsor**', with characteristic curved pods. *Zones 7–10.*

VIGNA

This genus of beans consists of about 150 species of leguminous plants found mostly in the tropical parts of the world. The leaves are divided into 3 leaflets and the pea-flowers are produced in terminal clusters on long stems. Seed pods can vary in size from 2 in to 36 in (5–90 cm) long and contain small kidney-shaped or round seeds in various colors. The seeds of all are edible and some species are grown for bean sprouts, especially in Asian countries. Several species are also cultivated for cattle food and for green manure.

Cultivation

All can be readily raised from seed in a warm climate. Sow seed in spring in fertile, moist but well-drained soil in full sun. Water well during the growing season, but less during winter. Frost-tender, vignas can be grown in a green-house in cooler climates.

Vigna radiata
Mung bean, bean sprout

Native to Burma and India, mung beans are popular as sprouting vegetables and have been an important part of the diet of the people in Asia for thousands of years. It is the green type of mung bean which is commonly used to sprout. They can be grown on a small scale at home and only take a few days to sprout. Mung beans are eaten raw in salads and lightly steamed in Oriental dishes. *Zones 10–11.*

Vigna unguiculata
Cowpea

Originally from tropical Africa, this species is now widely cultivated for its immature pods and seeds which are cooked as a green vegetable or dried and cooked like dried beans. *Vigna unguiculata* subsp. *susquipedalis* is the asparagus bean or yard-long bean with succulent pods sometimes reaching 3 ft (1 m) in length. It is popular as a green vegetable in some countries. With sufficient warm weather, cowpeas will thrive in a nitrogen- and lime-rich, well-drained soil. Sow seed in spring about 6 in (15 cm) apart in rows. Water thoroughly in dry weather. Harvest the beans in summer. *Zones 10–11.*

ZEA

The maize or sweet corn genus is now thought to include 4 species of annual and perennial grasses from Central America; the crop species may be an ancient hybrid, its grains found in archeological excavations up to 5600 years old. They bear terminal male panicles with solitary 'ears'; the female inflorescences have numerous spikelets in rows on a thick axis enclosed within a 'husk', from which only the long silky styles emerge; these are followed by a 'cob' of fleshy kernels. Ornamental cultivars are grown for their variegated leaves and multi-colored cobs.

Cultivation

Grow corn in full sun in fertile, moist, well-drained soil. Sow seed in spring or early summer in short rows 24 in (60 cm) apart. Water well in dry weather and stake as the stems grow taller. Harvest when the corn kernels are yellow by twisting the cobs firmly from the stem. They may be prone to aphids.

Zea mays cultivar

Zea mays cultivar

Zea mays
Sweet corn, maize, mealy

This robust annual grows to 12 ft
(3.5 m) tall with arching, lance-shaped,
waxy leaves. It produces terminal
panicles of male flowers to 8 in (20 cm)
long, and female inflorescences of the
same length. The flowers are followed in
late summer or early autumn by cobs
with usually yellow, sweet, edible grains.
Popular cultivars include 'Golden
Beauty'; 'Jubilee', an early-maturing
cultivar; 'Miracle' with particularly
sweet grains; and 'Rosella'. Supersweet
varieties have very sweet grains with a
high sugar content like 'Honey 'n' Pearl'
and 'Sweet Perfection'. *Zones 7–11.*

Zea mays cultivar

Zea mays cultivar

Herbs

Allium sativum cultivar

ALLIUM

Several species in this genus are used as vegetables for their edible leaves and bulbs, but some are used as herbs for adding flavor to food. See under 'Vegetables' for genus and cultivation information.

Allium sativum
Garlic

The common garlic is quite like an onion above ground but the bulb is compound, its tight papery sheath enclosing several to many daughter bulbs or 'cloves'. The pungent cloves are valued around the world for cooking and are also used medicinally to treat and prevent infections. It is unknown in the wild, but closely related plants are found in central Asia. Small umbels of dainty deep pink to white flowers are borne in summer on stalks about 18 in (45 cm) tall. Plant individual cloves 2 in (5 cm) deep in autumn in warmer areas or in spring in frosty areas. Garlic takes 5 or 6 months to mature; harvest when the leaves have turned yellow. Garlic planted near roses helps to keep aphids away. *Zones 7–10.*

Allium schoenoprasum 'Forescate'

Allium schoenoprasum
Chives

The narrow, cylindrical leaves of this perennial are used for flavoring and garnishing savory dishes. It forms small, neat clumps, to 10 in (25 cm) tall, and bears numerous balls of mauve flowers in late spring and summer, which are edible. Sow seed or divide and replant clumps in spring. Grow in full sun or part-shade and keep well watered. Lift and divide the clumps every 2 or 3 years to invigorate the tufts. Chives make attractive edging for the herb garden and can be grown in window boxes, troughs and flower pots. Frequent cutting stimulates bushy growth and more tender leaves. A vigorous cultivar, 'Forescate' has rose-pink flowers. *Zones 5–10.*

Allium schoenoprasum cultivar

Allium tuberosum
Chinese chives, garlic chives

Cultivated for centuries in India and China, this edible species is now widely grown for its leaves, used as a green vegetable. It grows up to 18 in (45 cm) high and has flat, narrow leaves and angled flowering stems. Fragrant, star-shaped white flowers are borne from summer to autumn. Although grown in the tropics, it is fairly frost tolerant. Sow seed in spring or divide and replant mature clumps. It prefers rich, moist soil. *Zones 7–11.*

ANETHUM
Dill

This genus consists of a single species, the commonly cultivated dill *(Anethum graveolens)*. Dill has a long wiry root, upright hollow stems and ferny foliage very similar to that of fennel *(Foeniculum vulgare)*. Umbels of tiny bright yellow flowers develop at the stem tips and are

Allium tuberosum cultivar

followed by the pungent seeds. The foliage and seeds of dill are widely used in pickling and fish dishes. The foliage is best used before flowering. It also has medicinal uses, most notably as an indigestion remedy.

Cultivation

Only moderately frost-hardy, dill is easily grown in any moist, well-drained, humus-rich soil in sun. The seed is best sown in spring where it is to grow, as seedlings are difficult to transplant. Dill often self-sows.

Anethum graveolens
Dill

Originally from southwestern Asia, this deliciously aromatic annual grows to about 3 ft (1 m) high with leaves divided into thread-like, fragile segments. Yellow flowers are borne in summer followed by the pungent dill seeds. Both leaves and seeds are used for flavoring. *Zones 5–10.*

ANGELICA

This genus of 50 or so species is mainly indigenous to the cooler parts of the northern hemisphere. One species, *Angelica archangelica*, has long been used as a medicinal herb and for cooking. Ornamental species are valued for the bold palm-like structure of their leaves, the bunches of pale green flowers on tall stems and the pleasant aroma.

Cultivation

Angelicas prefer moist, well-drained, rich soil in sun or shade. Plants die after flowering and setting seed and should then be removed. Sow seed in spring; it often self-sows.

Angelica archangelica

A robust fast-growing biennial, this species was for centuries valued for its medicinal uses — to relieve toothache, to dispel 'phrenzies of the head', and to

Angelica archangelica

protect against the plague. It is the young stems that are used, formerly cooked as a vegetable, nowadays most familiar as a candied green garnish for sweet dishes. It grows to 6 ft (1.8 m). Keep cutting back flowerheads to ensure leaf production. It has handsome, deeply divided, bright green leaves and umbels of small flowers in late summer. It does best in filtered sunlight with protection from strong winds. *Zones 4–9.*

ANTHRISCUS

A genus of 12 species of annuals, biennials and perennials from Europe and temperate Asia, one of which (chervil) is used as a culinary herb. They are typical umbellifers—members of the carrot family— with large, much-divided basal leaves and hollow, branched flowering stems terminating in umbels of tiny white or greenish flowers. The small dry fruits are narrow with a terminal 'beak'.

Anthriscus cerefolium

Cultivation

Chervil is best grown in a sheltered and moderately sunny position, in light, well-tilled soil. Sow seed directly into the beds in spring or late summer, harvesting leaves as soon as large enough and before the flowering stem begins to extend. If some plants are allowed to reach flowering size they will usually self-seed.

Anthriscus cerefolium
Chervil

Native to Europe and western Asia, chervil is grown as a cool-season annual. It resembles parsley and grows to about 24 in (60 cm) tall. The light green, finely textured leaves and stems are harvested 2–3 in (5–8 cm) above the crown; they are particularly used in French cooking to provide a delicate licorice flavor. *Zones 6–10.*

ARMORACIA
Horseradish

This is a genus of 3 species of vigorous, taproot-forming perennials found naturally from southeast Europe to Siberia, only one of which is cultivated. Horseradish is an extremely vigorous grower. The tough, white roots are used to prepare the well-known condiment and also have some medicinal properties.

Cultivation

Horseradish is very easily grown in temperate climates, in any soil in sun or light shade. Divide established clumps or plant root cuttings in spring, at least 24 in (60 cm) apart. Harvest the roots the following autumn. It replicates itself freely.

Armoracia rusticana
Horseradish

This is the only commonly grown species and the one used for horseradish sauce.

Native to southeast Europe, it has 12–18 in (30–45 cm) long, bright to deep green leaves with a puckered surface, sometimes lobed towards the base. Panicles of white flowers develop in summer but are usually removed to encourage root development. **'Variegata'**, as the name suggests, is a variegated form. Japanese horseradish, or wasabi, is a different plant, belonging to the genus *Wasabia*. *Zones 5–10*.

ARTEMISIA
Wormwood
This large genus of around 350 species of evergreen and deciduous perennials and shrubs from temperate regions of the northern hemisphere includes many species from arid and semi-arid environments. Some are popular herbs, others are grown as ornamentals for their decorative, feathery foliage, which is often aromatic, sometimes repellent to insects and may be coated with whitish hairs. The small greenish to yellowish flowerheads are not showy.

Armoracia rusticana

Armoracia rusticana 'Variegata'

Artemisia dracunculus

Borago officinalis

Cultivation

Mostly quite frost-hardy, they prefer an open, sunny situation with light, well-drained soil. Prune back lightly in spring to stimulate growth. Plant cuttings in summer or divide in spring. Transplant during winter.

Artemisia dracunculus
Tarragon

Native to central and eastern Europe and grown for its narrow, aromatic green leaves which have a delicate, peppery aniseed flavor, tarragon grows up to 3 ft (1 m) in the warmer months, dying back to a perennial rootstock over winter. It does not produce seed. To propagate, divide and plant in early spring. Harvest the leaves in summer and autumn before they die down for winter. The tarragon seed sometimes offered is the flavorless *Artemisia dracunculoides*, known as Russian tarragon. *Zones 6–9.*

BORAGO

This is a European genus of 3 species of annuals and short-lived perennials. The plants are generally erect with rather coarse growth and are covered with bristly hairs. They form clumps of lance-shaped basal leaves that rapidly develop in spring into branched, leafy flowering stems. By late spring the plants bear semi-pendulous, starry purple-blue or white flowers. The flowers are a rich source of nectar and are popular with beekeepers.

Cultivation

These plants are easily grown in any light, moist, well-drained soil in full sun. They often self-sow and may become invasive. Sow seed of the annual species in late winter for a spring crop. Protect from snails.

Borago officinalis
Borage

This annual herb is grown for its cucumber-flavored leaves and pretty, purplish blue star-shaped flowers. The plant grows to around 30 in (75 cm) high with clusters of flowers in spring and summer. The fresh young leaves are used raw in salads and cool drinks or cooked with vegetables. The edible flowers can also be used to decorate salads, or crystallized and used for cake decoration. *Zones 5–10.*

CALAMINTHA
Calamint

This genus of 7 species of aromatic
perennial herbs is native mainly to
Europe and temperate Asia, with 2
species from the USA. They are similar
in growth habit to the true mints
(Mentha), with creeping rhizomes and
leaves in opposite pairs on square stems,
but the white, pink or purplish flowers
are mostly larger and borne in looser
terminal sprays. The leaves of several
species are used in herbal medicine and
are also infused to make herbal teas. The
name *Calamintha* (beautiful mint) goes
back to ancient Greek, referring originally to an aromatic herb of this general
kind but now not identifiable.

Cultivation

Mostly fairly frost-hardy, calaminthas
are easily grown in moist but well-
drained soil in a sheltered position; some
species prefer woodland conditions in
part-shade, others thrive best in full sun.
Divide the rhizomes and replant or sow
seed in spring.

Calamintha nepeta
Lesser calamint

Native to much of Europe, North Africa
and western Asia, this unassuming plant,
12–24 in (30–60 cm) tall, favors dry,
well-drained conditions in full sun. Its
small leaves are shallowly toothed and
the small summer flowers, held in long,
erect, rather open sprays, are pale
mauve or almost white. The epithet
nepeta was presumably given to indicate
its resemblance to the catmint genus
Nepeta. **Calamintha nepeta** subsp.
glandulosa **'White Cloud'** and **'Blue
Cloud'** are popular cultivars. *Zones 4–10.*

CAPPARIS

This is a genus of around 250 species of
shrubs, small trees and scrambling,

Calamintha nepeta cultivar

prickly climbers, occurring in most
warm parts of the world. Only 2 species
extend into Europe; one of these is the
caper bush *(Capparis spinosa)* whose
flower buds are used as a condiment.
Capparis plants are distinctive for the
paired, hooked spines at the base of each
leaf, often only seen on juvenile plants,
and the attractive fragrant flowers with
delicate white, cream or pink petals and
brush of long showy stamens. The
knobby fruits usually develop on a stalk
that elongates above the persistent calyx.
Except for the caper, few species are
cultivated but they have some use as
hedge or barrier plants in hot, dry areas
and some are quite ornamental.

Cultivation

All species need a climate with long, hot
summers, though their frost-hardiness in
winter varies considerably (Zone 8
minimum). They need full sun and very
free-draining soil. Sow fresh seed or
plant semi-ripe cuttings in early spring.

Capparis spinosa
Caper, caper bush

Capers are the unopened flower buds of this low evergreen shrub, several subspecies of which occur in the wild from Mediterranean shores to southern Asia, Australia and the Pacific region. It has roundish, leathery leaves and pretty, fluffy cream flowers. In cold climates it is mostly grown as a container plant, overwintered under glass, but in frost-free zones it can be treated as a perennial. Harvest the flower buds in summer before they show any color. Often pickled in wine vinegar, capers are used as garnish and in sauces and butters. *Zones 8–12.*

CARUM

About 30 species belong to this genus of annuals, biennials and perennials, one of which is the well known herb caraway *(Carum carvi).* The species are scattered throughout the temperate regions of the world, but caraway is the only one grown as a garden plant. The plants have finely dissected basal leaves and hollow, branched stems bearing umbels of tiny white flowers, followed by aromatic, dry fruitlets. Caraway has been used as a condiment and medicinal herb since ancient Egyptian times. It is still widely cultivated for its aromatic seeds, used to flavor bread, cakes, sauces and pickles.

Cultivation

These frost-hardy plants grow well in deep, fertile, moist, well-drained soil in full sun. Sow seed in early autumn in mild winter areas, otherwise in spring.

Capparis spinosa

Carum carvi

Carum carvi
Caraway
This attractive biennial or perennial grows to about 3 ft (1 m) high with finely cut, lacy leaves. In its second year it bears umbels of small white flowers in early summer, followed by a crop of seeds. *Zones 5–10.*

CHAMAEMELUM

Four species of annuals and perennials from the Mediterranean region and Europe make up this genus, closely allied to *Anthemis* and *Matricaria*. They have aromatic, finely divided leaves and smallish daisy flowerheads with white rays and a large, domed disc. Only one, *Chamaemelum nobile*, is commonly cultivated as a medicinal herb and for herbal teas; it is also used as an ornamental and for ground cover.

Chamaemelum nobile

Cultivation
They need a sunny position and moist, well-drained soil of light texture. Sow seed or plant cuttings in spring or autumn.

Chamaemelum nobile
syn. *Anthemis nobilis*
Chamomile, Roman chamomile
There is debate as to whether this plant or *Matricaria recutita* (German chamomile) is the 'true' chamomile, but *Chamaemelum* is generally favored as it has a stronger aroma and greater herbal potency. It is a short-lived perennial growing to around 12 in (30 cm) high, though inclined to flop over. It has finely lobed leaves and bears white flowerheads, about 1 in (2.5 cm) across, from late spring to early autumn. Chamomile tea is made from the leaves and blossoms and has a mild sedative and soothing effect. Chamomile is also grown as a lawn substitute; the prostrate cultivar **'Treneague'** is best for this as it creeps along the ground by rooting runners and rarely flowers. A chamomile lawn emits a wonderful aroma when walked on. *Zones 5–10.*

CORIANDRUM

Only 2 species make up this western Mediterranean genus of annuals, one of them (coriander) renowned as a flavoring herb widely used in Southeast Asian and Middle Eastern cuisine. The plants have a fleshy taproot and much-divided leaves, the leaflets becoming much finer beneath the umbels of numerous small white flowers.

Cultivation
Coriander requires light but fertile, well-drained soil and full sun. Sow seed in early spring.

Coriandrum sativum
Coriander, ketumbar
This herb is grown mainly for its seeds and aromatic leaves, although in Thai cuisine the whole plant, including the roots, is used. It is a fast-growing annual

Coriandrum sativum cultivar

to 30 in (75 cm) high with parsley-like leaves. The umbels of tiny white flowers in summer are followed by small, round aromatic seeds in autumn. Fresh leaves provide an exotic tang in Asian dishes. The dried seeds are used in curry powders, chutneys, confectionery, cakes and sauces. *Zones 7–12.*

CUMINUM

Native to the Mediterranean region and west and central Asia, this genus contains only 2 species of annuals. They are slender plants with delicate, much-divided leaves and small umbels of tiny white or pink flowers. The small oval, dry fruits or 'seeds' are very aromatic. One species, *Cuminum cyminum* (cumin) is grown for its seeds, which are used as a flavoring herb, or sometimes classified as a spice.

Cultivation

Cumin is frost-tender and grows best in warm climates. Grow in a light, well-drained soil in a sunny position. Sow seed in spring in a warm situation.

Cuminum cyminum
Cumin

Cumin is grown commercially in India, China, Japan and the Middle East for its powerfully flavored seeds. It is a small annual, which grows to 12 in (30 cm) high, with leaves finely divided into thread-like segments. The small white flowers in summer are followed by aromatic seeds. The dried seed is an important ingredient in curry powders. The Dutch and the Germans also flavor cheese with cumin, and it is used in many Mexican and Middle Eastern dishes. *Zones 9–12.*

CURCUMA

This genus consists of about 40 species of tuberous and rhizomatous perennials, ranging from tropical Asia to northern Australia in regions of very seasonal

rainfall. The plants have tufts of broad canna-like leaves, which usually die back in the tropical dry season, and short erect spikes of small, often brightly colored flowers that emerge from between large bracts. Some are grown as ornamentals in tropical gardens or as curiosities in botanical garden greenhouses, but the genus is best known for the spices obtained from the rhizomes of several species, most notably turmeric from *Curcuma domestica.*

Cultivation

In tropical areas grow these plants in a well-tilled garden bed in moderately fertile soil. Plant rhizomes or tubers late in the dry season and water frequently when new leaves appear. Harvest turmeric rhizomes when the leaves die back.

Curcuma domestica
syn. *Curcuma longa*
Turmeric

Turmeric is grown throughout tropical Asia for its bright orange rhizomes, which apart from their mildly spicy flavor are valued as a food coloring, providing a substitute for the very expensive saffron. It is also used for dyeing cloth. The broadly

Curcuma domestica

Cymbopogon citratus

lance-shaped, bright green leaves can form large clumps up to about 3 ft (1 m) tall in hot areas. Short, dense spikes of pale yellow flowers are produced in summer. It prefers the warmth of the tropics but can be successfully grown in warm-temperate areas. The fresh or dried roots provide color and pungent fragrance to chutneys, pickles and curries; harvest the roots when the foliage begins to dry off in autumn. *Zones 10–12.*

CYMBOPOGON

This genus comprises at least 50 species of rather coarse grasses, native to warmer regions of Africa, Asia and Australia. Many species have aromatic foliage, from essential oils in the tissues. They form dense clumps, mostly with long, flattened leaves, and send up long-stalked seed heads with clustered spikelets that are woolly or silky-haired in some species. Several species are cultivated for their aromatic oils, others are used as ornamentals in warm-climate plantings.

Cultivation
Their main requirement is a climate with a long summer growing season, and a well-drained, light-textured but fertile soil. Some species, including lemongrass, may not overwinter successfully if winters are cool and wet, and should be replanted each year in late spring in such climates. Sow seed or divide established clumps in spring.

Cymbopogon citratus
Lemongrass
This valuable grass, believed to have originated in India, forms a dense clump of long gray-green leaves that can reach as much as 6 ft (1.8 m) high. It rarely flowers or produces seed in cultivation. The crushed or bruised leaves have a

Eruca sativa

strong lemon fragrance but are very tough and inedible; it is the fleshy white bases of the shoots that are collected in summer and used fresh in Southeast Asian cooking. The leaves can be dried to make a herbal tea. *Zones 10–12.*

ERUCA

Native to the Mediterranean region and northeastern Africa, this genus of cress relatives comprises 6 species of annuals. They form a rosette of deeply lobed leaves and bear flowers in terminal racemes. The narrow seed pod contains 2 rows of seeds. Only one species, *Eruca sativa* (rocket) is cultivated as a salad vegetable or herb and is now naturalized in various parts of the world.

Cultivation

Rocket needs cool weather and fast growth for tender, mild-tasting leaves. Grow in rich, evenly moist soil with good drainage.

Sow seed in spring or in early autumn in mild areas where the plants will overwinter. The plants are ready to harvest about 40 days after sowing. Remove the flowering stems to prevent the spread of unwanted seedlings.

Eruca sativa
Rocket, arugula, roquette

This low-growing annual, to around 24 in (60 cm) high, is native to southern Europe where it is very popular as a salad green. Young leaves have the best flavor and can be cooked like spinach or eaten raw. *Zones 7–10.*

FOENICULUM
Fennel

This genus of one species of aromatic biennial or perennial is grown for its yellow flower umbels and finely cut, aniseed-flavored leaves, which are used in cooking; it also has edible stems and seeds. Darker leafed cultivars provide attractive contrast in the herb garden or flower border.

Cultivation
Grow this frost-hardy plant in full sun in fertile, moist but well-drained soil. Sow seed in spring or autumn and remove spent flowers to prevent self-seeding. Harvest the leaves in summer and the seeds in autumn.

Foeniculum vulgare
Fennel
This tall, graceful perennial grows to 6 ft (1.8 m) tall with thick, hollow stems,

masses of feathery foliage and flat clusters of yellow flowers on tall, erect stems in summer. The flowers are followed by brown seeds. Both the leaves and seeds have a strong aniseed taste and are used for flavoring fish and other savory dishes. ***Foeniculum vulgare* var. *azoricum*** (syn. *F. v.* var. *dulce*), Florence fennel, has a crisp white 'bulb' with the texture of celery. ***F. v.* subsp. *piperitum*** has fleshy leaves with segments less than ½ in (12 mm) long. Its lateral clusters of flowers are longer than those produced terminally. **'Purpurascens'** has finely divided bronze-purple foliage when young. *Zones 5–10.*

Foeniculum vulgare cultivar

Foeniculum vulgare var. *azoricum*

Foeniculum vulgare 'Purpurascens'

GLYCYRRHIZA
Licorice

This genus consists of around 20 species of perennial legumes from the Mediterranean region, Asia, Australia and the Americas. The plants have pinnate leaves with oval leaflets and axillary spikes of small pea-like flowers. *Glycyrrhiza glabra* is cultivated for its soft, fibrous roots which are a source of licorice used for flavoring, confectionery and medicine. The wild licorice of North America is *G. lepidota*.

Cultivation

Moderately frost-hardy, they prefer full sun and deep, humus-rich, well-drained soil that should be kept evenly moist. Sow seed in spring or autumn or divide in early spring. Harvest the roots in autumn.

Glycyrrhiza glabra
Licorice

This perennial, native to the Mediterranean region and western Asia, has short, tough stems springing from a rather woody rootstock and grows to a height and spread of 3 ft (1 m). It has feathery, mid-green leaves and pea-like, bluish purple and white flowers on short upright spikes in late summer. *Zones 8–10.*

HELICHRYSUM
Everlasting, paper daisy, strawflower

Until recently, this genus comprised around 500 species of annuals, perennials and shrubs found mainly in southern Africa and Australia, with some from the Mediterranean, west and central Asia, and New Zealand. Members of the daisy family, they all have typical flowerheads but with papery, mostly whitish bracts instead of ray florets or 'petals'; these are long-lasting when dried, hence the common names. Botanists have now begun to reclassify species in this genus

into separate groups and rename them as distinct genera. *Helichrysum italicum*, the only species cultivated as a culinary herb, remains one of the 'true' helichrysums.

Cultivation

Helichrysum italicum will tolerate only light frosts and is best suited to mild climates with low summer humidity. It needs gritty, well-drained soil that is not too fertile and a warm, sunny position. Sow seed, or plant cuttings or rhizome divisions in spring.

Helichrysum italicum
syn. *Helichrysum angustifolium*
Curry plant

This clump-forming perennial herb from the Mediterranean grows 4–24 in (10–60 cm) tall with a spread of up to 3 ft (1 m). It has linear, grayish downy leaves with an intense curry aroma. The new, tender leaves can be used to flavor salads and cooked meat dishes. Dense, flattish sprays of very small, dark yellow flowerheads are borne at the end of the branches in spring and summer. *Zones 8–10.*

HYSSOPUS
Hyssop

This genus of aromatic culinary and medicinal herbs belongs to the mint family and includes about 5 species of herbaceous perennials and shrubs. All are found in poor soils around the northern Mediterranean coasts and also in Asia Minor. The leaves vary between the species from linear to ovate and may be green or blue-green in color. The flowers are small, tubular with protruding stamens and usually a shade of blue, although they may also be white or pink.

Cultivation

All species prefer full sun and although they will grow in dry sandy soil, they thrive in friable, fertile loam; good

Glycyrrhiza glabra

Hyssopus officinalis

drainage is essential. Ensure adequate water particularly in autumn and winter. Prune by shearing plants all over. Plant cuttings in early summer or sow seed in autumn.

Hyssopus officinalis
Hyssop

This bushy perennial herb grows to 24 in (60 cm) and has narrow, pointed, dark green leaves. Spikes of small violet-blue flowers, which attract bees and butterflies, are borne in late summer. White and pink flowering forms are also available. Fully frost-hardy, hyssop is evergreen in mild climates but dies down for winter in cool areas. The slightly bitter leaves are used in small quantities with fatty meats and fish. The essential oil made from the leaves has antiseptic properties and is used in the manufacture of perfumes. *Zones 3–11.*

LAURUS

This genus consists of 2 species of evergreen shrubs and trees from the Mediterranean region, Canary Islands and the Azores. The common laurel (*Laurus nobilis*) has been grown as an ornamental since ancient times and has always had great symbolic significance. Among other uses, its dark green foliage has been used in funeral and remembrance wreaths. The highly aromatic leaves are also dried and used as a culinary herb (an essential ingredient in bouquet garni). Both species are useful evergreen screen plants and tub specimens, and are often used for topiary.

Cultivation

Cool- to warm-climate plants, they are moderately frost-hardy and do best in sheltered positions in sun or part-shade in fertile, well-drained soil. They tolerate

coastal conditions. Sow seed in autumn
or plant cuttings in summer.

Laurus nobilis
Sweet bay, bay tree, bay laurel, laurel
A broadly conical tree, this species
grows up to 40 ft (12 m) high and 30 ft
(9 m) wide, but is generally smaller in
cultivation. Its glossy, dark green leaves
are smooth and leathery and in classical
times were used to make the victor's
'crown of laurels'. It produces small,
star-shaped, fragrant yellowish flowers
in late spring to early summer, followed
by small round green berries that ripen
to dark purplish black in autumn. This
tree is suited to clipping and shaping.
'Aurea' is a yellow-leafed form and
'Saratoga' is best suited to training as a
single-trunked tree. *Zones 7–10.*

LEPIDIUM
Peppercress, pepperwort
Like the related mustards and watercress, the 140 or so species of this
worldwide genus of annuals and perennials have sharp-tasting, peppery leaves
and even hotter tasting seeds. The genus
includes a number of weeds, but some
species are cultivated for use in salads.
Most are slender plants with narrow,
often toothed or lobed leaves and
terminal spikes of small white flowers
borne over a long period.

Cultivation
For salad use, sow peppercress seeds
densely at almost any time of year,
avoiding the hottest months, or winter in
cool climates. They can be grown in
almost any soil with frequent watering to
keep the shoots crisp and tender. The
tops can be cut off with scissors when
only 2–3 in (5–7 cm) high; several
successive harvests may be obtained
over the following few weeks. Alternatively, the seed can be sprouted without

Laurus nobilis

soil on wet paper towels or in a sealed
jar (after soaking) and used like bean
sprouts.

Lepidium sativum
Curled cress, garden cress
Native to Europe, this species often
grows wild as a weed. If allowed to
reach maturity, cress forms a slender
plant up to 24 in (60 cm) tall, with
narrowly lobed leaves and tiny white
flowers followed by reddish brown seed
pods. It may survive beyond the first
year and has tuberous roots. Used as a
salad herb, the leaves are always cut
when young as the adult foliage is tough
and bitter tasting. *Zones 4–10.*

Levisticum officinale

LEVISTICUM
Lovage
This genus consists of one species, a bright green perennial herb from the eastern Mediterranean with celery-like leaves divided into wedge-shaped segments. Umbels of small greenish yellow flowers are borne in summer, followed by ribbed aromatic seeds in early autumn. When crushed the leaves release a strong balsamic odor. This is a traditional cottage garden plant and its tall stature makes it a good background specimen in the herb garden.

Cultivation
Grow this fully frost-hardy plant in deep humus-rich soil with good drainage in full sun or part-shade. Keep soil evenly moist, especially when grown in full sun. Protect from strong winds. Plant root divisions or sow seed in spring.

Levisticum officinale
Lovage
This robust species grows up to 6 ft (1.8 m) high and has dark green leaves and a thick, erect, hollow stem. The roots and shoots are used in salads. *Zones 4–10.*

MATRICARIA
This extensively revised genus of aromatic annual herbs consists of 5 species, native to the temperate regions of the northern hemisphere. They have finely dissected leaves with numerous linear segments and produce terminal, white daisy-like flowerheads from spring to late summer. *Matricaria recutita* is valued for its herbal use; other species produce good cut flowers. They can be grown in a rockery, herb garden or as a border edging.

Cultivation
These fully frost-hardy plants prefer well-drained, light sandy soil in full sun. Sow seed in summer.

Matricaria recutita
syn. *Matricaria chamomilla*
German chamomile
This is an aromatic annual with stems to 24 in (60 cm) tall and finely divided, light green leaves. Its white daisy-like flowers with golden centers are borne in summer and autumn. The fully opened flowers can be harvested and dried. This species is used in similar ways to *Chamaemelum nobile* (chamomile). Use discarded tea flowers on the compost pile to activate decomposition. *Zones 6–10.*

MELISSA
Balm
This genus of 3 species of perennial herbs has representatives from Europe to central Asia. The name *Melissa* is derived from a Greek word meaning bee, because of the abundance of nectar

Matricaria recutita

in the flowers which attracts bees. Borne in opposite pairs on square stems, the crinkled, ovate or heart-shaped leaves emit a lemon odor when bruised. Axillary spikes of white or yellowish flowers appear in summer. These quick-growing, decorative foliage plants look good along paths, in herb gardens, among ferns and when grown in pots.

Cultivation
Very frost-hardy, they prefer full sun or light shade if summers are hot. Slightly moist, well-drained soil is best. Sow seed in spring; propagate variegated forms by root division or from young spring cuttings.

Melissa officinalis
Lemon balm, bee balm
This perennial, to 24 in (60 cm) high, is grown for its fresh lemon-scented and lemon-flavored leaves. Small white flowers are borne in late summer and attract pollinating bees to the garden. Lemon balm spreads rapidly, dies down in winter but shoots again in spring. The leaves are used to make a calming herbal tea. They also give a light, lemon flavor to fruit salads, jellies, iced tea and summer drinks, and can be used as a substitute for lemon peel in cooking. *Zones 4–10.*

MENTHA
Mint
This genus contains 25 species of aromatic perennial herbs, some ever-green and some semi-evergreen, from Europe, Asia and Africa. Most are cultivated for their fragrance, some for their flavor or ornamental appeal. Several species make attractive ground covers. They vary in size from tiny creeping forms to bushy plants, and vary in flavor from refreshing to very strong.

Cultivation
Most are very frost-hardy. They like sunshine and rich soil and need lots of moisture. Mint is invasive, spreading rapidly by runners; to keep the plants

Melissa officinalis

Mentha × *piperita*

under control, grow in large pots, watering regularly and repotting annually. Sow seed or divide roots in spring or autumn.

Mentha × piperita
Peppermint

This spreading perennial, grown for its aromatic foliage and culinary uses, grows to 24 in (60 cm) high and wide. Using underground stems, it forms a carpet of oval, toothed, mid-green and reddish green leaves. Purple flowers appear in spring. *Mentha* × *piperita* f. *citrata*, Eau de Cologne mint, is too strong and bitter for culinary use but is grown for its distinctive perfume. *Zones 3–10.*

Mentha × *piperita* f. *citrata*

Mentha spicata

Mentha spicata

Mentha suaveolens

Mentha suaveolens 'Variegata'

Mentha spicata
Spearmint
Growing to 24 in (60 cm), this fast-growing mint with dark, crinkly leaves thrives in a sunny or part-shaded position. It is the most popular mint for cooking and is used in mint sauce, mint jelly and to flavor and garnish new potatoes, green peas, fruit drinks and desserts. It is best grown in a container as it is highly invasive. *Zones 3–10.*

Mentha suaveolens
syn. *Mentha rotundifolia* of gardens
Apple mint
This vigorous suckering perennial grows to 3 ft (1 m) tall with felted, gray-green, apple-scented leaves. Its attractive, fragrant foliage can be used in the kitchen, but it is best grown in a container with no contact with the ground as it suckers strongly and is difficult to control. **'Variegata'** has white-variegated leaves with a particularly fruity aroma. *Zones 6–10.*

Mentha × villosa f. *alopecuroides*

Mentha × villosa f. alopecuroides
Bowles' mint, winter mint
This mint is a hybrid between *Mentha spicata* and *M. suaveolens*. It is a vigorous, erect plant to 3 ft (1 m) high and the ovate or rounded mid-green leaves have a distinct spearmint scent. Pink flowers are produced in dense spikes in autumn. This mint may be used in any dish where spearmint is called for. In warm-temperate climates it will keep growing through winter. *Zones 5–10.*

MURRAYA
Allied to the *Citrus* genus, this small genus of 4 species of evergreen trees and shrubs comes from India and Southeast Asia. They have aromatic foliage and attractive creamy white flowers which resemble those of their relative, the orange, and are often strongly scented. The fruits are small oval berries. The genus was named after John Andrew Murray, a pupil of Linnaeus.

Cultivation

Murraya species flourish in warm, frost-free climates in full sun or part-shade and humus-rich, moist but well-drained soil. When grown in borderline temperate situations, they need shelter. Early pruning ensures a shrub thickly branched from the ground up; clipping after the late flowering season will keep their shape. Sow seed or plant cuttings in spring.

Murraya koenigii

Murraya koenigii
Curry leaves, curry leaf tree, karapincha

This aromatic shrub from the Indian subcontinent grows to about 10 ft (3 m) tall. Its leaves are used in curries and other spicy dishes. Loose sprays of small, fragrant, creamy white flowers stand out against the fresh green foliage in summer and are followed by small black fruit. *Zones 10–12.*

Myristica fragrans

MYRISTICA

Native to tropical Asia, northern Australia and Pacific islands, this genus consists of about 80 species of tropical evergreen trees that may grow to 100 ft (30 m). Only the female trees produce the large succulent fruits, which are borne several times a year. The leaves are usually waxy white underneath.

Cultivation

They must be protected from frost and dry conditions, and planted in rich, moist, well-drained soil if they are to flourish outside their homelands. They need a hot, humid position away from sun, strong winds and pollution. Sow seed, plant cuttings or propagate by grafting in spring and autumn.

Myristica fragrans
Nutmeg

The fruit of this tree from Indonesia is nutmeg, now cultivated commercially mainly in Indonesia and Grenada. A slender, evergreen tree reaching 50 ft

(15 m), it has distinctive whorls of spreading branches, smooth gray bark, aromatic leaves and small, pale yellow flowers. Ripe nutmegs are fleshy, pear-shaped, brilliant scarlet berries. Their jackets are harvested to make mace, a milder spice. *Zone 12.*

MYRRHIS
Sweet Cicely, myrrh

This is a genus of only one species—an attractive long-lived perennial in the carrot family, native to southern Europe. It has aromatic, fern-like leaves and fragrant creamy white flowers in flattened heads in early summer, followed by ribbed, shiny brown seeds that have a very brief viability. The leaves and seeds have a sweet aniseed flavor and can be cooked with fruit as a sugar substitute. They are also good in raw vegetable juices.

Cultivation

Fully frost-hardy, sweet Cicely needs part-shade and moist but well-drained,

Myrrhis odorata

fertile soil. Sow fresh seed or divide in autumn or spring.

Myrrhis odorata

This graceful perennial to 6 ft (1.8 m) high is excellent as a background plant in the herb garden or mixed flower border. It will tolerate shade and can be sited beneath garden trees. It self-seeds readily and the strongest seedlings may be transplanted. *Zones 5–10.*

NASTURTIUM
Watercress

There are 6 species of watercress. The one most commonly cultivated is *Nasturtium officinale*, an aquatic plant with soft, hollow stems and dark green rounded leaf segments. White roots form on the leaf nodes. Originally a marsh plant from Europe and northern Asia, watercress is now a river weed in North America and temperate southern hemisphere regions. Rich in vitamins and minerals, watercress is popular as a sharp-tasting salad herb or is cooked as a vegetable in Asian dishes. It is also used for stimulating the digestion and to ease severe headaches.

Cultivation

Watercress must have clean running water or be watered copiously to grow well; an old laundry tub is ideal as the old water can be regularly drained and the tub refilled with fresh water when needed. These plants flourish in damp, shaded corners of the garden as well as in ponds. Sow seed in spring or plant cuttings about 4 in (10 cm) apart in early autumn, making sure the soil has been thoroughly and deeply manured. Water thoroughly and constantly, and prune the shoots to keep growth thick.

Nasturtium officinale
syn. *Rorippa nasturtium-aquaticum*
Common watercress

This species has creeping stems up to 30 in (75 cm) long, erect at the tips. The small white flowers appear in racemes, but should be cut back when they appear in order to promote vegetative growth. *Zones 6–10.*

OCIMUM
Basil

This genus of approximately 35 species of frost-tender annuals, perennials and shrubs is native to tropical Asia and Africa. They are now widely cultivated in many other countries for their highly aromatic leaves, which are used for medicinal purposes or in cooking. They have mostly oval leaves in opposite pairs and small tubular flowers borne in whorls towards the ends of the stems in late summer.

Cultivation

Grow in a protected, warm, sunny position in a moist but well-drained soil. Sow seed in mid-spring. Regularly pinch back plants to encourage bushy growth and to prevent them going to seed quickly. Protect from late frosts and check for chewing insects and snails.

Ocimum basilicum
Basil, sweet basil

This native of tropical Asia, together with its cultivars, is the most commonly grown basil, used widely in Mediterranean cooking. Fresh leaves are best; freeze them for the winter as they lose their flavor when dried. A tender annual, growing to about 18 in (45 cm) high, its oval, light green leaves have a delicious warm, spicy fragrance. Small white flowers are carried in whorls towards the ends of the stems in late summer. There are a number of varieties of basil including a compact small leaf type; a crinkled, lettuce leaf variety and the beautiful **'Dark Opal'**, which has rich purple stems and leaves. There are a number of perennial varieties, but their flavor is inferior. **'Minimum'** is a dwarf form with tiny leaves, used in the Greek Orthodox Church for sprinkling holy water. Basil can be grown in cooler climates as a summer annual. *Zones 10–12.*

Ocimum basilicum cultivar

Ocimum tenuiflorum
syn. *Ocimum sanctum*
Holy basil

This flavorsome aromatic herb from India is a sacred plant in the Hindu religion. It is a short-lived perennial that dies back to a few woody stems near ground level. It grows to about 3 ft (1 m) tall with many upright stems clothed in oval, toothed leaves. Small, not very showy flowers appear on a spike from the tips of the branches. It is not particularly frost-hardy and in cooler areas is usually raised as a summer annual. *Zones 10–12.*

Ocimum tenuiflorum cultivar

Origanum majorana cultivar

ORIGANUM
syn. *Majorana*
Marjoram, oregano
Native to the Mediterranean region and western Asia, the 36 species of perennials and subshrubs in this genus of the mint family have aromatic leaves and stalked spikes or heads of small tubular flowers with crowded, overlapping bracts. Some species are grown as culinary herbs, while others are grown for their decorative pink flowerheads. With arching or prostrate stems arising from vigorously spreading rhizomes, they make useful plants for trailing over rocks, banks and walls.

Cultivation
These plants like full sun and a moderately fertile, well-drained soil. Sow seed in spring or divide roots in autumn or spring. Trim excess growth regularly.

Origanum majorana
syns *Majorana hortensis*, *Origanum hortensis*
Sweet marjoram, sweet basil
A highly aromatic plant up to 24 in (60 cm) high, marjoram originates in the Mediterranean but has long been grown elsewhere in Europe for its sweet and spicy, small gray-green leaves. The tiny white flowers are borne in short spikes with very tightly packed bracts. The leaves are used fresh or dried for savory foods. Marjoram has a special affinity with tomatoes and goes well with many meats. *Zones 7–10.*

Origanum onites cultivar

Origanum vulgare cultivar

Origanum onites
syn. *Majorana onites*
French marjoram, pot marjoram
This small, rounded, aromatic shrub grows to around 18 in (45 cm) tall with wiry, hairy stems and bright green, heart-shaped leaves. White or pale pink flowers are borne in clusters at the ends of the branches in late summer. A native of Sicily, this popular herb is used in Mediterranean cooking. Taller than the species, **'Aureum'** has golden green foliage and pink flowers. *Zones 8–11.*

Origanum vulgare 'Aureum'

Origanum vulgare
Common oregano, wild marjoram
The common oregano has a sharper, more pungent flavor than marjoram. It has a sprawling habit and grows to 24 in (60 cm) high with dark green, oval leaves and small, white or pink flowers in summer. The leaves are used, fresh or dried, in many Mediterranean-inspired dishes. In Italy, oregano is used in pizza toppings and pasta dishes. **'Aureum'** has a less sprawling habit and bright greenish gold leaves. **'Thumble's Variety'** is a low, mound-forming selection with yellow-green leaves. *Zones 5–9.*

PANAX
Ginseng
This genus consists of 5 or so species of perennial herbs, 2 of which are commercially cultivated. Chinese or Asian ginseng *(Panax ginseng)* has been used for centuries by the Chinese and Koreans as a medicinal herb. North American ginseng *(P. quinquefolius)* has similar properties to the Asian species; both have a sweetish aromatic flavor. It is the roots that are valuable: graded according to age, color and their distinctive humanoid shapes; the older the root and the more human its shape, the more highly it is valued.

Cultivation

These plants require a humus-rich, well-drained soil. As woodlands are their native habitat, it is important to provide adequate shade, especially during the summer months. Also ensure good air circulation around the plants. Sow seed or plant root divisions in spring. The roots are normally harvested after about 5 years' growth.

Panax ginseng

syn. *Panax pseudoginseng*

Ginseng, Chinese ginseng, Asian ginseng

Native to northeastern China and Korea, this fully frost-hardy perennial grows to about 8 in (20 cm) tall. The dark green leaves are divided into 5 toothed leaflets. The small greenish white flowers have 5 petals and appear in late summer; these are followed by bright red berries in autumn. *Zones 6–9.*

PERILLA

This genus of 6 species of annuals, occurring from India to Japan, includes one species, *Perilla frutescens*, that is cultivated as a salad herb and foliage bedding plant. The plants have glossy, deep green, heavily veined and toothed, oval leaves, up to 6 in (15 cm) long. There are now many cultivars, mainly

Perilla frutescens cultivar

with purple foliage and various leaf shapes. The foliage is aromatic and is used as a garnish or flavoring. Spike-like inflorescences up to 4 in (10 cm) long develop at the stem tips and bear tiny white flowers; these are usually removed from cultivated plants to prevent seeding and to prolong plant life.

Cultivation
Grow in moist, well-drained soil in sun or part-shade. Sow seed in spring. Young plants tolerate light frost and may be planted in late winter to ensure a long season. Harvest the leaves in summer.

Perilla frutescens
Chiso, shiso
Found from the Himalayas to eastern Asia, this species, usually treated as a summer annual, grows to 3–5 ft (1–1.5 m) tall. Its coleus-like leaves are just over 4 in (10 cm) long, deeply serrated and sometimes spotted purple. The flower spike is about 4 in (10 cm) long and the tiny summer flowers are white or red tinted. The foliage is used as a herb in Japanese dishes and has medicinal properties. **'Atropurpurea'** is a purple-leafed form; *P. f. var. crispa* usually has dark purple or dark bronze, sometimes dark green, frilled leaves. *Zones 8–11.*

PERSICARIA
syns *Aconogonon, Bistorta, Tovara*
Knotweed
One species of this genus of 50 to 80 species of annuals, perennials or sub-shrubs is used as a culinary herb. They all have strong wiry stems with variously shaped leaves 1½–10 in (3.5–25 cm) long. The foliage often has purple-gray markings and may develop red and gold tints in autumn. The flowers, usually pink or cream, are small and are some-times borne in showy panicles or spikes.

Cultivation
Most are vigorous and very frost-hardy, easily cultivated in any well-drained soil in sun or part-shade. Some may become invasive: the stronger growers are best contained. Sow seed in spring or divide in spring or autumn.

Persicaria odorata
syn. *Polygonum odoratum*
Vietnamese mint
This tender perennial species from Southeast Asia grows to around 12 in (30 cm) tall, at which point the stems begin to bend down and take root at the tip. Its leaves have a pungent mint smell with a hint of curry and are used as a herb. In cool regions it is best treated as an annual. *Zones 10–12.*

PETROSELINUM
Parsley
This is a genus of 3 species of biennial herbs with long rootstocks and a rosette of bright green leaves, each divided into many leaflets with toothed margins. Flat open umbels of very small pale greenish yellow flowers are produced in the second year; these are followed by small, light brown seeds. Cultivated for thousands of years, parsley is still one of the most popular herbs and makes a decorative foliage plant for edging, either alone or mixed with colorful annuals. It is excellent for growing in containers.

Cultivation
Fully frost-hardy, these plants prefer full sun or light shade in warm climates. They like moist, well-drained soil and regular feeding. Sow seed from spring to late summer; in frost-prone areas, seedlings can be raised indoors. Seed may take up to 6 weeks to germinate and it is helpful to soak it in warm water overnight before sowing.

Petroselinum crispum cultivar

Petroselinum crispum var. *neapolitanum* cultivar

Petroselinum crispum
Parsley

This clump-forming species, which grows to 30 in (75 cm) in height and 24 in (60 cm) in spread, has triangular leaves and minute, star-shaped flowers. For the best flavor, harvest the leaves before the plant flowers. The most commonly used forms are curly-leafed parsley and the stronger, flat-leafed Italian variety or French parsley, ***Petroselinum crispum* var. *neapolitanum***. *Zones 5–11.*

PIMPINELLA

This is a genus of around 150 species of
mostly annuals and perennials from
Eurasia, Africa and South America.
They have entire or pinnate leaves and
umbrella-like heads of dainty, star-shaped
flowers. The blooms are followed by small,
oval-shaped fruits. *Pimpinella anisum* was
cultivated by the Egyptians, Greeks and
Romans for its aromatic seeds, used in
medicine and as a condiment.

Cultivation

All species are very frost-hardy and easy
to grow in a sunny, protected position.
Provide a moist but well-drained, fertile
soil for best results. Sow fresh seed
directly into the garden in mid- to late
spring. Germination may take up to 3
weeks.

Pimpinella anisum

Pimpinella anisum
Anise, aniseed

Native to the eastern part of the Mediterranean region, this aromatic annual to
24 in (60 cm) high has brilliant green,
fern-like leaves and umbels of tiny white
flowers in mid-summer. The light brown
seeds are used for flavoring cakes,
bread, confectionery and liqueurs. Cut
the whole plant back in autumn and
hang the branches in a dark, warm place
until the seeds are thoroughly dry.
Zones 6–10.

ROSMARINUS
Rosemary

Some botanists recognize up to 12
species in this genus, but most suggest
there is only one, an evergreen native to

Rosmarinus officinalis cultivar

the Mediterranean. It has been valued for centuries for its perfume and for medicinal and culinary uses. A small shrub, rarely growing more than 4 ft (1.2 m) tall, it has narrow, needle-like leaves that are dark green and aromatic. The blue flowers are held in short clusters.

Cultivation
Rosemary prefers a sunny site and thrives in poor soil if it is well drained; it is salt tolerant. Prune regularly to keep it compact and promote new growth. It can be grown as a specimen shrub or as a low hedge. Sow seed in spring or plant cuttings in summer.

Rosmarinus officinalis
Rosemary
Widely grown as a culinary herb, this species is also ornamental. It is upright with strong woody branches densely clothed with narrow, 1 in (2.5 cm), deep green leaves. Simple lavender-blue to deep blue flowers smother the bush in

autumn, winter and spring. Popular cultivars include **'Benenden Blue'** with vivid blue flowers; **'Huntingdon Carpet'**, a low spreading plant with bluish flowers; **'Lockwood de Forest'** with deep blue flowers and a spreading habit;

Rosmarinus officinalis cultivar

Rosmarinus officinalis 'Prostratus'

Rumex acetosa

Rumex scutatus

and '**Majorca Pink**', an upright plant with soft pink flowers. '**Miss Jessop's Upright**' grows vigorously to 6 ft (1.8 m); '**Prostratus**' (syn. *Rosmarinus lavandulaceus* of gardens), a ground-cover form, is ideal for spilling over walls or covering banks; and '**Tuscan Blue**' bears dark blue flowers. *Zones 6–11.*

RUMEX
Dock, sorrel

Chiefly found in northern temperate regions, this genus comprises around 200 species of annual, biennial and perennial herbs, usually with a deep tap root. Many species have been introduced to other parts of the world and have become invasive weeds. Docks are erect plants, usually with a basal rosette of simple leaves, with or without stem leaves. Whorls of flowers are borne in spikes or panicles, followed by small oval, pointed fruits. A few species are cultivated for their ornamental foliage or as herbs.

Cultivation

Most docks thrive in full sun in moderately fertile, well-drained soil. They are marginally to fully frost-hardy. Sow in spring or plant divisions in autumn, leaving 12 in (30 cm) between plants; broken pieces of root will also sprout. Remove flowers to encourage new, leafy growth. Protect young plants from slugs and snails.

Rumex acetosa
syn. *Acetosa sagittata*
Garden sorrel

This fast-growing, fully frost-hardy perennial grows to 3 ft (1 m) high and has bright green leaves shaped like arrowheads. Whorls of green flowers, which change to red, are borne during summer. The sour lemon-flavored leaves are eaten as a vegetable and in green salads. *Zones 3–9.*

Rumex scutatus
Sorrel, French sorrel

This low-growing perennial has pale green leaves and tiny flowers. French sorrel used to be eaten in the same way as spinach, but sorrel's tart flavor is more suitable for sauces, salads or in soups. Sorrel contains oxalic acid, which is toxic in large amounts. *Zones 6–10.*

RUTA
Rue

This genus consists of 8 species of subshrubs, shrubs and woody perennials from the Mediterranean region and Canary Islands, with deeply divided aromatic leaves and terminal sprays of small yellow flowers. Some are used as a medicinal and strewing herb or as an insect repellent, others are grown as ornamentals for their decorative blue-gray leaves and flowers. Take care when picking or weeding around rue as the foliage can cause an irritating rash in hot weather.

Cultivation

Marginally to fully frost-hardy, they prefer slightly alkaline, well-drained soil in full sun. Protect from strong winds and severe frost in cold climates. Plant divisions in spring or stem cuttings in late summer. Trim after flowering.

Ruta graveolens
Common rue

One of the bitter herbs of classical times believed to ward off disease, this species is also very decorative with pretty, blue-green, lacy leaves. It is a frost-hardy, evergreen shrub that grows 24 in (60 cm) high, with clusters of small yellow-green flowers in summer. Common rue has been used in the past for medicinal purposes, but can be dangerous if taken in large doses and during pregnancy. *Zones 5–10.*

Ruta graveolens

Salvia elegans cultivar

SALVIA
Sage

The largest genus of the mint family, *Salvia* consists of as many as 900 species of annuals, perennials and soft-wooded shrubs, from most parts of the world except very cold regions and tropical rainforests. Their tubular, 2-lipped flowers are very distinctive. The lower lip is flat but the upper lip helmet- or boat-shaped; the calyx is also 2-lipped and may be colored. The flowers come in a wide range of shades, including some of the brightest blues and scarlets of any plants, though yellows are rare. Species with aromatic leaves are grown primarily as culinary herbs, but most species make attractive ornamentals. The genus name goes back to Roman times and derives from the Latin *salvus*, 'safe' or 'well', referring to the supposed healing properties of *Salvia officinalis*.

Cultivation

Most of the shrubby Mexican and South American species will tolerate only light frosts, but some of the perennials are more frost-hardy. Sages generally do best planted in full sun in well drained, light-textured soil with adequate watering in summer. Sow seed in spring, plant cuttings in early summer or divisions of rhizomatous species at almost any time. Foliage of many species is attacked by snails, slugs and caterpillars.

Salvia elegans
Pineapple-scented sage

This open-branched perennial or subshrub from Mexico and Guatemala can reach 6 ft (1.8 m) in mild areas. It is grown for its light green foliage which has a distinctive pineapple scent and flavor. The leaves are used fresh but sparingly in fruit salads, summer drinks and teas. Whorls of small bright red flowers are borne in late summer and autumn. These are also delicious and may be added to desserts and salads for color and flavor. **'Scarlet Pineapple'** (syn. *Salvia rutilans*) is more free-flowering with larger scarlet flowers which, in milder areas, persist to mid-winter and attract honey-eating birds. *Zones 8–11.*

Salvia officinalis 'Purpurascens'

Salvia officinalis 'Tricolor'

Salvia officinalis 'Icterina'

Salvia officinalis
Common sage, garden sage

From Spain, the Balkans and North Africa, common sage is a decorative, frost-hardy, short-lived perennial that grows to 30 in (75 cm) high and wide, with downy gray-green oval leaves and short racemes of purple flowers in summer. Its culinary merits are well known, and it has entered folklore over the centuries for its real and supposed medicinal qualities. **'Berggarten'** is a low-growing form with large leaves and blue flowers; **'Icterina'** has gold and green leaves; **'Purpurascens'** has gray-green leaves with a purplish hue and pale mauve flowers; **'Tricolor'** is a garish combination of green, cream and beetroot red leaves. *Zones 5–10.*

SANGUISORBA
syn. *Poterium*
Burnet

This is a genus of about 18 species found over the northern temperate zones. They may be rhizomatous perennials or small shrubs, and all have coarsely ferny leaves. The flowerheads resemble small bottlebrushes, and often only the lower half of the bottlebrush has male and female parts to the flowers. Some species are grown for their ornamental foliage and flowers, which are good for cutting; *Sanguisorba minor* is grown in herb gardens for its edible leaves as well as its attractive flowers.

Cultivation
They prefer full sun or part-shade and moderately fertile, moist but well-drained soil that should not be allowed to dry out in summer. Sow seed or plant divisions in spring.

Sanguisorba minor
syn. *Poterium sanguisorba*
Garden burnet, salad burnet

This perennial occurs across Europe, western Asia and North Africa in dry rocky areas, often on limestone. It grows to 24 in (60 cm) tall and has 6 to 10 rounded toothed leaflets on each leafstalk. The flowers occur in terminal oblong heads to 1 in (2.5 cm). They are white, the upper ones female, the lower ones male, with the middle section comprised of both. The fresh leaves can be picked and used as a herb to flavor soups and salads. They taste rather like cucumber and are excellent in cold drinks. *Zones 5–9.*

SAPONARIA
Soapwort

The common name of this genus of 20 species of annuals and perennials from Europe and southwest Asia comes from the old custom of using the roots for washing clothes. They contain a glucoside called saponin, which is just as good as any detergent for dissolving grease and dirt and which, being edible, has been used as an additive to beer to ensure that it develops a good head when poured. Compact or taller, spreading plants, soapworts have narrow, variably shaped leaves and bear many 5-petaled flat, usually pink, flowers. They are good for rock gardens, banks and for trailing over walls.

Cultivation
Fully frost-hardy, they need sun and well-drained soil. Sow seed in spring or autumn or plant cuttings in early summer.

Sanguisorba minor

Saponaria officinalis

Saponaria officinalis
Bouncing bet, soapwort
While this species' pink flowers on their
24 in (60 cm) tall stems are not in the
first rank of beauty, they make a pretty
show in their summer season and the
plant grows almost anywhere; it is a very
nice old-fashioned flower for a cottage
garden. It has oval, smooth, mid-green
leaves. Keep an eye on adjacent plants,
as it spreads rapidly. *Zones 5–10.*

SATUREJA
Savory
This genus consists of 30 species of
annuals, semi-evergreen perennials and
subshrubs with many culinary uses.
Native to the northern hemisphere, they
were much loved by the Ancient Greeks
and Romans for their refreshing flavor.
They have aromatic leaves and tubular,
stalkless, 2-lipped flowers that appear in
summer and attract insects, especially bees.

Cultivation

These moderately to fully frost-hardy plants prefer full sun and well-drained soil. They are well suited to rock gardens or dry banks. Sow seed in winter or spring or plant cuttings in summer.

Satureja hortensis
Summer savory

This bushy annual grows 15 in (38 cm) tall and has narrow, dark green leaves and pale lavender flowers in late summer. The leaves have a sweet, spicy taste with a hint of thyme and are traditionally used to flavor bean dishes. They are also used for vinegar, salad dressings and butter. *Zones 8–11.*

Satureja montana
Winter savory

A spreading subshrub that grows to 18 in (45 cm), winter savory has dark green, pointed leaves and tiny white flowers with pink markings in summer. It may need winter protection in cold

climates and benefits from regular pruning to stimulate fresh growth and prevent legginess. A good edging or border plant, it is often grown to attract bees. The leaves, sharper and more peppery than those of summer savory, are used to flavor meat casseroles and roasts. *Zones 6–10.*

SESAMUM

This is a genus of about 15 species of annuals from Africa and tropical Asia, with leaves simple or palmately divided and white, pink, red or purple flowers that are tubular and 2-lipped. The fruits are oblong capsules that open when dry to release numerous small seeds. One species *(Sesamum orientale)* is the crop plant sesame, grown mainly for its seeds which are used to flavor bread, cakes and biscuits and from which sesame oil is extracted. The whole seed is used extensively in cooking in the Middle East and Asia. Tahini is a nut-like cream of ground sesame seeds much used in Lebanese food.

Satureja montana

Cultivation

Sesamum orientale requires a warm climate for the seeds to mature. It thrives in moderately rich soil in a sunny position. Sow seed in spring and allow a growing season of 90 to 120 days of hot weather. Harvest the seeds in autumn before they completely dry out and scatter.

Sesamum orientale

syn. *Sesamum indicum*

Sesame

This erect annual grows to 30 in (75 cm) tall and has dark green lance-shaped leaves and axillary, pink or white, tubular flowers. Capsules, containing the sesame seeds, follow the flowers in autumn. *Zones 9–12.*

THYMUS
Thyme

This genus consists of over 300 ever-green species of herbaceous perennials and subshrubs, ranging from prostrate to 8 in (20 cm) high. Natives of southern Europe and Asia, they are grown for their aromatic leaves and some species are used in cooking. The flowers are often tubular and vary from white through pink to mauve. Historically, thyme has been associated with courage, strength, happiness and well-being.

Thymus × citriodorus cultivar

Cultivation

These plants are mostly frost-hardy. They need a sunny site with moist, well-drained soil and will thrive in rockeries, between stepping stones or on banks. Sow seed or plant cuttings or divisions in summer. For thick, dense plants remove the flowerheads after flowering.

Thymus × citriodorus

syn. *Thymus serpyllum* var. *citriodorus*

Lemon-scented thyme

This delightful rounded, frost-hardy shrub grows 12 in (30 cm) high and has tiny oval lemon-scented leaves and pale lilac flowers. The leaves are used fresh or dry in poultry stuffings or to add lemon flavor to fish, meat and veg-etables. **'Anderson's Gold'** is a yellow-foliaged spreader that is inclined to revert to green; **'Argenteus'** has silver edges to the leaves; **'Aureus'** has golden variegated leaves; **'Doone Valley'** is prostrate with gold variegated leaves that develop red tints in winter; and **'Silver Queen'** has silvery white foliage. *Zones 7–10.*

Thymus herba-barona
Caraway thyme

With a species name meaning 'prince of herbs', this caraway-scented Corsican

Thymus herba-barona cultivar

Thymus vulgaris cultivar

native grows to 6 in (15 cm) tall with a spread of 10 in (25 cm). A subshrub, it has prostrate, woody, branching stems and lanceolate, deep green leaves. Tubular, rose-pink flowers with 2 lips are borne in terminal clusters in spring. It is marginally frost-hardy. *Zones 9–11.*

Thymus vulgaris
Common thyme

This is the most popular culinary thyme, producing the strongest flavored leaves. It is a frost-hardy subshrub that grows to 12 in (30 cm) high. White to pale purple flowers are produced in summer. The tiny, mid-green leaves are used in vinegars, butters and for a variety of meat or vegetable dishes. Thyme tea is used to aid digestion, sore throats and coughs. *Zones 7–10.*

TRIGONELLA
Fenugreek

This is a genus of about 80 species of slender annual legumes from the Mediterranean, southern Africa and Australia, with light green, trifoliate leaves and small, pea-like, white or pink flowers. These are followed by narrow sickle-shaped pods which contain up to 20 brownish yellow seeds. The dried seeds of *Trigonella foenum-graecum* have a strong spicy odor and have long been used as a food-flavoring and medicine. Fenugreek often appears as a spice in curry powders and chutneys, and is a herb much used in North African and Egyptian cooking. One kind of fenugreek is used to flavor special cheeses.

Cultivation

Although often sprouted year round for domestic use, fenugreeks are strictly summer annuals outdoors. Grow in moderately rich, well-drained soil in a sunny position. Sow seed directly into the soil in spring; thin the seedlings to 4 in (10 cm) apart.

Trigonella foenum-graecum
Fenugreek

This aromatic annual grows to 24 in (60 cm) high and has clover-like trifoliate leaves. Small white pea-flowers are borne in summer and are followed by a long narrow pod. This species is used as a fodder plant in central and southern Europe. It is also extensively cultivated as a spice in many countries, particularly in the Middle East and Asia. Pick the seeds when ripe and dry them in a warm, dry spot indoors. They can be used as a sprouting vegetable and will sprout in 3 to 4 days. They add spice to almost any kind of salad. *Zones 7–10.*

TROPAEOLUM
Nasturtium

The 87 species of annuals, perennials and twining climbers in this genus occur naturally from Chile to Mexico. They are often grown as ornamentals for their flowers, but some varieties produce edible tubers and the leaves and flowers of others can be used in salads. In warm areas, nasturtiums can survive for several years, self-sowing freely and flowering all year. The flowers can be single or double, about 2 in (5 cm) across, and come in red, orange, russet, yellow, cream and even blue. In the nineteenth century a white cultivar was bred, only to be lost.

Cultivation

Frost-hardy to frost-tender, most species prefer moist, well-drained soil in full sun or part-shade. Sow seed or plant basal stem cuttings or tubers in spring. Check for aphids and cabbage moth caterpillars.

Tropaeolum majus

Tropaeolum majus

Tropaeolum majus
Garden nasturtium, Indian cress

This vigorous, bushy annual has trailing
and climbing stems, spreading to 3 ft
(1 m) and a height of up to 18 in
(45 cm). It has rounded leaves marked
with radial veins and blooms in summer
and autumn. The 5-petaled flowers are
spurred, open and trumpet-shaped, and
come in many shades from deep red to
pale yellow. The hot-tasting leaves and
flowers can be added to salads. There
are several varieties with single or
double flowers, and a compact or trailing
habit. The **Alaska Hybrids** have single
flowers in a range of shades and variegated leaves. *Zones 8–11.*

ZINGIBER
Ginger

This genus consists of about 100 species of evergreen perennials with thick, branching, aromatic rhizomes and leafy, reed-like stems. They bear flowers in axils of colorful, waxy bracts in short spikes or globular heads on stalks arising from the rhizomes. One species produces the culinary root and stem ginger.

Cultivation

These frost-tender plants need a hot position with high humidity and plentiful water in summer, less in winter. Give them plenty of space to spread. Plant rhizome divisions in spring.

Zingiber officinale cultivar

Zingiber officinale
Common ginger, halia

Originating in southern Asia, this species can reach 6 ft (1.8 m) high in hot areas and has narrow lance-shaped leaves. Spikes of white flowers with purple streaks appear in summer. Harvest the roots after about 5 months, once the plant has developed a good set of leaves. The fresh root, peeled and finely chopped or grated, is used to flavor many Asian dishes, curries and chutneys. Dried and powdered ginger is used in sweet dishes and cakes. Also used medicinally, it was once thought to safeguard against marauding tigers. *Zones 10–12.*

Fruit &
Nuts

ACTINIDIA

In recent years, the fruit of this east Asian genus of about 40 species of woody climbers has been promoted as 'kiwi fruit' by New Zealand orchardists who export them to many countries. An older generation knew them as 'Chinese gooseberries', although the genus is not related to the gooseberry genus *Ribes*. The genus also contains some ornamental plants, treasured in regions with cool, moist climates. Mostly deciduous, they have tangled, twining branches with widely spaced, simple leaves. Both the branches and leaves are often covered with bristly hairs. Male and female flowers usually occur on separate plants, with white, green or reddish petals, and are quite showy in some species. The fruit is a fleshy oval berry containing numerous tiny seeds.

Cultivation

To obtain fruit, it is usually necessary to plant at least one male vine close to several females. The vines need either a

Actinidia deliciosa cultivar

strong trellis or support on which to climb. They prefer moist, fertile soil in a sheltered but sunny position. Plant cuttings in autumn or late winter.

Actinidia deliciosa
syn. *Actinidia chinensis*
Chinese gooseberry, kiwi fruit
This fruiting vine, introduced in 1900 from China's Yangtze valley, was once known as *Actinidia chinensis*, but research has revealed significant differences between this and the wild form. In ideal conditions, the plants can be very vigorous — the long, writhing canes can become as thick as a thumb in one season, forming a dense tangle. Both the oval leaves, up to 8 in (20 cm) long, and the stems are clothed in red bristles. The flowers, borne in late spring and early summer, have broad white petals: the male flowers also have a boss of gold stamens. The fruit, which follow in summer and autumn, vary in shape and

size, and a number of selected clones have been named as cultivars. Chinese gooseberries tolerate only moderate frosts and require abundant water and nitrogenous fertilizer in summer. In winter, the bare vines should be pruned back to a single branch along each trellis wire. *Zones 8–10.*

ANACARDIUM
Cashew
Although this genus includes 8 species of semi-deciduous small trees from tropical America, only *Anacardium occidentale*, the cashew, has been much cultivated. Both branches and foliage are untidy, so cashews are rarely grown as ornamentals. The stiff sprays of small pinkish flowers, which are fragrant at night, are followed in autumn by curious fruit, consisting of 2 parts. The 'cashew apple', actually a swollen, fleshy stalk, is colored, edible and up to 4 in (10 cm) long and 2 in (5 cm) in diameter. Sitting

Anacardium occidentale cultivar

in its hollowed apex is the true fruit, curved like the nut, with an outer fleshy husk containing an extremely acrid, resinous sap. This can badly burn the skin and must be removed (wearing gloves) before the edible kernel can be used. Most of the world's cashew crop comes from India, where the long, hot dry season suits its cultivation.

Cultivation
Fast growing when young, cashews grow in the tropics and the warmer subtropics. Sow seed directly into the ground in spring.

Anacardium occidentale
This species can grow to 25 ft (8 m), but usually reaches just half that height. It has a spreading, irregular crown that bears flowers early in the wet season, followed by the fruit. *Zones 11–12.*

ANANAS
Pineapple
This genus of 8 species of South American bromeliads includes several ornamental plants for subtropical and tropical gardens, but is more important as a commercial crop. The plants have large rosettes of narrow, tapering, tough leaves with sharply toothed or spiny edges. The flowers, which develop into the familiar compound fruit shape, are usually reddish purple, each backed by a bract and borne in a crowded head at the top of a short, stout stem that emerges from the center of the leaf rosette.

Cultivation
All *Ananas* species are very frost-tender, and can only be grown outdoors in climates that are tropical or subtropical. In cooler regions, they can be grown as indoor or conservatory plants, but they must have strong light. Grow in full sun in fertile, well-drained soil. Propagate by removing the basal suckers that develop on mature rosettes. Alternatively, remove the leafy top from the fruit and treat it as a cutting, either rooting it in soil or in water. Plant in early summer.

Ananas comosus
Pineapple
The pineapple was praised by early European explorers as the finest of all fruit. The leaf rosettes are up to 30 in (75 cm) high and 4 ft (1.2 m) wide. Each sword-shaped leaf is viciously edged with tiny thorns, but smooth-leafed cultivars have recently been developed. The inflorescence, up to 12 in (30 cm) long with yellow to red bracts, grows up to 4 ft (1.2 m) tall when in fruit. Fruit develop in the second year if conditions are suitable. '**Porteanus**' has leaves with a central yellow stripe, while '**Variegatus**' has leaves with cream marginal stripes and may develop red tints. *Zones 11–12.*

ANNONA
This genus of about 100 species of evergreen trees from the American tropics and subtropics includes some of the most delectably sweet tropical fruits, notably the cherimoya, custard apple and sweetsop. The trees have broad, oblong, strongly veined leaves, and curiously shaped flowers. These often have a pungent fruity aroma, and emerge from the old wood on short stalks. The fruit consist of many fused segments, and have tough green or brownish skin that may be covered in soft prickles or other protrusions. They contain many brown seeds embedded in a pulpy white flesh.

Cultivation
Mostly frost-tender, they are happiest in tropical and warmer subtropical areas.

Ananas comosus cultivar

Grow in a sheltered, sunny position and fertile, well-drained soil; fruit yield may be damaged by low temperatures. They may flower and fruit through much of the year. Plant trees in winter when dormant. Propagate from freshly extracted seed, or by grafting for selected varieties.

Annona muricata
Soursop

From northern South America, this plant grows to 15–20 ft (5–6 m), branching low with strongly ascending lateral growths. New growths have brownish silky hairs; older leaves are glossy bright green. The large green fruits are asymmetrically oval, covered in soft spines, and may be borne throughout the year. Despite the name, the fluffy white aromatic flesh is not very sour. *Zones 10–12.*

Annona squamosa
Custard apple, sugar apple

There are many varieties of custard apple, a popular, semi-deciduous fruit tree that grows to 15 ft (5 m). Its flowers are pale green and pleasantly scented. The large fruit has a custard-like texture and is delicious when eaten fresh. *Zones 10–12.*

ARTOCARPUS

Best known in the form of one of its many species, the breadfruit of Captain Bligh of the *Bounty* fame, *Artocarpus* is actually a very large tropical Asian

Annona muricata cultivar

Annona squamosa cultivar

genus of evergreen trees. It is closely related to *Ficus*, the fig genus, and in fact many of its species are hard to tell apart from figs when not in flower or fruit. The leaves, bark and twigs exude a milky sap when damaged. The minute, greenish, female flowers are crowded onto short, fleshy spikes, which after fertilization enlarge into aggregations of fleshy fruit, very large in the case of the species mentioned below.

Cultivation

Species with edible fruit are cultivated in the wet tropics, thriving best in deep, fertile, well-drained soil in sheltered positions. Propagate from seed, root cuttings or aerial layers (marcotts), which perpetuate desirable clones. Plant at any time, but preferably at the start of the wet season. Harvest the fruit in autumn.

Artocarpus altilis
syn. *Artocarpus communis, A. incisa*
Breadfruit

Believed to be native to the Malay region and carried into the Pacific by colonizing Polynesians, this species has handsome foliage, with ascending branches bearing deeply incised fresh green leaves up to 30 in (75 cm) long. Fast growing when young, it reaches 25 ft (8 m) in 10 years; old trees are not much taller but develop a rounded, bushy crown. The flower spikes are inconspicuous, the female ones developing into yellowish green globular fruit

Artocarpus heterophyllus cultivar

with starchy flesh that is eaten after
baking or boiling. *Zone 12.*

Artocarpus heterophyllus
Jackfruit, jaca

This Southeast Asian species is easily
confused with its close relative the
chempedak *(Artocarpus integer);* both
have similar gigantic, compound fruit
and leathery, unlobed leaves, but the
chempedak's fruit are sweeter. The
jackfruit grows to 30 ft (9 m) tall with a
single main trunk and dense, rounded
crown of dark green leaves. The fruit may
be up to 24 in (60 cm) long and weigh
up to 40 lb (18 kg). Their outer surface
is creamy brown with small conical
protuberances, and the sticky yellow or
pink flesh contains many large brown
seeds which are edible, as is the sweet
though malodorous flesh. *Zones 11–12.*

AVERRHOA

These tropical fruit trees are close
relatives of the *Oxalis* or wood sorrels,
some of which are hated weeds. Common to both are the flower structure of
5 overlapping pink or red petals and the
5-angled fruit, which in miniature in
Oxalis split open to scatter tiny seeds
rather than remaining fleshy as in
Averrhoa. The genus consists of only 2
species from Southeast Asia. These are
small trees with densely twiggy crowns
and short pinnate leaves, some of which
yellow and drop in the dry season. The
slightly fragrant flowers are borne in
short lateral clusters from the old wood
and the slow-ripening fruit hang in
clusters from the branches.

Cultivation

The trees are easily grown in full sun in
tropical and warmer subtropical, humid
climates, making fine small shade trees.
Propagate from seed, or by grafts or air-
layers (marcotts) which preserve

desirable clonal characteristics. Plant at
any time, but preferably at the start of
the wet season.

Averrhoa carambola
Carambola, star fruit, five-corner

In cultivation this upright species grows
to about 20 ft (6 m) high. The leaflets of
the compound leaves have the curious
habit of folding together after being
touched or at night. It flowers and fruits
through much of the year, but with
major flushes of flower in the middle of
both the wet and dry seasons. The large,
ornamental fruit ripen through pale
yellow, when their flavor is pleasantly
acid, to deep golden orange, when they
become sweet and deliciously tangy,
reminiscent of passionfruit. *Zones 11–12.*

Averrhoa carambola cultivar

Carica papaya cultivar

CARICA
Papaya, pawpaw

Large, succulent, edible fruit character-
ize this genus of 22 species from Central
and South America. One species, *Carica
papaya*, is grown throughout the tropics
for its large sweet fruit, and 2 or 3 others
with slightly smaller fruit are cultivated
to a lesser extent. Although ultimately
tree sized, they remain soft wooded and
are short lived. The very large leaves are
mostly deeply lobed in a snowflake-like
pattern. Male and female flowers are
normally borne on separate trees, but
hermaphrodite trees have been developed for cultivation. The small, cream,
male flowers are in long-stalked
panicles, while the larger, fleshy females
are stalkless and solitary. Female flowers
are followed by cylindrical or round
fruits in spring, with a second crop in
late summer.

Cultivation

Papayas can only be grown outdoors in
frost-free or near frost-free climates. The
lowland tropical species are not really
suitable for frost-free temperate regions,
but may be induced to ripen their fruits
against a hot wall or in a greenhouse.
Plant in spring in rich, moist, well-
drained soil in full sun or part-shade.
Propagate from seed, cuttings or by
grafting.

Carica papaya
Papaya, pawpaw

The true papaya is very much a tropical
plant, and will not tolerate freezing
temperatures or even prolonged cold. It

grows up to 20 ft (6 m) high with a single trunk and a palm-like head of foliage. The leaves are up to 24 in (60 cm) across and are carried on 24 in (60 cm) stems. Young plants bear the heaviest crops of fruit, and it is wise to keep a succession of plants coming on as replacements. *Zones 10–12.*

CARYA
Hickory

These medium to large deciduous trees are valued for their strong wood and edible nuts. Some 20 species occur in North America and Asia. They have large, pinnate leaves that turn yellow, orange or rich gold in autumn. Male and female flowers appear on the same plant in late spring. The nut is enclosed in a leathery husk that is neatly divided into 4 segments. *Carya illinoinensis* is the only commonly cultivated species, grown for its edible pecan nuts.

Cultivation

Hickories are fast growing and although quite frost-hardy, *Carya illinoinensis* needs long, hot summers to set fruit and for the wood to mature. It prefers a sheltered, fertile site with deep, moist soil in regions with cold winters and long, hot, humid summers. Many selections have been named, propagated by grafting. Plant when dormant in winter.

Carya illinoinensis
Pecan

This species produces one of the world's most popular edible nuts. From central USA, it occurs along broad river valleys and grows to 100 ft (30 m) tall with scaly gray bark. In cultivation, it grows quickly to become an open-crowned tree of about 30 ft (9 m) within 10 to 15 years. The leaves are long, with many glossy green leaflets, and the elongated nuts occur in clusters in autumn. *Zones 6–11.*

Carya illinoinensis cultivar

CASTANEA
Chestnut, chinquapin

A genus of 10 species of cool-climate deciduous trees, from temperate Eurasia and North America, all bearing edible nuts enclosed in a prickly, burr-like husk. The leaves are elliptical with regularly toothed margins and a feather-like arrangement of veins. In spring or early summer, showy catkins of male flowers appear, and the less conspicuous female flowers on the same tree develop into the nuts. The larger species are highly valued for the fine timber they produce.

Cultivation

In a cool climate, chestnuts are easily grown in full sun or part-shade in deep, fertile soil. Hot, dry summers suit them

Castanea sativa cultivar

well as long as ample soil moisture is available in winter and spring. Propagate from seed; plant out seedlings early to avoid disturbing the taproot. Plant in autumn or early spring. Collect the nuts in autumn.

Castanea sativa
Sweet chestnut, Spanish chestnut

This species comes from countries around the Mediterranean, Black and Caspian Seas, but has been planted throughout Europe for its edible nuts since time immemorial. Young trees are vigorous and have a pyramidal crown, but become massive and spreading with age, and the bark is deeply fissured. In autumn, the leaves turn from yellowish green to gold and russet. When planting for nuts, buy grafted named varieties from a source certified free of disease. *Zones 5–9.*

Castanea sativa cultivar

× *CITROFORTUNELLA*

This hybrid genus name includes any existing or potential hybrid between the genera *Citrus* and *Fortunella* (the kumquats), both of which are regarded as citrus fruits in a broad sense. The plants are intermediate in character between these, as might be expected, showing the influence of the *Fortunella* parent in a more shrubby habit, smaller leaves and less edible fruit than most *Citrus* plants.

The calamondin is the only well-known hybrid of this type, but there is also a less well-known cross between a lime and a sweet kumquat.

Cultivation

All are sensitive to frost. Like other citrus they need ample water all year round and regular feeding. They are usually propagated by grafting onto a *Poncirus trifoliata* rootstock. Plant in summer.

× *Citrofortunella microcarpa* cultivar

× *Citrofortunella microcarpa*
syn. *Citrus mitis*
Calamondin, Panama orange

A hybrid between a mandarin *(Citrus reticulata)* and a kumquat *(Fortunella margarita)*, this is the least edible of all citrus fruits. However, it makes an attractive ornamental shrub of up to about 8 ft (2.4 m) high with small bright orange fruits and is widely grown either as a tub specimen outdoors or, in cool climates, as a potted indoor plant. *Zones 10–12.*

CITRULLUS

This genus of 3 species is remarkable for having produced some of the sweetest of all melons, the watermelons, even though all its forms are very bitter and normally quite inedible. The plants are trailing annuals or perennials with very deeply lobed leaves and yellow flowers. The fruit, borne in summer, have smooth but hard skins and green, white or pink flesh in which is embedded brown to black seeds.

Cultivation

Grown in much the same way as pumpkins or cantaloupes, they require a friable, well-manured soil with good drainage and a long, warm growing season with plenty of water—the longer and hotter the summer the better the crop will be. In cool climates they may be grown in a greenhouse, but the space they need diminishes their value in terms of fruit production. Sow seed in spring. Watch for cucumber beetles.

Citrullus lanatus cultivar

Citrullus lanatus
syn. *Citrullus vulgaris*
Watermelon, camel melon
The original wild form of this species is believed to have come from southwestern Africa and is a prostrate annual vine with hairy stems, lobed leaves about 4 in (10 cm) long, and a spherical or oval melon 4–6 in (10–15 cm) long with moderately bitter flesh. It is a common weed in inland Australia. Apart from the watermelon, cultivated forms include some smaller melons with yellow or orange flesh, and the 'preserving melon' *(Citrullus lanatus* var. *citroides)* which is also small with white, hardly sweet flesh, used for pickling. *Zones 8–11.*

CITRUS
The number of original wild species in this genus of small evergreen trees, originally native to Southeast Asia, is very uncertain as many of the cultivated forms are probably ancient hybrids from their first domestication in China and India. While largely cultivated for their fruit, citrus plants have the bonus of looking attractive in the garden, with glossy evergreen leaves and fragrant flowers. Most species are frost-tender to some degree but a few tolerate light frosts: the lemon is the most cold resistant, especially when grafted onto the related *Poncirus trifoliata* rootstock, and the lime is the least cold resistant, best grown in subtropical locations. All citrus can also be grown in pots, as long as the containers are large and the citrus are grown on dwarf rootstocks.

Cultivation
Very well-drained, friable, slightly acid, loam soil is best. They need full sun, regular watering and protection from wind, especially during the summer months. Citrus also need regular feeding, including large amounts of nitrogen and potassium for good fruiting. Prune only to remove dead, diseased and crossing wood. Subject to a range of virus diseases, they are susceptible to many pests including scale, leaf miner, bronze orange bug, spined citrus bug and fruit fly. They are rarely propagated by home gardeners as this is done by grafting, a specialist task. Plant in spring or autumn.

Citrus aurantifolia
Lime
Best in tropical and subtropical climates, the lime is stronger in acidity and flavor than the lemon. It is an erect tree, to 15–20 ft (5–6 m) tall, with spiny, irregular branches, making it less ornamental than other citrus plants. The Tahitian lime, the most popular variety, bears fruit all year round. The Mexican lime has smaller fruit with high acidity and a stronger flavor, and is also a thornier tree. *Zones 10–12.*

Citrus aurantium
Sour orange, Seville orange
These marginally frost-hardy small trees are grown as ornamental shrubs or for

Citrus aurantifolia cultivar

Citrus aurantium cultivar

Citrus limon cultivar

their fruit, borne mainly in summer, which are used to make marmalade and jelly. They have spiny branches and glossy ovate leaves; the fragrant white flowers are followed by the reddish orange fruit, 2–3 in (5–7 cm) in diameter. The dwarf **'Bouquet de Fleurs'** is a very fragrant, ornamental shrub; **'Chinotto'** is excellent in containers or borders, with small, dark green leaves and a compact habit. The heavy-fruiting **'Seville'** is the premium marmalade orange. Watch for melanose (dark brown spots on the wood and fruit) and citrus scab. *Zones 9–11.*

Citrus limon
Lemon

This large shrub or small spiny tree, to around 20 ft (6 m) tall, has finely toothed, light green leaves and fragrant flowers that open from purple- or red-tinted buds. Flowers are followed by the yellow fruit. Lemons grow best in warm Mediterranean climates with mild winters. They are prone to collar rot, so plant with the graft union well above the soil and keep mulch away from the stem. **'Eureka'** is a one of the most commonly grown cultivars, bearing fruit and flowers all year round. It is an attractive, almost thornless tree, the best variety for temperate locations and coastal gardens. **'Lisbon'** is a popular commercial variety because it is reliable and heavy fruiting; it is good for hot areas but is thorny. The smaller and hardier **'Meyer'** bears smaller fruit and is ideal for growing in pots. *Zones 9–11.*

Citrus medica
Citron, cedrat

This was the first citrus to reach the Mediterranean, some saying it came with Alexander's returning armies from India. It was believed to have medicinal properties in earlier times and was also used to make perfume. A tall shrub of rather ungainly habit, it has purple-tinged young foliage and flowers. The fruit, borne in autumn, is like a giant

Citrus medica cultivar

Citrus limon 'Eureka'

Citrus limon 'Meyer'

Citrus × *paradisi* cultivar

lemon, 6–12 in (15–30 cm) long, but of more irregular shape and with a rougher, highly fragrant skin. It has little juice and is used mainly for marmalade and candied peel. The smaller-fruited **'Etrog'** has been grown in Israel for many centuries and has become part of Jewish religious custom. *Zones 9–11.*

Citrus × *paradisi*
Grapefruit

Easily grown in mild areas, the grape-fruit can make a dense, rounded tree to 20–30 ft (6–9 m) or more, similar to the orange but larger and with larger leaves. The large, golden-skinned summer fruits grow in clusters like grapes (hence its common name). The fruits usually have white flesh, but some varieties with pink flesh are available. **'Golden Special'** is a frost-hardy cultivar. Seedless grapefruits are particularly popular and include

Citrus × *paradisi* cultivar

'Marsh' and **'Morrison's Seedless'**. **'Ruby'**, another seedless variety has sweet pink flesh. **'Wheeny'**, a popular Australian hybrid, thrives in climates too cold for other cultivars and has very juicy fruit. All are usually grown from cuttings or grafts. *Zones 10–12.*

Citrus reticulata cultivar

Citrus sinensis cultivar

Citrus reticulata
Mandarin, tangerine

This is the most varied citrus species, and has a wide range of climate tolerance: some varieties can survive an occasional light frost. It grows to 12–20 ft (4–7 m) or so high, and is a good fruit tree for the suburban garden, producing fruit from autumn to spring. Similar to oranges, the fruit are smaller and looser skinned. It is slow growing and has heavily perfumed flowers. *Zones 9–11.*

Citrus sinensis
Orange

This species forms an attractive, round-headed tree, to 15 ft (5 m) or more tall, with glossy foliage and sweet-scented white flowers. It can be grown in most non-tropical climates and will even tolerate very light frosts. **'Joppa'** is a good variety for tropical gardens. **'Ruby Blood'** has oblong fruit with a reddish color to its rind, flesh and juice; it is the best known and best tasting of the 'blood oranges'. **'Valencia'** is perhaps the most frost-hardy of all oranges; it produces fruit in spring and summer which is usually used for juice but can also be eaten fresh. Navel oranges are mutated forms with a 'navel' at the fruit apex, and no seeds: **'Washington Navel'**, which fruits through winter, has very large and sweet, bright orange fruit and is best suited to slightly cooler areas. New varieties available to commercial growers may be found at specialist nurseries. *Zones 9–11.*

Citrus sinensis 'Valencia'

Citrus × tangelo
Tangelo

This evergreen tree grows 20–30 ft (7–9 m) high and 10 ft (3 m) wide and bears fruit in summer. Derived from a cross between the tangerine *(Citrus reticulata)* and the grapefruit *(C. × paradisi)*, the tangelo is renowned for its juice and as a superb dessert fruit with a tart, yet sweet flavor. Plant in a warm site sheltered from frost. *Zones 9–11.*

Citrus × *tangelo* cultivar

CORYLUS
Hazel, filbert

The 10 or more deciduous trees and large shrubs in this genus from northern temperate regions are best known for their edible nuts. The commonly grown species have massed stems that spring from ground level, but some others have a well-developed trunk. The branches are tough and supple, and bear broad, toothed leaves that are somewhat heart-shaped and strongly veined. Male and female flowers grow on the same plant, the males in slender catkins that appear before the leaves expand; the females are inconspicuous. The catkins develop into the distinctive nuts, each enclosed in a fringed green husk and ripening in summer.

Cultivation

Provide ample space, full sun or part-shade and fertile, moist but well-drained, chalky soil. Propagate by detaching suckers, or by fresh nuts. Plant in spring. For fruit set, there is a cold requirement of about 1000 hours below 45°F (7°C). Cool, moist summers also assist nut production.

Corylus avellana
Common hazel, cobnut, European filbert

This species occurs throughout Europe, western Asia and northern Africa. It typically makes a broad mass of stems about 12–15 ft (4–5 m) high. In winter, the bare twigs are draped with a striking display of yellow catkins. The nuts are half enclosed in a fringed tube. In autumn the leaves turn pale yellow. **'Cob'** produces large, long nuts in a thin shell. **'Contorta'** is a bizarre cultivar with branches that twist and wriggle in all directions; when leafless they are cut for sale by florists. **'Cosford'** is a good pollinator, producing many male flowers. **'Halls Giant'**,

another popular pollinator because of its fairly low yields bears large, sweet-tasting nuts with smooth kernels. *Zones 4–9.*

CUCUMIS
Cucumber, gourd, melon

As well as the cucumber (see under 'Vegetables'), this genus includes most of the melons except watermelon, which is *Citrullus*. The melons are mostly scrambling vines, with large, lobed leaves and white or yellow flowers. They produce rounded fruit with many seeds and white, yellow or orange flesh in summer.

Cultivation

All melons need a long, hot growing season to produce sweet fruit, and in a

Corylus avellana cultivar

Cucumis melo, Cantalupensis Group cultivar

Cucumis melo, Inodorus Group cultivar

cooler climate the vines grow best over concrete or rocks, or trained over black plastic so heat can circulate around the plant. Plant in humus-rich soil and water generously. Hand pollinate if growing melons on a small scale. Propagate from seed sown in spring.

Cucumis melo
Melon

The wild forms of this species occur over the whole range of the genus, producing 2 in (5 cm) long melons that are barely edible. Long domestication has given rise to the sweet, delicious melons we know today. They have evolved into several major cultivar groups, according to the characteristics of their fruit. The **Cantalupensis Group** includes the cantaloupes, or rockmelons: compact plants with oval or round fruit with netted rinds and orange flesh. The **Inodorus Group** are the honeydew melons: small bushy plants producing melons with a hard rind making them suitable for long storage. The greenish white skin is often smooth and the flesh pale green or yellow. The **Reticulatus Group** are the netted melons, with net-like markings on the rind and orange flesh; they are widely grown in the USA. *Zones 8–11.*

CYDONIA
Quince

This genus contains one species of quite unusual and ornamental, decidu-ous tree. Native to temperate Asia, it belongs to the pome-fruit group of the rose family. The small, crooked, very woody trees have smooth bark and simple, oval leaves, downy at least on the underside and clustered on short spur-shoots (as in apples) except on the long summer growths. Solitary flowers with downy calyces and pink petals are

Cydonia oblonga cultivar

borne at the ends of the spur shoots. The large, pear-shaped fruits have waxy or almost greasy skins that are pleasantly aromatic. The fruit is usually cooked and is good for preserving and pickling.

Cultivation

Quinces will only thrive in cool-temperate climates. They require moist, deep soil and a sunny position. Propagate from seed (easily obtained from over-ripe fruit) or by grafting for named varieties. Plant in autumn or late winter. The aromatic fruit can be left on the tree for a few weeks after they ripen in autumn.

Cydonia oblonga
Common quince

A spreading, bushy tree of 12–15 ft (4–5 m), this species forks low down on its trunk into crooked limbs. The leaves are moderately large and deep green above but downy on the undersides and on young twigs. In late spring it bears very attractive flowers, about 2 in (5 cm) in diameter and usually a clear pale pink. The fruit, edible when cooked, ripen to pale or deep yellow and are up to 6 in (15 cm) long with hard flesh. *Zones 6–9*.

CYPHOMANDRA

This genus of about 30 species of evergreen shrubs, climbers and small trees from tropical America is closely related to *Solanum*. They have thin, usually hairy leaves, 5-petaled pink to purple flowers in branched sprays in the leaf axils, and berry-like fruits of varying size, which are edible in some species. *Cyphomandra betacea*, the tamarillo, is grown for its fruit.

Cultivation

The tamarillo is best suited to subtropical or frost-free, warm-temperate climates. Train against a wire fence or stake to protect from wind, as it is inclined to be top-heavy. It is a shallow-rooted plant that prefers moist but not wet soil. Prune lightly after fruiting and pinch out growing tips at 3 ft (1 m) high to encourage branching. Propagate from cuttings, and plan to replace it after 5 years or so because it is short lived. Plant in spring.

Cyphomandra betacea cultivar

Cyphomandra betacea
Tamarillo, tree tomato

This large shrub from South America grows to about 10 ft (3 m) tall with a tree-like form and a wide crown. It bears large green leaves and small sprays of pinkish flowers in the branch forks over much of the year. A succession of egg-shaped fruits follow, mainly in summer; they are about 2–3 in (5–8 cm) long with shiny dark red skin (yellow-orange in some varieties). Tamarillos can be used for jam or the pulp can be eaten as a dessert. *Zones 9–11*.

DIOSPYROS
Persimmon, ebony

This genus consists of several hundred species of mostly evergreen trees from the tropics and subtropics, as well as several deciduous species from temperate Asia and America. Some species bear edible fruit in summer, notably the black sapote *(D. digyna)* and the Japanese and American persimmons. *Diospyros ebenum* from Sri Lanka provides the now rare timber ebony. All have strong branches, smooth-edged leaves, and flowers with rolled-back petals and a leaf-like calyx that enlarges as the pulpy fruit develops; the fruits of most species are edible. For good crops, grow plants of both sexes.

Cultivation

Fully frost-hardy to frost-tender, these trees prefer well-drained, moist soil, with ample water in the growing season and, being brittle, need shelter from strong wind. Propagate from seed. Plant trees in autumn or late winter.

Diospyros digyna
Black sapote

This evergreen tree grows to 60 ft (18 m) tall in the wild in Mexico and Central America; it has also naturalized in tropical Asia. The leaves reach 8 in

(20 cm) long; the flowers are small, white and fragrant. The fruit, about 4 in (10 cm) across, ripen quickly from olive green to black and are high in vitamin C. *Zones 11–12.*

Diospyros kaki
Japanese persimmon, kaki
This native of China that has been cultivated in Japan for centuries, is a deciduous tree, which grows to about 20 ft (6 m) tall with spreading branches. Its dark green, oval leaves turn yellow to deep orange in autumn. It has small cream flowers, which are followed by orange or yellow fruit about 3 in (8 cm) across. The fruit have delicious sweet flesh when ripe. There are many cultivars. *Zones 8–10.*

Diospyros kaki cultivar

Diospyros kaki cultivar

Diospyros virginiana cultivar

Diospyros virginiana
American persimmon, possum wood
This spreading tree can reach over 100 ft (30 m) in its native eastern USA, in alluvial river valley forests, but in cultivation it usually reaches 20–30 ft (6–9 m). It has cream flowers and sweet edible fruit, 1½ in (35 mm) across, ripening to orange or purple-red. The timber (white ebony) is valued for its durability. *Zones 5–9.*

DURIO
There are 20 or more species in this genus of tall evergreen trees, native to tropical Southeast Asia. They have elliptical, dull green, scaly leaves and their usually creamy white, heavily scented flowers are borne on the old wood, often twice a year. Some flowers develop into large, prickly fruits in autumn that fall and split open when ripe to reveal a strong-smelling, edible pulp.

Cultivation
As tropical plants, they do not thrive where temperatures fall much below 65°F (18°C). They prefer moist, humus-rich soil with full sun or dappled shade. Plants may be propagated from seed but the best fruiting cultivars are grafted or budded. Plant at any time.

Durio zibethinus
Durian
The durian, notorious for its putrid smell, is widely cultivated as a fruit tree in Asia. The tree grows to 120 ft (37 m) in the wild. The leaves are 8 in (20 cm)

long, dark green above and paler on the undersides. The greenish white or pink flowers, in clusters of 3 to 30, grow directly on the trunk and branches. The large, spiny, green to yellow fruits are up to 15 in (38 cm) long. *Zone 12.*

ERIOBOTRYA

This genus, which belongs to the rose family, includes 30 species of evergreen shrubs and trees. Only the loquat, *Eriobotrya japonica*, is commonly grown. Widely distributed through eastern Asia, from the eastern Himalayas to Japan, they include trees growing to 30 ft (9 m). All bear leathery, deeply veined leaves with silvery or felty undersides. The creamy white, scented flowers are held in loose sprays at the tips of the branches during autumn, and are followed by edible, decorative fruits.

Cultivation
Easily grown, they are marginally frost-hardy and will tolerate dry as well as coastal conditions. Grow in a fertile, well-drained soil in a sunny position. Propagate from seed or cuttings in early summer.

Eriobotrya japonica
Loquat
Native to China and Japan, the loquat can grow to 20–30 ft (7–10 m) tall. It forms a shapely conical tree, but in gardens it can be kept considerably more compact if pruned after the golden yellow fruit have been harvested. The large, deep green leaves are pale and felty underneath. Flowers are borne in late autumn and the fruit, which set in winter, ripen in spring. It is very susceptible to fruit fly, and birds can also damage the crop. This is a plant for temperate areas where ample moisture is available as the fruit mature. *Zones 8–10.*

FEIJOA
Pineapple guava
Named after Brazilian botanist de Silva Feijo, this genus of 2 species from subtropical Brazil and Argentina consists of evergreen shrubs that reach about 15 ft (5 m) tall with a similar spread. The plants are grown for their showy, edible flowers and guava-like fruits. The fruits appear only after a hot summer and may be damaged by autumn frosts. The oval, glossy green leaves have a silvery underside. Some botanists prefer to classify this genus as *Acca.*

Cultivation
Feijoas prefer a mild, temperate climate and are moderately frost-tolerant. Plant in well-drained, humus-rich soil and

Eriobotrya japonica cultivar

Feijoa sellowiana cultivar

provide ample water while the fruits
mature. They are easily propagated from
seed but grafted plants of named
cultivars produce better fruits. Fruit fly
is a problem in some areas. Plant in
autumn or late winter.

Feijoa sellowiana
syn. *Acca sellowiana*
Pineapple guava, feijoa
This species, with pruning, can be
formed into a single-trunked small tree
or it can be clipped as a hedge. The
flowers, carried on the new season's
growth, have red petals that are white
underneath and almost overshadowed
by prominent, dark red stamens. The
elongated fruit have a tangy flavor
and are eaten raw or made into jam.
Zones 8–11.

FICUS
Fig
This genus consists of about 800 species
of evergreen and deciduous trees, shrubs
and climbers from tropical and subtropical areas of the world. It includes the
common fig, *Ficus carica*, which bears
edible fruit, but most species are grown
for their ornamental foliage and for
shade. The tiny flowers are enclosed in
hollow fruit-like receptacles which
develop in the leaf axils.

Cultivation
Some grow to great heights in gardens
and most have vigorous, invasive root
systems. Moderately frost-hardy to
frost-tender, many make good pot plants
when young. Figs prefer full sun to part-
shade, humus-rich, moist but well-

drained soil and shelter from cold winds. Water potted figs sparingly. Propagate from seed, cuttings, or aerial layering. Plant edible figs in winter when leafless.

Ficus carica
Common fig

The edible fig, with its distinctive 3-lobed leaves, is indigenous to Turkey and western Asia and has been cultivated for millennia. A small deciduous tree, it reaches 30 ft (9 m) and needs a sunny site in a warm climate with dry summers, as rain can split the ripening fruit, usually harvested in summer and autumn. There are many named cultivars. **'Black Mission'** is the well-known black fig grown in California; the fruit is of excellent quality and in warm regions it bears two crops per year. **'Brown Turkey'** is a productive, vigorous tree with large, purplish brown fruit with pink flesh and a rich flavor. **'Genoa'** bears greenish yellow fruit with a rich

flavor and amber flesh. **'San Pedro'** is prized for its large and early first crop of fruit, which may be followed by a second, smaller crop. *Zones 8–11.*

Ficus carica cultivar

Ficus carica 'Black Mission'

FORTUNELLA
Kumquat, cumquat

The renowned Scottish plant collector Robert Fortune (1812–80) introduced the kumquat to the conservatories of the UK, where it has flourished ever since. The genus comprises 5 evergreen shrubs or small trees from south China to Malaysia. Originally they were included in the *Citrus* genus, to which they are closely related. They make compact, small shrubs and most have a small spine at the junction of leaf and branch. The fragrant white flowers are borne in spring followed by the small, edible orange fruits in summer and autumn. They make perfect container plants for small gardens or sunny patios.

Cultivation

Frost-tender, kumquats require an open position in full sun and fertile, moist but well-drained soil. Apply fertilizer in spring and water during the growing season, especially when the fruits are forming. In frost-prone areas grow in containers and overwinter in a greenhouse. Propagate species from seed or cuttings and varieties by budding onto rootstock in autumn or spring.

Fortunella japonica cultivar

Fortunella japonica
Kumquat, round kumquat, marumi cumquat

Reaching 8–12 ft (2.5–4 m), or smaller when container grown, this species from China bears decorative, small, golden orange fruit. They persist for a considerable time, but are best picked as they ripen to maintain the tree's vigorous growth. *Zones 9–11.*

FRAGARIA
Strawberry

The dozen or so species in this genus are mostly native to temperate areas of the northern hemisphere. They are low-growing, creeping or tufted perennials popular as ornamental ground covers and for their fleshy red fruit borne mainly in summer. They have palmate leaves with 3 toothed leaflets and cymes of white or pink, 5-petaled flowers. The

Fragaria × *ananassa* cultivar

Fragaria × *ananassa* cultivar

Fragaria × *ananassa* cultivar

strawberry itself is a false fruit; a large fleshy receptacle covered with tiny pips. Modern, more robust cultivars can fruit for 6 months, or all year round in a warm climate. There are many named varieties with varying flavors.

Cultivation

Grow these frost-hardy plants in containers or beds lined with straw in free-draining, acidic soil. The plants need full sun or light shade and protection from wind; in cold climates grow them in slits in sheets of plastic. Propagate from seed in spring or autumn or by runners and replant with fresh stock every few years. Protect them from snails, strawberry aphids and birds. Botrytis can be a problem in high rainfall areas.

Fragaria × *ananassa*
Garden strawberry

The name ananassa means 'pineapple-flavored', a curious description for this modern, large-fruited hybrid that arose from crossing American species. It has ovate leaflets that are glaucous above and white beneath. A wide range of garden strawberry cultivars have been developed to suit differing climates. Some, like **'Aromel'**, are repeat-fruiting and will produce a number of crops in one season; others, like **'Honeoye'**, produce only one main crop. *Zones 4–10.*

Fragaria vesca
Strawberry, woodland strawberry

Prior to their cultivation, which began in the sixteenth century, this strawberry was gathered from European woodlands. It is a spreading perennial with white flowers and grows to 12 in (30 cm) high. **'Semperflorens'** (syn. *Fragraria alpina*) has few runners and bears small, tangy, red or yellow fruit from early summer to autumn. **'Sweetheart'** and **'Temptation'** are just two of the many popular garden forms of this species. *Zones 4–10.*

GARCINIA

This is a genus of some 200 species of slow-growing evergreen trees and shrubs mostly from tropical Asia with a few from Africa. They are grown for their thick foliage and edible fruits. The mangosteen, *Garcinia mangostana*, is considered by many to be one of the world's most delicious fruits. Some species are cultivated for the yellow latex in their stems, which has been used in dyeing and is said to have medicinal properties.

Cultivation

Plant in part-shade in moist, well-drained soil and water regularly. Male and female flowers are borne on separate trees, but male trees are rare and most fruits are formed without fertilization (they thus contain no seeds). Propagation from cuttings or by layering is difficult and the trees bear fruit only in equatorial climates, so they are rarely seen away from their origins. Plant at any time.

Garcinia mangostana
Mangosteen
A slow-growing evergreen tree, about 30 ft (10 m) tall, the mangosteen is thought to have originated somewhere in Indonesia or Malaysia. It bears distinctive, glossy deep purple fruit, 3–4 in (7.5–10 cm) in diameter, which have a large leathery calyx attached to the base. The fruit has a thick, tough shell; inside the edible part consists of 5 to 8 glistening white segments, some containing a large seed. One or two crops of fruit are produced each year, usually in the tropical wet season. *Zones 11–12.*

JUGLANS
Walnut
This genus of 15 species of deciduous trees is found from the Mediterranean region and the Middle East to East Asia and North and South America. The name *Juglans* is derived from the Latin *Jovis glans*, meaning 'Jupiter's acorn'. All species bear edible nuts—usually produced within 12 years—and several yield fine timber used in furniture making. They are also grown for their handsome form and elegant, aromatic foliage. Greenish yellow male catkins and inconspicuous female flowers appear on the same tree in spring before the large pinnate leaves. They are followed by the hard-shelled nuts which can be collected from the ground when they have fallen in autumn. The fallen leaves are said to be toxic to other plants, so do not put them on the compost heap. These are excellent ornamental trees for parks and large gardens.

Cultivation
Cool-climate trees, they prefer a sunny position. Although quite frost-hardy, young plants and the new spring growth are susceptible to frost damage. They prefer deep, rich alluvial soil of a light, loamy texture and need regular water. Walnuts can be propagated from freshly collected seed in autumn but seedling trees produce nuts inferior to those of named varieties available as grafted plants. Plant in winter when leafless.

Juglans cinerea
Butternut, white walnut
From the rich woodlands and river valleys of eastern North America, this species reaches 60 ft (18 m) and has gray, furrowed bark. The dark green pinnate leaves are up to 18 in (45 cm) long and hairy on both sides. Male and female catkins, borne from late spring to early summer, are followed by clusters of 2 to 5 strongly ridged, edible, sweet-tasting, oily nuts, each enclosed in a sticky green husk. Native Americans used this tree as a digestive remedy and it was also widely used as a laxative in the nineteenth century. *Zones 4–9.*

Juglans regia
Common walnut, Persian walnut, English walnut
From southeastern Europe and temperate Asia, this slow-growing tree reaches 50 ft (15 m) tall with a spread of 30 ft (10 m). It has a sturdy trunk, a broad, leafy canopy and smooth, pale grey bark. The leaves are purplish bronze when young, and yellow-green catkins are borne from late spring to early summer. They are followed by the edible nut, enclosed in a green husk that

Juglans regia cultivar

withers and falls. The timber is valued for furniture making. Cultivars include **'Wilson's Wonder'**, which fruits younger than most at about 7 years old. *Zones 4–10.*

LITCHI
Lychee

This genus consists of just one evergreen tree from southern China and Southeast Asia, which is grown throughout the subtropics for its foliage and delicious fruit. The lychee is grown commercially by air layering or grafting the best varieties.

Cultivation

It requires full sun and shelter from wind and cold, although it can withstand an occasional light frost. Deep, moist soil is best, with regular water. Propagate from seed in summer or by budding or air-layering in spring. Trees raised from seed start to bear fruit after about 5 years.

Litchi chinensis cultivar

Litchi chinensis
Lychee

A graceful, slim-trunked tree, the lychee reaches a height of 30 ft (9 m) and a spread of 10–15 ft (3–4.5 m). Bright green pinnate leaves, gold or pink when young, form a low-spreading crown. Clusters of small, greenish yellow, petal-less flowers are borne in abundance in spring, followed by the bright red, edible fruit in summer which contain a sweet, whitish pulp and a brown seed. The pulp is reminiscent in texture and flavor to grapes. *Zones 10–11.*

MACADAMIA

Consisting of 11 species, this relatively small genus from Australia, Sulawesi in Indonesia and New Caledonia is made up of small to medium evergreen rainforest trees. Their leathery, narrow leaves, usually in whorls of 3 or 4 on the twigs, have smooth or toothed edges. They bear small flowers, crowded on cylindrical spikes, and nuts that take up to 9 months to mature.

Cultivation

These frost-tender trees require sun, plenty of water and fertile, moist but well-drained soil. They flower and fruit year-round in the tropics and in summer in temperate climates, with the nuts ripening in late summer, usually 5 to 8 years after planting. The best crops come from selected cultivars commonly grafted onto seedlings. Propagate from ripe seed in autumn.

Macadamia integrifolia
Smooth shell macadamia nut, Queensland nut

This spreading tree has whorls of leathery, glossy leaves and produces panicles of small, creamy white flowers 4 in (10 cm) long. It reaches 70 ft (21 m) in height and has edible round, brown nuts. *Zones 9–11.*

Macadamia tetraphylla cultivar

Macadamia tetraphylla
Rough shell macadamia nut, bopple nut

Growing to about 40 ft (12 m) in height with a bushy habit when given room, this handsome tree bears long, pendulous spikes of pink or white flowers. Its toothed, dark green leaves may be prickly. The new leaves are pinkish red before darkening with age. *Zones 10–11.*

MALUS

Apple, crabapple

This genus of 35 species of deciduous flowering and fruiting trees from the northern temperate zones contains a diverse range of crabapples as well as the many cultivars of edible apple, probably derived from crosses between several species and usually named *Malus × domestica*. The leaves are simple and toothed, sometimes lobed, and the flower clusters vary from white to deep rose pink or deep reddish purple. Best known

Malus × *domestica* 'Delicious'

Malus × *domestica* 'Discovery'

for their fruit, they are also valued for their shapely form and delicate spring blossom.

Cultivation
Very frost-hardy, they prefer a cool, moist climate and full sun (but tolerate part-shade) and need fertile, well-drained, loamy soil with protection from strong winds. They grow in poorer soils if fertilized occasionally. Cut out dead wood in winter and thin out branches to allow plenty of air and light round the fruit. Apples are not completely self-fertile and for good fruit production a different cultivar should be grown nearby. Advice on compatible pollinating cultivars should be obtained before buying apple trees. Propagate by budding in summer or grafting in winter. Plant trees in early spring in cool climates, in autumn in warmer areas. Watch for aphids and fireblight.

Malus × *domestica*
Common apple
This large hybrid group contains upright, spreading trees, usually with dark, gray-brown scaly bark and gray to reddish brown twigs. They can grow 30 ft (9 m) tall and 15 ft (5 m) wide. Their leaves are usually downy underneath and the white flowers are often suffused with pink. The sweet fruit are green or yellow to red. These common orchard trees are distinguished from the wild crab *(Malus sylvestris)* by their downy shoots, blunter leaves and juicy fruit that sweeten on ripening. There are hundreds of cultivars; some of the best known are **'Cox's Orange Pippin'**, **'Crofton'**, **'Delicious'**, **'Discovery'** and **'Fuji'**. Some apples have been bred specifically for their taste like **'Gala'**, a small dessert fruit with excellent flavor and good storage qualities. Other popular eating applies include **'Golden**

Malus × *domestica* 'Golden Delicious'

Delicious', **'Golden Harvest'**, **'Granny Smith'**, **'Gravenstein'**, and **'James Grieve'**. Some established cultivars like **'Jonathan'** have been used extensively for breeding new varieties; it is the parent of **'Jonagold'** (a cross with 'Golden Delicious') which has large, yellow, red-striped fruit with excellent flavor and a crisp texture, and **'Jonamac'**, a tall variety that can be trained over a path to make an arch. Many relatively new varieties are grown for their greater disease resistance, such as **'Liberty'**, a highly productive and especially disease-resistant tree; **'McIntosh Rogers'** has been used to breed other scab-resistant cultivars. **'Melrose'** produces good dessert apples

Malus × *domestica* 'Granny Smith'

Malus × *domestica* 'Jonathan'

Malus × *domestica* 'James Grieve'

Malus × *domestica* 'Melrose'

Malus × *domestica* 'Jonagold'

Malus × *domestica* 'McIntosh Rogers'

Malus × *domestica* 'Jonagold'

that store well. Apples good for cooking include **'Newtown Pippin'**, bearing large green, quite tart apples, and **'Rome Beauty'** which bears large red fruit with greenish white flesh.

All the apples mentioned so far are varieties that are grown commercially to supply year-round fruit. But there are many fine old varieties that are worthwhile growing in home gardens and small orchards with special markets. **'Adam's Pearman'** is a quality dessert apple with golden yellow skin flushed bright red; **'Ashmead's Kernel'** is an upright spreading tree with light greenish yellow fruit and sweet white flesh; **'Blenheim Orange'** has yellow fruit with one half flushed dull orange red; **'Bramley's Seedling'** has large, late-ripening fruit best suited to cooking; and **'Ellison's Orange'** bears light greenish yellow fruit with soft juicy flesh and a rich flavor.

Some apple varieties have been bred as single-stemmed columnar forms, enabling the trees to be grown close together in a row without occupying a lot of ground. Named varieties include **'Starkspur Compact Mac'** and **'Starkspur Supreme Red Delicious'**. *Zones 3–9.*

Malus × domestica 'Bramley's Seedling'

Malus × domestica 'Ashmead's Kernel'

Malus × domestica 'Blenheim Orange'

Malus × *domestica* 'Starkspur Compact Mac'

Malus × *domestica* 'Ellison's Orange'

Malus × *domestica* 'Starkspur Supreme Red Delicious'

Malus pumila 'Dartmouth'

Malus pumila

This name was once applied to the eating apples, now regarded as *Malus* × *domestica*, but its use still lingers for a group of crabapple varieties of uncertain origin. Their small, attractive fruit are ideal for stewing and have been used for generations for jellies and jams.
'Dartmouth' is an open, spreading tree to 25 ft (8 m) with white flowers that open from pink buds and large crimson fruit. *Zones 3–9.*

MANGIFERA

This is a genus of 40 or more species of evergreen trees from India and Southeast Asia. Their dense, glossy leaves are drooping and tinged strongly with red when young; this feature of tropical trees is thought to protect them from sun and heavy rain. The fruits, which are drupes, consist of a big central stone usually containing 3 embryos: the first 2 result from pollination, the third arises entirely from the mother tree. If the first two are removed as the seed germinates, the third grows and replicates the parent fruit. Nonetheless, it is customary to graft selected varieties.

Cultivation

These trees tolerate subtropical conditions, but prefer tropical monsoonal climates with a marked dry season. Rain at flowering time can rot the blossoms and ruin the crop. Plant in full sun in deep, rich soil; they need protection from strong winds. Prune when young to develop a single trunk. In addition to grafting, they can be propagated from ripe seed from summer to autumn. Check for fruit fly and fungal diseases.

Mangifera indica
Mango

The mango can grow 80 ft (25 m) tall and wide, although grafted trees are normally smaller. The tiny, greenish spring flowers are borne in large sprays. The fruit resemble enormous peaches, though the skin is smooth, and ripens to orange or red. Seedling trees tend to have furry seeds, making juice extraction awkward, and their flavor is often marred by a bitter aftertaste. Selected cultivars have superior fruit, sweet to the last, with smooth pits; **'Alphonso'** is universally regarded as the finest mango. **'Kensington Pride'** is the main commercial crop mango in Australia and is a vigorous tree bearing large, very sweet, almost round yellow fruit with a pink blush. **'Nam Doc Mai'** bears subtletasting, elongated deep yellow fruit. Other popular cultivars include **'Peach'**; **'R2E2'** with very large fruit; and **'Strawberry'**. *Zones 11–12.*

Mangifera indica cultivar

MORUS
Mulberry

There are about 10 species of deciduous shrubs and trees in this genus from the northern hemisphere. They bear broad, roughly heart-shaped leaves with closely toothed margins; the leaves on seedlings may be deeply lobed. Catkins of inconspicuous greenish flowers develop into tiny fruits, closely packed together to appear like a single fruit, the mulberry. Some species have been cultivated for centuries for their edible fruit and for silk production, as silkworm larvae feed on the leaves.

Cultivation

Mulberries thrive under a wide range of conditions, but do best in fertile, well-drained soil in a sunny, sheltered position. Propagate from cuttings, which can be quite large branches, in autumn or winter.

Morus alba
White mulberry

This species is mainly used for silk production in China and Japan, but is

Morus alba cultivar

Morus nigra cultivar

commonly grown on the eastern coast of Australia for its fruit. A vigorous, low-branching tree, it grows to 40 ft (13 m) tall with a broad, spreading crown and pendulous smaller branches. The leaves, almost hairless, are fresh green to yellow with strong veins and sharp, marginal teeth. The rather rubbery, summer fruit are cylindrical, sometimes long and narrow, and can vary in color from white through pink or red to purple-black. *Zones 5–10.*

Morus nigra
Black mulberry

Grown primarily for its fruit, this is the common mulberry of Britain and northern Europe, believed to have come from China or central Asia. It is similar to *Morus alba*, but has a thicker trunk, a more compact crown and darker leaves with velvety down underneath and blunt teeth. The dark red or almost black fruit ripen in early summer, becoming sweet when ripe. *Zones 6–10.*

MUSA
Banana, plantain

Bananas, native to Southeast Asia, are now cultivated throughout the tropics. Since they can ripen in transit, they have become a very familiar fruit in most temperate countries. Nearly all the edible varieties, including red and green fruit, lack seeds entirely. Most are grown for their fruit, but the genus also includes *Musa textilis*, which yields strong fiber known as Manila hemp, and other species grown for their enormous leaves or colored flowers. The flowers are borne in large spikes, erect or pendulous depending on species, the buds enclosed in large purplish bracts. Female flowers are borne at the base of the spikes, male ones further up. Although they often grow to tree size,

they are really giant herbaceous perennials: each 'trunk' is composed of leaf bases and, when the flowering shoot has risen and borne fruit, it dies.

Cultivation

Some of the smaller species can be grown as house plants or in greenhouses in temperate climates. Banana crops require fertile, moist soil and full sun. Protect from winds, which will cause new growth to shred. Propagate from ripe seed or by division of clumps. Plant at any time in tropical areas, in spring in cooler areas.

Musa acuminata
Banana

One of the most widespread wild species in tropical Asia, this plant normally forms a clump of several false stems up to about 20 ft (6 m) tall with long arching leaves. The pendulous flower spike has dull reddish bracts and the

Musa × paradisiaca cultivar

Musa × paradisiaca cultivar

fruit are long and curved, seedless in cultivated forms. **'Dwarf Cavendish'** grows only 6–10 ft (1.8–3 m) high with short, broad leaves. *Zones 10–12.*

Musa × paradisiaca

This hybrid name covers all the banana cultivars derived from the cross of *Musa acuminata* and *M. balbisiana*. They grow to 25 ft (8 m) tall, often flowering and bearing fruit less than 18 months after the shoot emerges from the rootstock. **'Lady Finger'**, 15 ft (5 m) tall, is well suited to domestic gardens, and is less vulnerable to bunchy top virus; it also tolerates more temperate climates. *Zones 10–12.*

NEPHELIUM

Related to the lychee *(Litchi chinensis)*, this Southeast Asian genus contains about 35 species of evergreen trees, with densely foliaged spreading crowns.

Nephelium lappaceum cultivar

Olea europaea subsp. *europaea*

Some species are grown in subtropical and tropical regions for their sweet-tasting, edible fruits.

Cultivation

These frost-tender plants require a tropical climate with even rainfall through the year. Provide full sun, and fertile, well-drained soil enriched annually with plenty of compost and well-rotted manure. Propagate from seed, or by grafting for named varieties. Plant in spring.

Nephelium lappaceum
Rambutan

This tree grows to 15 ft (4.5 m) tall, and bears clusters of white flowers in spring. The blooms are followed by orange-red fruit in summer, which are similar to lychees; they have a more delicate flavor, and are among the sweetest and most delicious of all tropical fruit, with a translucent flesh encased by a soft, prickly skin. *Zone 12.*

OLEA
Olive

There are about 20 species in this genus, all long-lived, evergreen trees. They have leathery, narrow to broad leaves and tiny, off-white flowers that are followed by the fruit, known botanically as drupes. The most important species is the common olive *(Olea europaea)*, which has many cultivars and is the source of olive oil. Since ancient times it has been cultivated around the Mediterranean for its nourishing, oil-rich fruit. The fruit are too bitter to be eaten fresh: they must be treated with lye (sodium hydroxide) before being pickled or preserved in their own oil. The wood of the olive tree is prized for carving and turning.

Cultivation

Generally, these plants require a mild climate, but winters need to be sufficiently cool to induce flowering, while the summers must be long and hot to ensure fruit development. Although olives can survive on poor soils, better crops will result if the trees are given a well-drained, fertile loam with ample moisture when the fruits are forming. Propagate from seed in autumn, from heel cuttings in winter or from suckers.

Olea europaea
Common olive

Olea europaea is a tree of wide distribution in Africa, Arabia and Himalayan Asia. The cultivated olive, *O. e.* **subsp.** *europaea*, is believed to have derived from smaller fruited plants thousands of years ago. A slow grower to about 30 ft (9 m), it is very long lived and does not bear fruit fully until it is at least 10 years old. Its picturesque habit, rough, gray bark and gray-green leaves, touched with silver on their undersides, make it a beautiful tree. *O. e.* **subsp.** *africana* has pea-sized black fruit and glossy dark green leaves, brown on the undersides. It makes a handsome small shade tree with a thick, gnarled trunk, but seeds itself so profusely as to become a problem weed in subtropical climates. There are numerous cultivars developed for eating or oil production: **'Barouni'** is grown mainly for eating and bears a good crop of large fruit, often called queen olives. **'Manzanillo'** is a popular commercial variety as it produces a heavy crop of olives with a high oil content; its low, spreading habit makes it easy to harvest. **'Mission'** has small olives with a high oil content and is very cold-resistant. **'Sevillano'** is a popular eating variety; it has good crops of large, fleshy olives with a low oil content. *Zones 8–11.*

PACHIRA

From tropical America, this genus consists of 24 species of evergreen and deciduous trees that can reach 90 ft (28 m). They are grown for their large, compound leaves and unusual flowers, which are followed by big, woody pods. The flowers have a large number of protruding stamens and are borne throughout the year, though each bloom lasts only a short time. These trees make excellent bonsai or container specimens.

Cultivation

Frost-tender, they need moist soil, full sun and preferably a tropical environment. Propagate from seed or cuttings in late summer.

Pachira aquatica
Guiana chestnut, shaving brush tree, provision tree

This evergreen tree can vary in height from 15 ft (5 m) to 60 ft (18 m). *Pachira aquatica* is grown for its fruit, which can be roasted and eaten in the same way as sweet chestnuts. This species has compound leaves consisting of up to 9 leaflets to 12 in (30 cm) long, and greenish or cream flowers with red-tipped stamens resembling long brushes. Its large brown fruit are 12 in (30 cm) long and 6 in (15 cm) round. This tree is suitable for boggy areas. *Zones 10–12.*

PASSIFLORA
syn. *Tacsonia*
Passionfruit, passion flower, granadilla

This genus contains over 400 species of mostly evergreen or semi-evergreen, tendril-climbing vines, primarily native to tropical South America. They are grown for their ornamental blossoms and their pulpy fruit, notably the passionfruit. Flowers range from pale pink to purple-red and fruit from pale yellow through to purple-black, depending on the species.

Cultivation

Very frost-hardy to frost-tender, these climbers are best suited to warm areas. Plant in rich, well-drained soil in full sun and provide support. Water regularly in summer. Prune congested or overgrown plants in spring. Propagate from seed in spring, or from cuttings or by layering in summer. Watch for nematodes.

Pachira aquatica cultivar

Passiflora edulis cultivar

Passiflora edulis
Passionfruit

This frost-tender species is valued for its glossy, bright green leaves, purple-white flowers and flavorsome fruit. It grows to 15 ft (5 m) and has white flowers that are green beneath. Train on a pergola or trellis and prune to prevent tangling, which can lead to insect infestation. Pick fruit in autumn when the skin has turned purple and is still smooth, but do not eat until the skin is wrinkled. This species is self-fertile. There are a number of vigorous cultivars and hybrids available, including **'Lacey'**, a popular Australian variety valued for its sweet-tasting fruit, and **'Nellie Kelly'**, a grafted cultivar bearing large fruit and large, dark green leaves. **'Panama Gold'** is a very popular passionfruit for commercial production with golden skin and flesh; **'Panama Red'** is a red-skinned form. **'Purple Gold'** bears a heavy crop of purple-skinned fruit with golden flesh. *Zones 10–12.*

Passiflora laurifolia
Yellow granadilla, Jamaica honeysuckle

This species, found through much of northern South America and the West Indies, has oval 4 in (10 cm) long leaves and flowers to 3 in (8 cm) wide. The sepals have red upper surfaces, green below. The petals are a similar color but with red, blue or white banding. The summer flowers are followed by ovoid yellow fruit, 3 in (8 cm) long. *Zones 11–12.*

Passiflora laurifolia cultivar

Passiflora quadrangularis
Giant granadilla

This vigorous, scrambling vine grows to 50 ft (15 m) or more tall. It has bright green, oval leaves and bears large, deep red flowers with a conspicuous ring of purplish filaments from mid-summer to autumn. The oblong to oval fruit, to 12 in (30 cm) long, have a yellowish rind with a very thick, spongy white inner layer and a sweet pulp. This frost-tender plant needs both high temperatures and high humidity to set fruit. *Zones 10–12.*

Passiflora quadrangularis cultivar

Persea americana cultivar

PERSEA

This genus consists of about 150 species of evergreen trees and shrubs mostly from tropical parts of Central and South America with a few from Asia and one, *Persea indica*, indigenous to the Azores and Canary Islands. The best known member of the genus is the avocado. They are large trees with deep green, elliptical leaves and inconspicuous unisexual flowers followed by the familiar large, rough-surfaced, pear-shaped fruits, which have a very high fat content.

Cultivation

Frost-tender and fast growing, they can be untidy trees as they drop leaves constantly. Although self-fertile, at least two trees are required for good crops. Avocados demand rich soil, perfect drainage, ample moisture and full sun when fruiting and are best sheltered from strong winds. Cutting-grown or grafted plants are superior to seedlings. Plant in spring.

Persea americana
syn. *Persea gratissima*
Avocado

This species is an evergreen tree that can reach a height of 60 ft (18 m). On a usually erect stem, it bears glossy, dark green, leathery leaves and small, green-ish flowers, held in the axils. Pear-shaped, nutritious, green or black fruit follow, ripening at most times of the year depending on the variety and region. The avocado is tender to both frost and drought, but can be nurtured in mild climates well outside the tropics. There are many named cultivars, each with different growth patterns and require-ments. *Zones 10–11.*

PHOENIX

These evergreen feather palms are native to subtropical and tropical parts of Asia, Africa and the Canary Islands. There are 17 very different species; some are an important source of food (dates and palm sugar), others are popular as house plants or avenue trees. *Phoenix* includes species with a single trunk as well as some that form clumps of stems. The long fronds have stiff, sharp spines at the base and form a dense crown. The small yellow flowers are of different sexes on different trees and are followed by the fruits on female trees.

Cultivation

Male and female plants are needed to ensure pollination. The plants prefer full sun, although they will tolerate part-shade, hot winds and poor soil if given good drainage. Hybrids between species are common. Trim off dead fronds. Propagate from seed in spring.

Phoenix dactylifera
Date palm

Native to the Middle East and North Africa, where they have been cultivated for over 5000 years, date palms grow to 60 ft (18 m) tall and 20 ft (6 m) wide with slender trunks. The fronds have a grayish tinge; those at the top point upwards, the lower ones curve down-wards to make a spherical crown. The dates, borne in autumn and early winter, are 1–3 in (2.5–8 cm) long, cylindrical and yellowish when fresh. Production of good quality fruit requires a climate with fierce summer heat and a dry atmo-sphere. *Zones 10–12.*

PHYSALIS
Ground cherry

This is a genus of about 80 species of annuals and perennials with a wide distribution, especially in the Americas. Most form a clump of upright leafy stems 2–4 ft (0.6–1.2 m) tall. The leaves are variable in shape, often with lobes or shallow-toothed edges. The flowers are small, usually white or yellow blotched purple, and are backed by calyces that enlarge to enclose the fruit as they develop in summer. The fruit are yellow, orange or red berries, and are often edible. They are ripe when the calyces start to dry out.

Cultivation
Hardiness varies, but most species tolerate moderate frosts. They prefer moist, well-drained soil and a position in sun or part-shade. Propagate from seed or by division. Plant in spring.

Physalis peruviana
Cape gooseberry, ground cherry
This perennial South American species grows to around 3 ft (1 m) tall. It is often treated as an annual and is grown for its crop of bright yellow to purple,

edible berries. Its leaves are oval to heart-shaped and up to 4 in (10 cm) long. The yellow-blotched purple flowers are ½ in (12 mm) wide and are quickly enveloped by the calyces. *Zones 8–11.*

PINUS
Pine
This important genus of conifers consists of around 120 species of needle-leafed evergreens, found in most parts of the northern hemisphere, especially in the Mexican highlands, southern USA and China. Most are medium to tall forest trees but a few are small and bushy. All have needles grouped in bundles of 2 to 7. Male (pollen) and female (seed) cones are borne on the same tree. *Pinus* species are divided into **white pines** (soft pines), which have 5 needles and

Physalis peruviana cultivar

non-woody cone scales, and **black pines** (hard pines), with 2 to 4 needles and woody cone scales that take 2 years or more to mature their seeds. Particularly valued for their wood, used for construction and paper pulp, the seeds of several species (pine nuts) are also an important food in some cultures. The nuts can be eaten whole, scattered in salads or other dishes, or may be pressed for oil or ground.

Cultivation
Most pines tolerate a range of conditions, will thrive on soils of moderate to low fertility, and are very wind resistant. They may need a symbiotic soil fungus to assist nutrient uptake on poorer soils. These fungi are likely to be already present in the pines' native regions, so a handful of decaying needles from a pine forest can be added if planting pines where none have grown before. The majority of pines require well-drained soil, and resent soil disturbance. Propagate from seed; cultivars may be grafted. Plant in winter.

Pinus edulis
Pine nut, Rocky Mountain piñon
Native to southwest USA, this species grows to around 50 ft (15 m) and has a compact domed crown with silver-gray, scaly bark. Its stiff needles are in pairs, 1½ in (3.5 cm) long and dark green. In autumn, it produces small, light brown cones which contain sweet-tasting, oily nuts. It thrives in hot, dry areas. *Zones 5–9.*

Pinus pinea
Roman pine, stone pine, umbrella pine
From southern Europe and Turkey, this species can reach 80 ft (24 m) in the wild and has a flattened crown and straight, but often leaning trunk with furrowed reddish gray bark. The rigid, paired

needles are 4–8 in (10–20 cm) long and bright green. It has shiny, brown, globe-shaped cones and contain edible seeds — the pine nuts. Once established this pine copes with most conditions, including dryness and heat. *Zones 7–8.*

PISTACIA
Pistachio
This small genus consists of 9 species of deciduous and evergreen trees and shrubs occurring naturally in the warm-temperate regions of the northern hemisphere. It includes the familiar edible pistachio nuts as well as ornamental deciduous species that develop vivid foliage tones in autumn, and species grown for their resins and oils. The tallest species grow to 80 ft (24 m). The leaves are compound, usually composed of an even number of leaflets. The

Pinus pinea

flowers are generally inconspicuous, male and female flowers occurring on separate plants. Female plants display clusters of small berries or fleshy fruits in autumn and early winter.

Cultivation

A well-drained soil in full sun is preferred. Propagate from seed sown in autumn and winter, or by budding or grafting.

Pistacia vera
Pistachio nut

This small deciduous tree reaching a height and spread of 30 ft (9 m) is native to western Asia and the Middle East, but is cultivated worldwide. The leaves consist of 1 to 5 pairs of oval leaflets and turn red-gold in autumn. Red male and white female flowers are borne on separate trees; at least one of each is needed for a crop of nuts in autumn. These are reddish, fleshy and oval with a green or yellow kernel. Hot, dry summers followed by mild to cold winters give the best yield. *Zones 8–10.*

PRUNUS

This large genus, mostly from the northern hemisphere, includes the edible stone fruits—cherries, plums, apricots, peaches, nectarines and almonds—but also ornamental species and cultivars with beautiful flowers. There are several shrubby species, but most are trees growing on average to 15 ft (5 m), although some can reach 100 ft (30 m). Most of the familiar species are deciduous and bloom in spring (or late winter in mild climates) with scented,

Pistacia vera cultivar

Prunus armeniaca cultivar (sun-drying)

5-petaled, pink or white flowers and simple, often serrated leaves. All produce a fleshy fruit containing a single hard stone. Many have attractive autumn foliage, and others have interesting bark. Cherry and plum timber is sometimes used commercially.

The 430 species in the genus are divided among 5 or 6 subgenera. They are: *Prunus* in the narrow sense, which includes all the plums and sometimes *Armeniaca*, the apricots; *Amygdalus* includes peaches, nectarines, almonds and a few ornamental species; *Cerasus* includes all the cherries and flowering cherries with few-flowered umbels; while *Padus* includes the bird cherries, mainly North American, with small flowers in long racemes; finally, the evergreen *Laurocerasus*, also with flowers in racemes and including the cherry laurel and tropical rainforest trees from Asia and the Americas.

Cultivation

Plant when dormant in winter in moist, well-drained soil in full sun but with protection from strong wind for spring blossom. Keep the base of trees free of weeds and long grass. Feed young trees with a high-nitrogen fertilizer. Many fruiting varieties respond well to espaliering. Propagate by grafting or from seed—named cultivars must be grafted or budded onto seedling stocks. Pests and diseases vary with locality.

Prunus armeniaca
Apricot

Now believed to have originated in northern China and Mongolia, the apricot was introduced to the Middle East more than 1000 years ago and from there to Europe. It grows to no more than about 25 ft (8 m) tall, the trunk becoming characteristically gnarled with age. White or pinkish blossoms are

Prunus armeniaca 'Story'

borne in early spring before the leaves appear. The twigs are reddish, and the smooth, heart-shaped leaves are about 3 in (8 cm) long. The yellow-orange fruit contains a smooth, flattened stone that separates easily from the sweet-tasting flesh. Prune moderately after flowering to encourage a good fruit crop. **'Glengarry'** bears the earliest maturing fruit, so is best grown in frost-free areas; the apricots are small but have good flavor. **'Morocco'** produces large, round fruit in mid-season that are good for drying. **'Story'** is another popular mid-season cultivar. **'Trevatt'** is often grown commercially for its large, sweet fruit that are good for drying. *Zones 5–10.*

Prunus avium
Sweet cherry, gean, mazzard, wild cherry

Native to Europe and western Asia, this species is the major parent of the cultivated sweet cherries. It can reach 60 ft (18 m) tall, with a rounded crown and a stout, straight trunk with banded reddish brown bark. The pointed, dark green leaves are up to 6 in (15 cm) long and turn red, crimson and yellow before they drop. Profuse white flowers appear in late spring before the leaves and are followed by black-red fruit. The cultivated cherries are rarely self-fertile, so trees of two or more different clones are often necessary for fruit production. Cherry wood is prone to fungus, so

Prunus avium cultivar

Prunus cerasus cultivar

Prunus avium cultivar

Prunus cerasus var. *austera* cultivar

avoid pruning in winter or in wet weather. **'Napoleon'** is an old French variety, valued for its large yellowish fruit, which are excellent for preserving. The ornamental cultivar **'Plena'** carries a mass of drooping, double white flowers. There are a number of popular, high-yielding cultivars, including the self-fertile **'Stella'**, which bears large, heart-shaped, dark red cherries, and **'Van'** with its large crops of very sweet, shiny black fruit. *Zones 3–9.*

Prunus cerasus
Morello cherry, sour cherry

The fruiting cherries of Europe and western Asia have been the subject of much botanical confusion. Many have been placed under this species, characterized by a smaller, more bushy habit than that of *Prunus avium*, suckering from the roots, and acid fruit. Its wild origin is unknown and botanists suspect it may have a common ancestry with *P. avium*. It is self-fertile, so an isolated tree can set fruit, but like the sweet cherry, it needs cold winters for successful growth. *P. c.* var. *austera*, the morello cherry, has pendulous branches and bears blackish fruit with purple juice; the red amarelle cherries with clear juice belong to *P. c.* var. *caproniana*, while the famous maraschino cherries with very small blackish fruit are *P. c.* var. *marasca*, which grows in Dalmatia. *Zones 3–9.*

Prunus × domestica
Plum, European plum

The common plum of Europe is believed to be an ancient hybrid, its probable ancestors thought to include the

Prunus × domestica 'President'

Prunus × domestica 'Stanley'

blackthorn, *Prunus spinosa*, and the cherry plum, *P. cerasifera*. It has numerous cultivars, most grown for their sweet fruit but some for their display of blossom. It is a vigorous grower to a height of 30 ft (9 m) or even more, with a tangle of strong branches spreading into a broad, dense crown of foliage. Only the vigorous new growths are sometimes spiny. Profuse, small clusters of white flowers are borne in spring, and the summer fruits are spherical to elongated with a yellow, red or blue-black skin and green or yellow flesh; they range in length from 1¼ to 3 in (3–8 cm). Not as juicy as the red-fleshed Japanese plums (*P. salicina*), the fruit of most cultivars are best cooked or dried for prunes. A popular cultivar for commercial production, **'Angelina Burdett'** bears small purple plums with a heavy bloom in mid-season. Cultivars with crops later in the season include **'Coe's Golden Drop'**, one of the best plums for eating with sweet, juicy, amber-yellow fruit with red spots; **'Grand Duke'**, which has large, oval, deep purple fruit; and **'President'**, which bears very sweet and juicy, purple oblong fruit with a heavy bloom.

'Stanley' bears large, purple-black, sweet and juicy, yellow-fleshed fruit in mid-season. **P. × domestica subsp. insititia**, the damson plum or bullace, is a thornier tree that often succeeds in districts too cold for large-fruited varieties; the small purple-black fruit with tart acid flesh are used for jams and jellies. *Zones 5–9.*

Prunus dulcis
syn. *Prunus amygdalus*
Almond
Closely related to the peach, the almond is believed to have originated in the eastern Mediterranean region, needing a climate with warm dry summers and cool winters to bear well. Growing to over 20 ft (6 m) high, it has a moderately spreading habit. Stalkless pink blossoms are borne in clusters of 5 to 6 on the leafless branches in late winter or early spring. These are followed in summer by flattened, furry fruit which dries and splits to release the weak-shelled stone; this contains the almond kernel. Almonds need well-drained, salt-free soil and the young trees are frost-tender; they are not self-fertile and two varieties that blossom at the same time are needed

to produce fruit. They are prone to shot-hole disease, which appears on the fruit as purple spots, spoiling the nut inside. Prune to an open vase shape to encourage 3 or 4 main branches. *Zones 6–9.*

Prunus persica
Peach, flowering peach, nectarine

Believed to have originated in China but introduced to the Mediterranean region over 1000 years ago, the peach grows to 12 ft (3.5 m) or more tall. It bears an abundance of pinkish red flowers in early spring (or late winter in mild climates). The narrow, 6 in (15 cm) long, mid-green leaves appear after the blossoms. Its delicious mid-summer fruit, which vary from cream and pale pink to yellow or scarlet, are covered with a velvety down and contain a stone that is deeply pitted and grooved. The many cultivars include both fruiting and flowering types; the latter mostly have small, hard fruit that are of little use for eating, but the fruiting cultivars can also have showy flowers. Fruiting cultivars include **'Anzac'**, grown for its heavy crops of red-flushed cream and green

Prunus persica 'Dixired'

fruit with soft juicy white flesh; **'Dixired'**, which bears smaller red-flushed, yellow-fleshed fruit; **'Flordaprince'**, another yellow-fleshed peach with large red and yellow fruit; and **'Golden Queen'**, which bears a very late crop of completely yellow fruit, often used commercially for canning. Other popular cultivars are **'Kernechter von Vorgebirge'**; **'Maravilha'**, with small, white-fleshed fruit colored dark red and cream; **'Orion'**, which bears a good crop of very juicy, white-fleshed, dark maroon and cream fruit; **'Red Haven'**, which bears medium-sized, yellow-fleshed peaches over a long season; **'Rekord aus Alfter'**; and **'Robert Blum'**. **'Sherman's Early'** is the

Prunus persica cultivar

Prunus persica 'Red Haven'

Prunus persica 'Rekord aus Alfter'

Prunus persica 'Kernechter von Vorgebirge'

Prunus persica 'Robert Blum'

Prunus persica var. nectarina cultivar

earliest fruiting peach, bearing small dark red fruit. *P. persica* **var.** *nectarina*, the nectarine, is almost identical to the peach in habit and flowers, but its fruit are smooth skinned, mostly smaller and with a subtly different flavor. There are several named varieties and their seedlings often revert to the normal, downy-skinned peaches. *Zones 5–10.*

Prunus salicina
Japanese plum

Including many of the best varieties, this plum may be an ancient hybrid of Chinese parentage and is not known in the wild. It makes a moderately large, spreading, deciduous tree up to 30 ft (9 m) tall with broad, slightly bronze-tinted leaves. The profuse white blossom is borne in early spring, or even in late winter in some climates, and is prone to damage from late frosts. Most varieties need cross-pollination with a compatible variety (not necessarily Japanese) for good fruit production. The late summer fruit are mostly very sweet and juicy with red or yellow flesh and thin purple or slightly greenish skin. Japanese plums do best in climates with a cold winter and a long, hot summer. Popular cultivars include **'Friar'** with juicy, deep purple to almost black fruit; **'Mariposa'**, bearing very sweet, dark red-fleshed plums with red-mottled skin; **'Narrabeen'**, which flowers early and bears large red, yellow-fleshed fruit; **'October Purple'** with large, very sweet, purple plums; and **'Queen Rosa'**, which has large, deep red fruit with a bloom on the skin. One of the most well known cultivars, **'Santa Rosa'** is unusual in being self-fertile; it bears juicy, red-fleshed, dark purple fruit. **'Satsuma'** bears good crops of large, juicy, slightly tangy tasting, dark red fruit. *Zones 5–10.*

PSIDIUM
Guava

This genus has about 100 species of evergreen trees and shrubs, which can

Psidium guajava cultivar

grow to 30 ft (9 m) tall. Native to
Central and South America, they are
grown for their fruits and foliage. Their
simple leaves are arranged in opposite
pairs. The clusters of 5-petaled white
flowers are followed by fruit in summer
and autumn. The fruit are globular to
oval with a thin, aromatic skin and soft
white or pinkish flesh in which small,
woody seeds are embedded. They are
used to make jellies, jams and juice, and
are available fresh in tropical and
subtropical areas.

CULTIVATION

Guavas need a warm to hot climate, a
sheltered site and rich, moist but well-
drained soil. Tip prune for compactness.
Propagate from seed or cuttings, or by
layering or grafting. Plant in spring or
summer.

Psidium cattleianum
Cherry guava

This shrub, which grows to 20 ft (6 m),
takes its common name from its deep red
to purplish fruit which are about 1 in
(2.5 cm) across. It has an upright trunk
with smooth, beautifully mottled bark.
The rounded, shiny green leaves, 3 in

Psidium cattleianum cultivar

(8 cm) long, are leathery and form a
canopy to 12 ft (4 m) across. Its single
flowers are 1 in (2.5 cm) across. ***Psidium
cattleianum* var. *littorale*** has yellow
fruit; **'Lucidum'** has sweet purplish fruit.
Zones 9–11.

Psidium guajava
Yellow guava

Grown in all tropical and subtropical
regions for its nutritious abundant fruit,
this tree reaches 30 ft (9 m) with a
dense, bushy canopy. It has scaly,
greenish bark and leathery leaves, 6 in
(15 cm) long, with prominent veins and
downy undersides. Spring flowers
bunched in the leaf axils are followed by
round, 3 in (8 cm) diameter fruit with
pink flesh and yellow skins. *Zones 10–12.*

Punica granatum cultivar

Punica granatum 'Nana'

Punica granatum cultivar

PUNICA
Pomegranate

This genus, originating from the Mediterranean region and southern Asia,
consists of just two species of deciduous
shrubs or trees. They have opposite,
entire leaves and trumpet-shaped, bright
red flowers. *Punica granatum*, the only
species cultivated, has been valued for
centuries for its edible fruit.

Cultivation

Pomegranates can be grown in a wide
range of climates, from tropical to warm-
temperate, but the red or orange fruit
will ripen only where summers are hot
and dry. Plant in deep, well-drained soil
preferably in a sheltered, sunny position.
They can be pruned as a hedge and are
also good in tubs. Propagate from seed
in spring, from cuttings in summer or by
suckers.

Punica granatum
Pomegranate

This species, growing to 15 ft (4.5 m)
tall and 10 ft (3 m) wide, has blunt-
tipped, glossy leaves, 3 in (8 cm) long.
Its large, 8-petaled, red-orange flowers
are borne at the branch tips in spring
and summer. These are followed by the
apple-like fruit, which have a thick rind
and a mass of seeds, each enclosed in a
reddish, acid-sweet envelope. Many
cultivars are available, the fruit varying
from very sweet to acidic and the
flowers from red to pink or white.
Punica granatum **'Nana'**, a dwarf
cultivar to 3 ft (1 m) high, has single
orange-red flowers and small fruit. The
commercially grown **'Wonderful'** has
double, orange-red flowers and large
fruit. *Zones 9–11.*

Pyrus communis 'Beurre Bosc'

Pyrus communis cultivar

Pyrus communis 'Packham's Triumph'

PYRUS
Pear

These 30 or so species from temperate Eurasia and North Africa are related to the apple *(Malus)*. Slow-growing, deciduous and semi-evergreen trees, they can reach 80 ft (24 m) but are often smaller. They have been cultivated since antiquity for their grainy textured, sweet, juicy, yellowish green fruits, not all of which are pear-shaped. They are also valued for their attractive autumn foliage, which needs plenty of sun, and their clusters of fragrant, 5-petaled, white flowers, sometimes tinged pink, which appear with the leaves, or just before them, in spring. The glossy leaves vary from almost round to quite narrow.

Cultivation

Having modest moisture needs they suit coastal areas with heavy, sandy loams and good drainage in a sunny position. They are ideal for cool-temperate climates. Cross-pollinate for fruit. Prune to remove damaged branches and for shape in late winter or early spring. Propagate from seed or by grafting. Plant in autumn or early spring.

Pyrus communis
Common pear

The parent of many garden cultivars, the wild pear is grown for its beautiful single, pinkish white flowers with red stamens. Long lived, the tree reaches 50 ft (15 m) with short branches and dark grey or brown bark that cracks into small plates. The dark green, leathery leaves have serrated margins and long stalks. The greenish summer fruit, up to 2 in (5 cm) long, ripen to yellow and are usually gritty with a dull flavor—the fruit of the cultivars are much sweeter and best when picked before fully ripe. **'Beurre Bosc'** is cultivated for its heavy crops of large, soft, sweet, brown-skinned pears that are good for baking. **'Bon Chrétien'** has been cultivated since medieval times for its medium-sized, succulent, musky-flavored fruit: it is the parent of the famous English **Williams** pear, known in North America,

Australia and New Zealand as the Bartlett pear and grown for canning—the red-skinned cultivar is known as **'Red Bartlett'**. **'Conference'**, an early-flowering pear from Europe, produces the best quality fruit if cross-pollinated; the fruit start to ripen in mid-autumn and should be picked before fully ripe. **'Corella'** is a South Australian cultivar that bears small, greenish yellow fruit flushed with red late in the season. Another late-cropping pear is **'Josephine de Malines'**, an old European cultivar bearing very sweet and juicy, small, conical, yellow-green fruit flushed with red. **'Packham's Triumph'** is an Australian cultivar with large, sweet, green-skinned fruit. Other popular cultivars include **'Triumph von Vienne'** and **'Winter Cole'**, an Australian cultivar bearing a large, late crop of small, almost round, slightly blushed yellow pears with very smooth, juicy flesh; and **'Winter Nelis'**, a late-ripening variety, producing small, sweet and juicy fruit with greenish skin spotted red. *Zones 2–9.*

Pyrus communis 'Triumph von Vienne'

Pyrus communis 'Triumph von Vienne'

Pyrus pyrifolia
Nashi pear, Japanese pear, sand pear

This compact tree, grown for centuries in China and Japan, grows to 50 ft (15 m) and is valued for its beauty and for its fruit. Abundant white flowers appear either just before or at the same time as the oblong, sharply toothed leaves. Glossy green when young, the leaves turn a rich orange-bronze in autumn. The small, round, brown fruit are hard and have a gritty texture. *Pyrus pyrifolia* var. *culta* is the name used for all the cultivated forms with larger, edible fruit, including the modern nashi pears. **'Kosui'** is a Japanese cultivar with russet-skinned, globular fruit. *Zones 4–9.*

RIBES
Currant

This genus, from cool-temperate regions in the northern hemisphere, contains some 150 species of evergreen and deciduous, ornamental and fruiting shrubs. The white, scarlet, purple, green or black berries, borne in early summer, are usually edible. They can grow to 10 ft (3 m) and have long, arching stems. Some species have reddish brown branches, and some have prickles on the stems or on the fruits, or on both. The lobed, mid-green leaves, sometimes with downy or felted undersides and toothed edges, may turn red and orange before dropping. Masses of yellow, red or pink blossoms, which are sometimes fragrant, are borne in late winter or early spring.

Cultivation

These unisexual plants must be planted in groups to ensure vigorous fruiting. They are fully frost-hardy and need to be grown in moist, rich soil with a site in full sun or semi-shade. In the USA, some species are host to white pine blister rust. Propagate from seed in spring or cuttings in winter.

Ribes nigrum cultivar

Ribes nigrum
Blackcurrant

Native to Europe and temperate Asia, this shrub reaches 6 ft (1.8 m) and bears greenish white flowers and sweet, black fruit. It thrives if fertilized with potash and nitrogen. Prune old shoots to promote new growth and pick fruit when the upper berries start to fall. Watch for currant borer moth, mites and leaf spot. **'Ben Lomond'** is late-ripening, with a high yield of large fruit; **'Jet'** has a heavy crop of big fruit. **'Baldwin'** is another popular cultivar. *Zones 5–9.*

Ribes nigrum 'Baldwin'

Ribes silvestre 'Jonkheer van Tets'

Ribes silvestre cultivar

Ribes silvestre
syns *Ribes rubrum, R. sativum*
Redcurrant, white currant
Native to western Europe, this deciduous, prickle-free species is an erect 6 ft (1.8 m) shrub with 2½ in (6 cm) long, lobed leaves that have silvery undersides. Racemes of small flowers open in spring, followed by clusters of small, very juicy, round red or pale amber (white) fruit. They are rather tart and are excellent fresh or cooked. Noteworthy cultivars include the very popular **'Fays Prolific'** which bears large, sweet, deep red berries; **'Jonkheer van Tets'**, a vigorous,

Ribes silvestre cultivar

Ribes silvestre 'Viking'

Ribes uva-crispa 'Invicta'

open-bushed redcurrant that flowers and fruits very early; **'Raby Castle'**; and **'Red Dutch'**, a very old Dutch cultivar bearing loose clusters of glossy, bright red fruit. Other cultivars include: **'Red Lake'**, vigorous, densely branched and disease-resistant with an early crop of dark red, rather small fruit; **'Viking'**; and **'White Grape'**, which bears large clusters of pale pinkish yellow fruit. *Zones 6–9.*

Ribes uva-crispa
syn. *Ribes grossularia*
Gooseberry, European gooseberry

This stiff, spiny, deciduous shrub is native to central Europe and North America. It grows about 3 ft (1 m) tall, with upright canes and small green leaves held at stiff angles from the stems. Pinkish green flowers are followed by greenish fruit covered with soft bristles. This species rarely fruits well in frost-free climates. There are many cultivars in a variety of sizes and shapes, bearing green, russet green or yellow green fruit. **'Careless'** is a spreading bush with few thorns and elongated, yellow, fairly bland-tasting fruit; **'Crown Bob'** bears heavy crops of hairy berries that ripen from yellow to deep red; **'Invicta'** (syn. 'Malling Invicta') is an early ripener with a heavy crop of large yellow fruit; and **'Leveller'** has good-flavored fruit and is fairly vigorous. ***Ribes uva-crispa* var. *reclinatum*** has bristly, round to slightly elongated fruit that may be yellow or red when ripe; **'Roaring Lion'** is a popular, vigorous cultivar producing a good crop of red berries; and **'Whinham's Industry'** is a slow-growing bush with a good crop of tasty, round, yellow berries with purple red bristles. *Zones 5–9.*

RUBUS

This large genus of 250 or more species of deciduous and evergreen shrubs and scrambling climbers occurs in most parts of the world. The plants range from the tiny cloudberry *(Rubus chamaemorus)* through to viciously armed, 12 ft (4 m) high thickets and high forest climbers. Their cane-like stems bear flowers and fruits in their second year. The leaves, usually felted underneath, are mostly compound with 3 to 7 leaflets arranged pinnately or palmately. The early summer flowers are white, pink or purple, resembling those of a small single rose, for example those of *Rubus* 'Navajo'. They are followed by the sweet, juicy fruits, a mass of tiny, usually red or black drupes.

Cultivation

These moderately to fully frost-hardy plants prefer moist, well-drained, moderately fertile soil in a sunny position. Some forms naturalize freely and can become an invasive menace. After fruiting, cut the canes back to ground level. Propagate by root division in winter, or from seeds, cuttings or suckers.

Rubus 'Navajo'

Rubus 'Navajo'

Rubus fruticosus 'Thornfree'

Rubus chamaemorus
Cloudberry

A native of the arctic and subarctic regions, this creeping perennial grows to about 10 in (25 cm) high and bears white flowers followed by edible yellowish berries in autumn. The berries have a sweet flavor and can be eaten fresh or used in preserves, pastries, sweets and vinegar. *Zones 2–8.*

Rubus fruticosus
Blackberry, bramble

This widespread, northern European bramble grows wild in woods and hedgerows. It is an aggregate, consisting of over 2000 microspecies, all differing in small details. The cultivated

Rubus fruticosus 'Thornfree'

Rubus fruticosus cultivar

Rubus idaeus cultivar

Rubus idaeus cultivar

blackberry's prickly, arching stems grow to 10 ft (3 m) with a similar spread. They bear deep green leaves with 3 to 5 leaflets, white or pink flowers 1 in (2.5 cm) across, and delicious blackberries with purple juice at the end of summer. **'Himalayan Giant'** (syn. 'Himalaya') is very vigorous with very dark, medium-sized berries which are produced over a long season; **'Loch Ness'** has spineless semi-erect canes. **'Thornfree'** has almost no thorns and produces a heavy crop of fruit late in the season. A number of the microspecies are troublesome weeds in Australia and New Zealand, and cultivation of *R. fruticosus* is prohibited in some Australian states. *Zones 5–10.*

Rubus idaeus
Raspberry, red raspberry

The northern hemisphere raspberry is a cool-climate, deciduous, perennial shrub 5 ft (1.5 m) tall and wide. It has smooth, reddish brown stems bearing many or few prickles and serrated leaflets 6 in (15 cm) long. The small, 5-petaled white flowers are borne in early summer on

Rubus idaeus cultivar

Rubus idaeus 'Killarney'

the side shoots of the branches produced over the previous summer. The succulent, aromatic berries, borne from mid-summer to mid-autumn (depending on the variety and the region) are usually red, but can occasionally be white or yellowish in color. The many cultivars include: **'Autumn Bliss'**, an easily grown, repeat-fruiting cultivar with medium-sized red berries; **'Bicentennial'**; and **'Canby'**, which has almost no prickles on its stems and small, early-ripening fruit. **'Chilcotin'** produces a large crop of fruit over a long period from mid-season onwards, and fruits again in autumn; **'Chilliwack'** is a rot-resistant, Canadian cultivar with thornless, erect canes; **'Everbearer'** is one of the few cultivars to bear fruit in

autumn, with large, dark red berries. **'Glen May'** and **'Killarney'** produce full-flavored fruit in early summer; **'Nootka'** is a mid-season cultivar with a large crop of fruit and another later crop. **'Skeena'** is popular for its early fruit production, bearing small, good-flavored berries on sturdy, almost spineless canes; at the other end of the fruiting season, **'Taylor'** bears bright red, medium-sized fruit on large, strong canes late in the season. **'Willamette'** is a popular commercial variety bearing heavy crops of large, good-flavored berries and another smaller, later crop. *Zones 4–9.*

Rubus × loganobaccus
Boysenberry, loganberry

This evergreen shrub grows to 15 ft (5 m) in height with upright stems and has broadly oval leaves that are white beneath. The white flowers are borne in prickly corymbs. **'Boysen'** (syn. *Rubus* 'Boysen'), the boysenberry, is a rampant grower with long canes that are either thorny or smooth and large, purple-red berries that take 6 weeks to ripen. **'Logan'** (syn. *Rubus* 'Logan'), the loganberry, is a hybrid between a blackberry and a garden raspberry, said to have originated in the garden of Judge Logan in California in 1881; its crimson, tart fruit is excellent for cooking. *Zones 5–10.*

Rubus parviflorus
Thimbleberry

Growing to over 15 ft (4.5 m) tall, this deciduous shrub comes from North America and northern Mexico. It has upright stems which are thornless. The young growth is covered with fine hairs, and when mature the stems have peeling bark. The kidney-shaped leaves are lobed and large, up to 8 in (20 cm) wide.

Rubus × *loganobaccus* 'Boysen'

Vaccinium corymbosum 'Blue Ray'

Vaccinium corymbosum 'Earliblue'

The flowers, which are borne in racemes, are 2 in (5 cm) wide and are followed by red berries. *Zones 3–10.*

VACCINIUM

This is a large and varied genus of about 450 species of deciduous and evergreen shrubs and occasionally small trees and vines. They are found mainly in the northern hemisphere in a wide range of habitats, stretching from the Arctic to the tropics. The species seen in gardens are shrubs valued for either their edible berries or their notable autumn color. The berries, known according to the species as bilberry, blueberry, cranberry, huckleberry or whortleberry, are red or blue-black and are often covered with a bloom when ripe. They are grown commercially for fresh fruit, as well as for juicing and canning. The leaves are bright green, often leathery and sometimes coppery red when young; their edges can be toothed or smooth. Small bell-shaped flowers, pale pink, white, purple or red, are borne in late spring or early summer.

Cultivation

Vaccinium species are generally frost-hardy and shade loving; many form dense, thicket-like shrubs. The plants need acidic, well-drained soil with plenty of humus and regular water; some even prefer boggy ground. Propagate by division or from cuttings in autumn.

Vaccinium corymbosum
Blueberry, highbush blueberry

This deciduous species from New England, USA, has a preference for boggy soils. It is grown mainly for its edible, blue-black berries but also has fine scarlet autumn foliage. The new leaves are bright green and it forms a dense thicket of upright stems with a height and spread of 6 ft (1.8 m). The clusters of pendulous flowers are pale pink. **'Blue Crop'** is very popular in the USA and has heavy crops of light blue berries. **'Blue Ray'** has delicious, sweet, juicy fruit. **'Earliblue'** is tall and vigorous with very large berries. For heavier cropping, grow two cultivars together. *Zones 2–9.*

VITIS
Grape vine, vine

This genus of around 65 deciduous, tendril-climbing shrubs and vines has huge commercial significance as the source of grapes. Only a few species yield fruits suitable for wine or the table, and almost all wine grapes are derived from *Vitis vinifera.* The foliage is standard through much of the genus—the roughly heart-shaped leaves have 3 to 7 lobes and often color well in autumn. Spring-borne sprays of small, 5-petaled flowers develop into the familiar fruits in late summer and early autumn.

Cultivation

Grow in humus-rich, moisture-retentive, deep but well-drained soil in full sun or part-shade. Fully to marginally frost-hardy, they need cool winters and low summer humidity or mildew will become a problem. Train on a sturdy pergola or fence. To protect the grapes from birds, cover the vines with bird netting or put paper bags around the grape clusters. Cut the grapes with sharp scissors when fully ripe. Vines need annual pruning in mid-winter to control their growth and encourage heavy fruiting. Propagate from cuttings in late winter. Wine grape cultivars are often grafted onto *Vitis labrusca* rootstock, resistant to the *Phylloxera* root aphid.

Vitis labrusca
Fox grape

The parent of most of the non-*Vitis vinifera* grapes cultivated in the USA,

Vitis labrusca cultivar

Vitis vinifera cultivar

Vitis vinifera cultivar

this native of the eastern seaboard produces long, felty young shoots that require trellising for support. The large, shallowly 3-lobed leaves are deep green above and felty white beneath. Full sun and well-drained, fertile soil are ideal for the production of the large, purple-black fruit, which have a musky or 'foxy' flavor. Popular cultivars include **'Carolina Black'** and particularly **'Concord'**, **'Catawba'** and **'Niagara'** which are commonly grown in areas where winters are cold and summers are cool and short. **'Isabella'** is a mildew-resistant cultivar grown widely in Australia on the coast of New South Wales. *Zones 4–9.*

Vitis vinifera
Grape

This species is native to Europe and the Mediterranean and has been cultivated since antiquity. A vigorous, fully frost-hardy vine, it has given rise to a multitude of varieties with either black or white (pale green or yellow) fruit; some are better for wine, others for eating fresh or dried. It is best grown where summers are dry. **'Albany Surprise'** is a sweet white eating grape; **'Cabernet Sauvignon'** is a black wine grape used for some of the best quality red wines; **'Chardonnay'** is a very popular white wine grape; **'Early Muscat'** is a white grape for eating and wine, with a strong muscat flavor; **'Festivee'** is another wine cultivar. Some grapes like the well known **'Flame Seedless'** have been bred especially for eating; it has early-ripening, juicy, light red fruit. **'Ganzin Glory'** is widely grown for its brilliant crimson autumn foliage which colors reliably even in mild-winter areas. **'Golden Chasselas'** is an old French cultivar with sweet white grapes for eating and wine. **'Italia'** is a white muscat grape with large golden fruit. Other popular wine grapes include: **'Merlot'**, a black grape often blended with 'Cabernet Sauvignon'; **'Müller Thurgau'**, a white grape used for bulk production wines; and **'Muscat Hamburg'**, a black grape used for wine and also drying and eating. **'Perlette'** is good for hot, tropical areas. **'Pinot Noir'** is a black grape used to make red wine and also champagne, in which it is fermented without its skin to prevent the wine reddening—some skin contact is allowed for pink champagne. **'Purpurea'** has spectacular bright crimson foliage in autumn; **'Riesling'**, and its derivatives, are popular white wine grapes, especially in Germany. **'Schiava Grossa'** (syn. 'Black Hamburgh') is a black eating grape; **'Semillon'** is a well known white wine grape; and **'Shiraz'** (syn. 'Syrah') is a black wine grape widely grown in Australia. **'Sultana'** is a popular eating grape with small white fruit; while **'Waltham Cross'**, grown mainly for drying, has large white fruit. *Zones 6–10.*

ZIZIPHUS

This genus of about 80 or so species of deciduous or evergreen trees and shrubs occurs naturally in warm- to hot-climate areas of both the northern and southern hemispheres. Some have spiny branches. Their leaves are usually marked with three veins and there are spines at the base of each leaf stalk. The insignificant flowers are small, greenish, whitish or yellow, and arranged in clusters in the leaf axils. The small, fleshy fruit of some species are edible.

Cultivation

Ziziphus species are frost-tender, and should be grown in open, loamy, well-

Vitis vinifera 'Festivee'

Vitis vinifera cultivar

drained soil in full sun. Provide plenty of water, and tip prune to maintain compact growth. Propagate from seed or root cuttings in late winter, or by grafting.

Ziziphus jujuba
Chinese date, jujube

This deciduous tree, which is distributed from western Asia to China, grows to 40 ft (12 m) tall. It bears oval to lance-shaped green leaves, 1–2 in (2.5–5 cm) long, with 2 spines at the base of each leaf stalk, one of which is usually bent backwards. Small greenish flowers are borne in spring. The dark red, oblong to rounded fruit grow to 1 in (2.5 cm) long: they ripen from autumn to winter on the bare branches and are apple-like in taste. They may be stewed, dried or used in confections. *Zones 7–10.*

Ziziphus jujuba

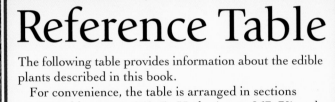

Reference Table

The following table provides information about the edible plants described in this book.

For convenience, the table is arranged in sections on Vegetables (pages 260–7), Herbs (pages 267–70) and Fruit & Nuts (pages 270–8). Each plant featured in the book is listed, with a summary of its cultivation details, including hardiness zone, when to plant, when to harvest, and a note of which part or parts are edible.

To indicate a crop that can be planted (or harvested) over an extended season we have used a dash (–), for example, summer–autumn, meaning it can be planted (or harvested) from summer to autumn. To indicate a crop that can be planted (or harvested) in two separate seasons we have used a solidus (/), for example, spring/autumn, meaning it can be planted (or harvested) in spring or alternatively in autumn.

NAME	COMMON NAME	ZONES	EDIBLE PART	PLANTING TIME	HARVESTING TIME
VEGETABLES					
Abelmoschus esculentus	okra, gumbo, lady's fingers	9–11	flower buds, pods	spring	summer–autumn
Agaricus campestris	mushroom, button mushroom	5–11	all	any	any
Allium ampeloprasum	wild leek, kurrat	6–10	bulbs, leaves, stems	spring–summer	late winter–early summer
Allium cepa	onion, spring onion	4–11	bulbs, stems	spring/autumn	summer/spring
A. cepa, Aggregatum Group	shallot, scallion	4–11	bulbs, leaves, stems	spring/autumn	summer/spring
Allium fistulosum	Welsh onion, Japanese bunching onion	6–9	leaves, stems	spring/autumn	when young
Allium porrum	leek	5–10	leaves, stems	spring/summer	spring/summer
A. porrum 'Giant Winter Wila'	leek	5–10	leaves, stems	spring/summer	spring/summer
A. porrum 'Mammoth Blanche'	leek	5–10	leaves, stems	spring/summer	spring/summer
A. porrum 'Musselburgh'	leek	5–10	leaves, stems	spring/summer	spring/summer
Apium graveolens var. *dulce*	celery	5–10	stalks	spring–summer	summer
A. graveolens var. *rapaceum*	celeriac	5–10	roots	spring	summer
A. graveolens var. *secalinum*	leaf celery	5–10	leaves	spring	summer
Asparagus officinalis	asparagus	4–9	shoots	spring	spring
A. officinalis 'Mary Washington'	asparagus	4–9	shoots	spring	spring
Atriplex hortensis	mountain spinach, orache	6–10	leaves	spring/autumn	spring/summer
A. hortensis var. *rubra*	mountain spinach, orache	6–10	leaves	spring/autumn	spring/summer
Barbarea vulgaris	water cress, winter cress, yellow rocket	6–10	leaves	summer	autumn–winter
Beta vulgaris subsp. *vulgaris*	beetroot, chard, silver beet	5–10	leaves, roots	spring/autumn	autumn/spring
B. vulgaris subsp. *vulgaris* 'Bolthardy'	beetroot	5–10	roots	spring/autumn	autumn/spring
B. vulgaris subsp. *vulgaris* 'Golden'	sugar beet	5–10	roots	spring/autumn	autumn/spring
B. vulgaris subsp. *vulgaris* 'Pablo'	beetroot	5–10	roots	spring/autumn	autumn/spring
Brassica juncea	Indian mustard, mustard greens	6–11	seeds, leaves	summer–autumn	autumn–winter
B. juncea 'Red Giant'	mizuna	6–11	seeds, leaves	summer–autumn	autumn–winter
Brassica napus	rape	5–9	seeds	spring	summer
B. napus, Napobrassica Group	swede, Swedish turnips, rutabaga	5–9	roots	spring	autumn–winter
Brassica nigra	black mustard	7–10	leaves, seeds	spring	summer, autumn
Brassica oleracea, Acephala Group	kale	6–11	leaves	spring/summer	autumn
B. oleracea, Acephala Group, 'Chou Palmier'	kale	6–11	leaves	spring/summer	autumn

NAME	COMMON NAME	ZONES	EDIBLE PART	PLANTING TIME	HARVESTING TIME
B. oleracea, Acephala Group, 'Moss Curled'	kale	6–11	leaves	spring/summer	autumn
B. oleracea, Acephala Group, Osaka Series	kale	6–11	leaves	spring/summer	autumn
B. oleracea, Acephala Group, 'Tall Scotch'	kale	6–11	leaves	spring/summer	autumn
Brassica oleracea, Botrytis Group	cauliflower	6–11	flower buds	spring/autumn	autumn/summer
B. oleracea, Botrytis Group, 'Early Purplehead'	cauliflower	6–11	flower buds	spring/autumn	autumn/summer
B. oleracea, Botrytis Group, 'Mini'	cauliflower	6–11	flower buds	spring/autumn	autumn/summer
B. oleracea, Botrytis Group, 'Snowball'	cauliflower	6–11	flower buds	spring/autumn	autumn/summer
B. oleracea, Capitata Group	cabbage	6–11	leaves	spring/autumn	autumn/summer
B. oleracea, Capitata Group, 'Golden Acre'	cabbage	6–11	leaves	spring/autumn	autumn/summer
B. oleracea, Capitata Group, 'Green Coronet'	cabbage	6–11	leaves	spring/autumn	autumn/summer
B. oleracea, Capitata Group, 'Greengold'	cabbage	6–11	leaves	spring/autumn	autumn/summer
B. oleracea, Capitata Group, 'Hardora'	cabbage	6–11	leaves	spring/autumn	autumn/summer
B. oleracea, Capitata Group, 'Hawke'	cabbage	6–11	leaves	spring/autumn	summer/autumn
B. oleracea, Capitata Group, 'Mammoth Red Rock'	red cabbage	6–11	leaves	spring/autumn	autumn/summer
B. oleracea, Capitata Group, 'Primax'	cabbage	6–11	leaves	spring/autumn	autumn/summer
B. oleracea, Capitata Group, Sabauda Subgroup	Savoy cabbage	6–11	leaves	spring/autumn	autumn/summer
B. o., Capitata Group, Sabauda Subgroup, 'Drumhead'	Savoy cabbage	6–11	leaves	spring/autumn	autumn/summer
B. oleracea, Capitata Group, Sabauda Subgroup, 'Karvoi'	Savoy cabbage	6–11	leaves	spring/autumn	autumn/summer
B. oleracea, Capitata Group, Sabauda Subgroup, 'Ludessa'	Savoy cabbage	6–11	leaves	spring/autumn	autumn/summer
B. oleracea, Capitata Group, Sabauda Subgroup, 'Ormskirk'	Savoy cabbage	6–11	leaves	spring/autumn	autumn/summer
B. oleracea, Capitata Group, Savoy Hybrid, 'Santana'	cabbage	6–11	leaves	spring/autumn	autumn/summer
B. oleracea, Capitata Group, 'Sugarloaf'	cabbage	6–11	leaves	spring/autumn	autumn/summer
Brassica oleracea, Cymosa Group	broccoli	6–11	flower buds, stalks	spring	spring/summer

NAME	COMMON NAME	ZONES	EDIBLE PART	PLANTING TIME	HARVESTING TIME
B. oleracea, Cymosa Group, 'De Cicco'	broccoli	6–11	flower buds, stalks	spring	spring/summer
B. oleracea, Cymosa Group, 'Green Duke'	broccoli	6–11	flower buds, stalks	spring	spring/summer
B. oleracea, Cymosa Group, 'Italian Green Sprouting'	sprouting broccoli	6–11	flower buds, stalks	spring	spring/summer
B. oleracea, Cymosa Group, 'Waltham 29'	broccoli	6–11	flower buds, stalks	spring	spring/summer
Brassica oleracea, Gemmifera Group	Brussels sprouts	6–11	shoots	spring/summer	autumn/winter
B. oleracea, Gemmifera Group, 'Icarus'	Brussels sprouts	6–11	shoots	spring/summer	autumn/winter
B. oleracea, Gemmifera Group, 'Jade Beauty'	Brussels sprouts	6–11	shoots	spring/summer	autumn/winter
B. oleracea, Gemmifera Group, 'Long Island'	Brussels sprouts	6–11	shoots	spring/summer	autumn/winter
B. oleracea, Gemmifera Group, 'Lunet Hybrid'	Brussels sprouts	6–11	shoots	spring/summer	autumn/winter
B. oleracea, Gemmifera Group, 'Ruby Red'	Brussels sprouts	6–11	shoots	spring/summer	autumn/winter
B. oleracea, Gemmifera Group, 'Troika'	Brussels sprouts	6–11	shoots	spring/summer	autumn/winter
B. oleracea, Gongylodes Group	kohlrabi	6–11	roots	spring/summer	autumn–winter
B. oleracea, Gongylodes Group, 'Earliest Erfurt'	kohlrabi	6–11	roots, leaves	spring/summer	autumn–winter
B. oleracea, Gongylodes Group, 'Early Purple'	kohlrabi	6–11	roots, leaves	spring/summer	autumn–winter
B. oleracea, Gongylodes Group, 'Purple Vienna'	kohlrabi	6–11	roots, leaves	spring/summer	autumn–winter
B. oleracea, Gongylodes Group, 'White Vienna'	kohlrabi	6–11	roots, leaves	spring/summer	autumn–winter
Brassica rapa, Chinensis Group	bok-choi, pak-choi	7–11	leaves, stalks	autumn–spring/ spring–summer	after 8 weeks
B. rapa, Michihili Group, 'Hong Kong'	Chinese cabbage	7–11	leaves, stalks	spring–summer	autumn–winter
B. rapa, Michihili Group, 'Jade Pagoda'	Chinese cabbage	7–11	leaves, stalks	spring–summer	autumn–winter
Brassica rapa, Pekinensis Group	Chinese cabbage, pe-tsai, wom-bok	7–11	leaves, stalks	spring–summer	autumn–winter
Brassica rapa, Rapifera Group	turnip	7–11	roots	spring/autumn	summer/winter
Brassica rapa, Rapifera Group, 'Purpletop White Globe'	turnip	7–11	roots	spring/autumn	summer/winter

NAME	COMMON NAME	ZONES	EDIBLE PART	PLANTING TIME	HARVESTING TIME
B. rapa, Rapifera Group, 'Scots Yellow'	turnip	7–11	roots	spring/autumn	summer/winter
B. rapa, Rapifera Group, 'Shogrin'	turnip	7–11	roots	spring/autumn	summer/winterautumn
B. rapa, Rapifera Group, 'Tokyo Cross'	turnip	7–11	roots	spring/autumn	summer/winter
B. rapa, Rapifera Group, 'White Stone'	turnip	7–11	roots	spring/autumn	summer/winter
Capsicum annuum	capsicum, pepper	8–12	fruit	spring	summer–autumn
Capsicum annuum, Cerasiforme Group	cherry pepper	8–12	fruit	spring	summer–autumn
Capsicum annuum, Conoides Group, 'Red Missile'	pepper	8–12	fruit	spring	summer–autumn
Capsicum annuum, Cubanelle Group, 'Gypsy'	cubanelle pepper	8–12	fruit	spring	summer–autumn
Capsicum annuum, Fasciculatum Group	red cone pepper	8–12	fruit	spring	summer–autumn
Capsicum annuum, Grossum Group, 'Golden Belle'	bell pepper	8–12	fruit	spring	summer–autumn
Capsicum annuum, Grossum Group, 'Purple Belle'	bell pepper	8–12	fruit	spring	summer–autumn
Capsicum annuum, Longum Group	cayenne pepper, paprika, banana pepper	8–12	fruit	spring	summer–autumn
Capsicum annuum, Longum Group, 'Long Sweet Yellow'	banana pepper	8–12	fruit	spring	summer–autumn
Capsicum frutescens	tabasco pepper, chilli pepper	9–12	fruit	spring	summer–autumn
Capsicum frutescens, Tabasco strain	tabasco pepper	9–12	fruit	spring	summer–autumn
Capsicum frutescens, Thai Hot strain	chilli pepper	9–12	fruit	spring	summer–autumn
Chenopodium bonus-henricus	Good King Henry, blite	4–9	leaves, roots	spring	summer
Cichorium endivia	endive, escarole	4–10	leaves	summer	autumn
C. endivia 'Batavian'	endive, escarole	4–10	leaves	summer	autumn
C. endivia 'Green Curled'	endive, escarole	4–10	leaves	summer	autumn
C. endivia 'Sally'	endive, escarole	4–10	leaves	summer	autumn
Cichorium intybus	chicory, witloof, radicchio	4–10	leaves, shoots, roots	summer/winter	autumn/spring
C. intybus 'Palo Rosa Bella'	chicory, witloof, radicchio	4–10	leaves, shoots, roots	summer/winter	autumn/spring
C. intybus 'Witloof'	chicory, witloof, radicchio	4–10	leaves, shoots, roots	summer/winter	autumn/spring
Colocasia esculenta	taro	10–12	tubers, shoots	spring	after 8 months
C. esculenta var. *antiquorum*	eddoe	10–12	tubers, shoots	spring	after 8 months
C. esculenta 'Fontanesii'	taro	10–12	tubers, shoots	spring	after 8 months

NAME	COMMON NAME	ZONES	EDIBLE PART	PLANTING TIME	HARVESTING TIME
Cucumis sativus	cucumber, gherkin	9–12	fruit	spring–summer	summer–autumn
Cucurbita maxima	pumpkin, autumn squash, winter pumpkin, winter squash	9–11	fruit	spring/summer	autumn
C. maxima 'Crown Prince'	pumpkin	9–11	fruit	spring/summer	autumn
C. maxima 'Golden Nugget'	squash	9–11	fruit	spring/summer	autumn
C. maxima 'Laternenkürbis St Martin'	pumpkin	9–11	fruit	spring/summer	autumn
Cucurbita moschata	crookneck squash, pumpkin, winter squash	8–11	fruit	spring/summer	autumn/winter
C. moschata 'Butternut'	squash	8–11	fruit	spring/summer	autumn/winter
Cucurbita pepo	gourd, pumpkin, summer squash, vegetable marrow	8–11	fruit	spring/summer	summer/autumn
C. pepo 'Atlantic Giant'	vegetable marrow	8–11	fruit	spring/summer	summer/autumn
C. pepo 'Rouge Vif d'Etampes'	vegetable marrow	8–11	fruit	spring/summer	summer/autumn
Cynara scolymus	globe artichoke	6–10	flowerheads	spring	spring/summer
Daucus carota subsp. *sativus*	carrot	3–11	roots	spring–autumn	winter
D. carota subsp. *sativus* 'Nantes'	carrot	3–11	roots	spring–autumn	winter
D. carota subsp. *sativus* 'Touchon'	carrot	3–11	roots	spring–autumn	winter
Dioscorea alata	greater yam	10–12	tubers	any	after 7–12 months
Eleocharis dulcis	water chestnut, Chinese water chestnut	9–12	tubers	spring	autumn
Glycine max	soya bean, soybean	9–11	seeds	spring	summer/autumn
Helianthus tuberosus	Jerusalem artichoke	4–10	tubers	spring	autumn
Ipomoea batatas	sweet potato, kumara	9–12	tubers	spring	autumn
Lactuca sativa	lettuce	7–12	leaves	spring/summer/autumn	spring/summer/autumn
L. sativa var. *augustana*	celtuce	7–12	leaves, stems	spring/summer/autumn	spring/summer/autumn
L. sativa 'Black Seeded Simpson'	lettuce	7–12	leaves	spring/summer/autumn	spring/summer/autumn
L. sativa 'Bubbles'	lettuce	7–12	leaves	spring/summer/autumn	spring/summer/autumn
L. sativa 'Buttercrunch'	lettuce	7–12	leaves	spring/summer/autumn	spring/summer/autumn
L. sativa 'Frisby'	lettuce	7–12	leaves	spring/summer/autumn	spring/summer/autumn
L. sativa 'Great Lakes'	lettuce	7–12	leaves	spring/summer/autumn	spring/summer/autumn
L. sativa 'Green Salad Bowl'	lettuce	7–12	leaves	spring/summer/autumn	spring/summer/autumn
L. sativa 'Lakeland'	lettuce	7–12	leaves	spring/summer/autumn	spring/summer/autumn
L. sativa 'Lolli Bionda'	lettuce	7–12	leaves	spring/summer/autumn	spring/summer/autumn
L. sativa 'Lollo Rossa'	lettuce	7–12	leaves	spring/summer/autumn	spring/summer/autumn
L. sativa 'New Red Fire'	lettuce	7–12	leaves	spring/summer/autumn	spring/summer/autumn

NAME	COMMON NAME	ZONES	EDIBLE PART	PLANTING TIME	HARVESTING TIME
L. sativa 'Red Oak Leaf'	lettuce	7–12	leaves	spring/summer/autumn	spring/summer/autumn
L. sativa 'Red Sails'	lettuce	7–12	leaves	spring/summer/autumn	spring/summer/autumn
L. sativa 'Red Salad Bowl'	lettuce	7–12	leaves	spring/summer/autumn	spring/summer/autumn
L. sativa 'Rouge d'Hiver'	lettuce	7–12	leaves	spring/summer/autumn	spring/summer/autumn
L. sativa 'Saladini'	lettuce	7–12	leaves	spring/summer/autumn	spring/summer/autumn
L. sativa 'Simpson Flute'	lettuce	7–12	leaves	spring/summer/autumn	spring/summer/autumn
L. sativa 'Target'	lettuce	7–12	leaves	spring/summer/autumn	spring/summer/autumn
Lycopersicon esculentum	tomato	8–12	fruit	spring	summer
L. esculentum 'Beefsteak'	tomato	8–12	fruit	spring	summer
L. esculentum 'Black Russian'	black tomato	8–12	fruit	spring	summer
L. esculentum var. *cerasiforme*	cherry tomato	8–12	fruit	spring	summer
L. esculentum 'Grosse Lisse'	tomato	8–12	fruit	spring	summer
L. esculentum 'Plumito'	Roma tomato	8–12	fruit	spring	summer
L. esculentum 'Red Pear'	tomato	8–12	fruit	spring	summer
L. esculentum 'Rouge de Marmande'	tomato	8–12	fruit	spring	summer
L. esculentum 'Super Roma'	Roma tomato	8–12	fruit	spring	summer
L. esculentum 'Tiny Tim'	tomato	8–12	fruit	spring	summer
L. esculentum 'Yellow Pear'	tomato	8–12	fruit	spring	summer
Lycopersicon pimpinellifolium	currant tomato	8–12	fruit	spring	summer
Manihot esculenta	cassava, tapioca	10–12	roots	any	any
Maranta arundinacea	arrowroot, Bermuda arrowroot	11–12	root	summer	after 6–12 months
Medicago sativa	alfalfa, lucerne	6–10	seeds, shoots	autumn/spring	summer/autumn
Oxalis tuberosa	oca	7–10	tubers	spring	winter
Pastinaca sativa	parsnip	7–10	roots	spring	winter
Phaseolus coccineus	scarlet runner bean	9–11	pods	spring	summer
P. coccineus 'Achievement'	scarlet runner bean	9–11	pods	spring	summer
Phaseolus lunatus	Lima bean, oca	10–12	seeds	spring	summer
Phaseolus vulgaris	French bean, kidney bean, string bean, haricot bean	7–11	pods, seeds	spring–summer	summer
P. vulgaris 'Blue Lake'	green bean	7–11	pods, seeds	spring–summer	summer
P. vulgaris 'Bountiful'	green bean	7–11	pods, seeds	spring–summer	summer
P. vulgaris 'Gourmet's Delight'	green bean	7–11	pods, seeds	spring–summer	summer
P. vulgaris 'Hawkesbury Wonder'	green bean	7–11	pods, seeds	spring–summer	summer
P. vulgaris 'Kentucky Wonder Wax'	green bean	7–11	pods, seeds	spring–summer	summer
P. vulgaris 'Majestic'	green bean	7–11	pods, seeds	spring–summer	summer

NAME	COMMON NAME	ZONES	EDIBLE PART	PLANTING TIME	HARVESTING TIME
P. vulgaris 'Pioneer'	green bean	7–11	pods, seeds	spring–summer	summer
P. vulgaris 'Purple King'	green bean	7–11	pods, seeds	spring–summer	summer
P. vulgaris 'Royal Burgundy'	green bean	7–11	pods, seeds	spring–summer	summer
P. vulgaris 'Slenderette'	green bean	7–11	pods, seeds	spring–summer	summer
P. vulgaris 'Tendercrop'	green bean	7–11	pods, seeds	spring–summer	summer
Phyllostachys edulis	edible bamboo, moso-chiku	8–11	shoots	spring/autumn	spring
Pisum sativum	garden pea	3–10	seeds	spring	summer
P. sativum 'Alderman'	garden pea	3–10	seeds	spring	summer
P. sativum var. *macrocarpum*	snow pea, mange-tout pea	3–10	seed pods	spring	summer
P. sativum var. *macrocarpum* 'Mammoth Sugar'	snow pea, mange-tout pea	3–10	seed pods	spring	summer
P. sativum var. *macrocarpum* 'Oregon Sugar Pod'	snow pea, mange-tout pea	3–10	seed pods	spring	summer
P. sativum 'Melbourne Market'	garden pea	3–10	seeds	spring	summer
P. sativum 'Snow Flake'	garden pea	3–10	seeds	spring	summer
P. sativum 'Sugar Bon'	garden pea	3–10	seeds	spring	summer
P. sativum 'Telephone'	garden pea	3–10	seeds	spring	summer
Raphanus sativus	radish	6–10	roots	summer–autumn	summer–winter
R. sativus 'French Breakfast'	radish	6–10	roots	summer–autumn	summer–winter
R. sativus 'Rex'	radish	6–10	roots	summer–autumn	summer–winter
R. sativus 'Round Red'	radish	6–10	roots	summer–autumn	summer–winter
R. sativus 'Tarzan'	radish	6–10	roots	summer–autumn	summer–winter
Rheum × *cultorum*	rhubarb	3–9	stalks	spring	summer
Sechium edule	chayote, choko, chow chow, christophine, vegetable pear	10–12	fruit, shoots	spring	spring/summer
Solanum melongena	eggplant, aubergine, mad apple	9–12	fruit	spring	summer
Solanum tuberosum	potato	6–11	tubers	spring	summer–autumn
S. tuberosum 'Desiree'	potato	6–11	tubers	spring	summer–autumn
S. tuberosum 'King Edward'	potato	6–11	tubers	spring	summer–autumn
S. tuberosum 'Kipfler'	potato	6–11	tubers	spring	summer–autumn
S. tuberosum 'Pink Fir Apple'	potato	6–11	tubers	spring	summer–autumn
S. tuberosum 'Pontiac'	potato	6–11	tubers	spring	summer–autumn
Spinacia oleracea	English spinach	5–10	leaves	spring/autumn	summer/spring
Taraxacum officinale	common dandelion, pissenlit	3–10	roots, leaves, flowers	spring	spring–summer
Tetragonia tetragonioides	New Zealand spinach	8–10	leaves	spring	summer
Tragopogon porrifolius	salsify, oyster plant	5–10	roots, shoots	spring	autumn–spring
Valerianella locusta	corn salad, lamb's lettuce	4–9	leaves	autumn	winter/spring

NAME	COMMON NAME	ZONES	EDIBLE PART	PLANTING TIME	HARVESTING TIME
Vicia faba	broad bean, fava bean	7–10	seeds	autumn	winter–spring
V. faba 'Aquadulce Claudia'	broad bean, fava bean	7–10	seeds	autumn	winter–spring
V. faba 'Early Long Pod'	broad bean, fava bean	7–10	seeds	autumn	winter–spring
V. faba 'Exhibition Longpod'	broad bean, fava bean	7–10	seeds	autumn	winter–spring
V. faba 'Green Windsor'	broad bean, fava bean	7–10	seeds	autumn	winter–spring
V. faba 'Leviathan Longpod'	broad bean, fava bean	7–10	seeds	autumn	winter–spring
V. faba 'Red Epicure'	broad bean, fava bean	7–10	seeds	autumn	winter–spring
Vigna radiata	mung bean, bean sprout	10–11	shoots	all year	after a few days
Vigna unguiculata	cowpea	10–11	pods, seeds	spring	summer
Zea mays	sweet corn, maize, mealy	7–11	cobs	spring	summer–autumn
Z. mays 'Golden Beauty'	sweet corn, maize, mealy	7–11	cobs	spring	summer–autumn
Z. mays 'Honey 'N' Pearl'	sweet corn, maize, mealy	7–11	cobs	spring	summer–autumn
Z. mays 'Jubilee'	sweet corn, maize, mealy	7–11	cobs	spring	summer–autumn
Z. mays 'Miracle'	sweet corn, maize, mealy	7–11	cobs	spring	summer–autumn
Z. mays 'Rosella'	sweet corn, maize, mealy	7–11	cobs	spring	summer–autumn
Z. mays 'Sweet Perfection'	sweet corn, maize, mealy	7–11	cobs	spring	summer–autumn

HERBS

NAME	COMMON NAME	ZONES	EDIBLE PART	PLANTING TIME	HARVESTING TIME
Allium sativum	garlic	7–10	bulbs	spring/autumn	after 5–6 months
Allium schoenoprasum	chives	5–10	leaves	spring	any
Allium tuberosum	Chinese chives, garlic chives	7–11	leaves	spring	any
Anethum graveolens	dill	5–10	leaves, seeds	spring	summer–autumn
Angelica archangelica	angelica	4–9	stems	spring	summer
Anthriscus cerefolium	chervil	6–10	leaves	spring–summer	summer
Armoracia rusticana	horseradish	5–10	roots	spring	autumn
A. rusticana 'Variegata'	horseradish	5–10	roots	spring	autumn
Artemisia dracunculus	tarragon	6–9	leaves	spring	summer–autumn
Borago officinalis	borage	5–10	leaves, flowers	winter	spring
Calamintha nepeta	lesser calamint	4–10	leaves	spring	summer
C. nepeta subsp. *glandulosa* 'Blue Cloud'	lesser calamint	4–10	leaves	spring	summer
C. nepeta subsp. *glandulosa* 'White Cloud'	lesser calamint	4–10	leaves	spring	summer
Capparis spinosa	caper, caper bush	8–12	flower buds	spring	summer
Carum carvi	caraway	5–10	seeds	spring/autumn	summer
Chamaemelum nobile	chamomile, Roman chamomile	5–10	leaves, flowers	spring/autumn	summer

NAME	COMMON NAME	ZONES	EDIBLE PART	PLANTING TIME	HARVESTING TIME
C. nobile 'Treneague'	chamomile, Roman chamomile	5–10	leaves, flowers	spring/autumn	summer
Coriandrum sativum	coriander, ketumbar	7–12	seeds, leaves	spring	summer–autumn
Cuminum cyminum	cumin	9–12	seeds	spring	summer
Curcuma domestica	turmeric	10–12	rhizomes	spring	autumn
Cymbopogon citratus	lemongrass	10–12	shoots	spring	summer
Eruca sativa	rocket, arugula, roquette	7–10	leaves	spring/autumn	after 40 days
Foeniculum vulgare	fennel	5–10	leaves, stems, seeds	spring/autumn	summer, autumn
F. vulgare var. *azoricum*	Florence fennel	5–10	leaves, stems, seeds	spring/autumn	summer, autumn
F. vulgare subsp. *piperitum*	fennel	5–10	leaves, stems, seeds	spring/autumn	summer, autumn
F. vulgare 'Purpurascens'	fennel	5–10	leaves, stems, seeds	spring/autumn	summer, autumn
Glycyrrhiza glabra	licorice	8–10	roots	spring/autumn	autumn
Helichrysum italicum	curry plant	8–10	leaves	spring	spring–summer
Hyssopus officinalis	hyssop	3–11	leaves	summer/autumn	spring–summer
Laurus nobilis	sweet bay, bay tree, bay laurel, laurel	7–10	leaves	summer/autumn	any
Laurus nobilis 'Aurea'	sweet bay, bay tree, bay laurel, laurel	7–10	leaves	summer/autumn	any
Laurus nobilis 'Saratoga'	sweet bay, bay tree, bay laurel, laurel	7–10	leaves	summer/autumn	any
Lepidium sativum	curled cress, garden cress	4–10	shoots, leaves, seeds	any	any
Levisticum officinale	lovage	4–10	roots, shoots, seeds	spring	summer–autumn
Matricaria recutita	German chamomile	6–10	leaves, flowers	summer	summer–autumn
Melissa officinalis	lemon balm, bee balm	4–10	leaves	spring	summer–autumn
Mentha × *piperita*	peppermint	3–10	leaves	spring/autumn	any
Mentha spicata	spearmint	3–10	leaves	spring/autumn	any
Mentha suaveolens	apple mint	6–10	leaves	spring/autumn	any
M. suaveolens 'Variegata'	apple mint	6–10	leaves	spring/autumn	any
Mentha × *villosa* f. *alopecuroides*	Bowles' mint, winter mint	5–10	leaves	spring/autumn	any
Murraya koenigii	curry leaves, curry leaf tree, karapincha	10–12	leaves	spring	any
Myristica fragrans	nutmeg	12	fruit	spring/autumn	any
Myrrhis odorata	sweet Cicely, myrrh	5–10	leaves, seeds	spring/autumn	summer
Nasturtium officinale	common watercress	6–10	leaves	spring/autumn	spring/summer
Ocimum basilicum	basil, sweet basil	10–12	leaves	spring	summer
O. basilicum 'Dark Opal'	basil, sweet basil	10–12	leaves	spring	summer
O. basilicum 'Minimum'	basil, sweet basil	10–12	leaves	spring	summer
Ocimum tenuiflorum	holy basil	10–12	leaves	spring	summer

NAME	COMMON NAME	ZONES	EDIBLE PART	PLANTING TIME	HARVESTING TIME
Origanum majorana	sweet marjoram, sweet basil	7–10	leaves	spring/autumn	any
Origanum onites	French marjoram, pot marjoram	8–11	leaves	spring/autumn	any
O. onites 'Aureum'	French marjoram, pot marjoram	8–11	leaves	spring/autumn	any
Origanum vulgare	common oregano, wild marjoram	5–9	leaves	spring/autumn	any
O. vulgare 'Aureum'	common oregano, wild marjoram	5–9	leaves	spring/autumn	any
O. v. 'Thumble's Variety'	common oregano, wild marjoram	5–9	leaves	spring/autumn	any
Panax ginseng	ginseng, Chinese ginseng, Asian ginseng	6–9	roots	spring	after 5 years
Perilla frutescens	chiso, shiso	8–11	leaves	winter–spring	summer
P. frutescens 'Atropurpurea'	chiso, shiso	8–11	leaves	winter–spring	summer
P. frutescens var. *crispa*	chiso, shiso	8–11	leaves	winter–spring	summer
Persicaria odorata	Vietnamese mint	10–12	leaves	spring/autumn	summer
Petroselinum crispum	parsley	5–11	leaves	spring–summer	summer
P. crispum var. *neopolitanum*	French parsley	5–11	leaves	spring–summer	summer
Pimpinella anisum	anise, aniseed	6–10	seeds	spring	autumn
Rosmarinus officinalis	rosemary	6–11	leaves	spring/summer	any
R. officinalis 'Benendon Blue'	rosemary	6–11	leaves	spring/summer	any
R. officinalis 'Huntingdon Carpet'	rosemary	6–11	leaves	spring/summer	any
R. officinalis 'Lockwood de Forest'	rosemary	6–11	leaves	spring/summer	any
R. officinalis 'Majorca Pink'	rosemary	6–11	leaves	spring/summer	any
R. officinalis 'Miss Jessop's Upright'	rosemary	6–11	leaves	spring/summer	any
R. officinalis 'Prostratus'	rosemary	6–11	leaves	spring/summer	any
R. officinalis 'Tuscan Blue'	rosemary	6–11	leaves	spring/summer	any
Rumex acetosa	garden sorrel	3–9	leaves	spring/autumn	summer
Rumex scutatus	sorrel, French sorrel	6–10	leaves	spring/autumn	summer
Ruta graveolens	common rue	5–10	leaves	spring–summer	any
Salvia elegans	pineapple-scented sage	8–11	leaves	spring–summer	any
S. elegans 'Scarlet Pineapple'	pineapple-scented sage	8–11	leaves	spring–summer	any
Salvia officinalis	common sage, garden sage	5–10	leaves	spring/summer	any
S. officinalis 'Berggarten'	common sage, garden sage	5–10	leaves	spring/summer	any
S. officinalis 'Icterina'	common sage, garden sage	5–10	leaves	spring/summer	any
S. officinalis 'Purpurascens'	common sage, garden sage	5–10	leaves	spring/summer	any
S. officinalis 'Tricolor'	common sage, garden sage	5–10	leaves	spring/summer	any
Sanguisorba minor	garden burnet, salad burnet	5–9	leaves	spring	summer

NAME	COMMON NAME	ZONES	EDIBLE PART	PLANTING TIME	HARVESTING TIME
Saponaria officinalis	bouncing bet, soapwort	5–10	leaves	spring–autumn	summer
Satureja hortensis	summer savory	8–11	leaves	winter–summer	summer
Satureja montana	winter savory	6–10	leaves	winter–summer	any
Sesamum orientale	sesame	9–12	seeds	spring	autumn
Thymus × citriodorus	lemon-scented thyme	7–10	leaves	summer	any
T. × citriodorus 'Anderson's Gold'	lemon-scented thyme	7–10	leaves	summer	any
T. × citriodorus 'Argenteus'	lemon-scented thyme	7–10	leaves	summer	any
T. × citriodorus 'Aureus'	lemon-scented thyme	7–10	leaves	summer	any
T. × citriodorus 'Doone Valley'	lemon-scented thyme	7–10	leaves	summer	any
T. × citriodorus 'Silver Queen'	lemon-scented thyme	7–10	leaves	summer	any
Thymus herba-barona	caraway thyme	9–11	leaves	summer	any
Thymus vulgaris	common thyme	7–10	leaves	summer	any
Trigonella foenum-graecum	fenugreek	7–10	seeds	spring	summer
Tropaeolum majus	garden nasturtium, Indian cress	8–11	leaves, flowers	spring	summer
T. majus, Alaska Hybrids	garden nasturtium, Indian cress	8–11	leaves, flowers	spring	summer
Zingiber officinale	common ginger, halia	10–12	root	spring	autumn

FRUIT & NUTS

NAME	COMMON NAME	ZONES	EDIBLE PART	PLANTING TIME	HARVESTING TIME
Actinidia deliciosa	Chinese gooseberry, kiwifruit	8–10	fruit	autumn–winter	summer–autumn
Anacardium occidentale	cashew	11–12	nuts	spring	wet season
Ananas comosus	pineapple	11–12	fruit	summer	summer
A. comosus 'Porteanus'	pineapple	11–12	fruit	summer	summer
A. comosus 'Variegatus'	pineapple	11–12	fruit	summer	summer
Annona muricata	soursop	10–12	fruit	winter	any
Artocarpus altilis	breadfruit	12	fruit	wet season	wet season
Artocarpus heterophyllus	jackfruit, jaca	11–12	fruit	wet season	wet season
Averrhoa carambola	carambola, star fruit, five-corner	11–12	fruit	wet season	any
Carica papaya	pawpaw, papaya	10–12	fruit	spring	spring–summer
Carya illinoinensis	pecan	6–11	nuts	winter	autumn
Castanea sativa	sweet chestnut, Spanish chestnut	5–9	nuts	spring/autumn	autumn
× Citrofortunella microcarpa	calamondin, Panama orange	10–12	fruit	summer	summer
Citrullus lanatus	watermelon, camel melon	8–11	fruit	spring	summer
C. lanatus var. citroides	preserving melon	8–11	fruit	spring	summer
Citrus aurantifolia	lime	10–12	fruit	spring/autumn	any
Citrus aurantium	sour orange, Seville orange	9–11	fruit	spring/autumn	summer
C. a. 'Bouquet de Fleurs'	sour orange, Seville orange	9–11	fruit	spring/autumn	summer

NAME	COMMON NAME	ZONES	EDIBLE PART	PLANTING TIME	HARVESTING TIME
C. aurantium 'Chinotto'	sour orange, Seville orange	9–11	fruit	spring/autumn	summer
C. aurantium 'Seville'	sour orange, Seville orange	9–11	fruit	spring/autumn	summer
Citrus limon	lemon	9–11	fruit	spring/autumn	any
C. limon 'Eureka'	lemon	9–11	fruit	spring/autumn	any
C. limon 'Lisbon'	lemon	9–11	fruit	spring/autumn	any
C. limon 'Meyer'	lemon	9–11	fruit	spring/autumn	any
Citrus medica	citron, cedrat	9–11	fruit	spring/autumn	autumn
C. medica 'Etrog'	citron, cedrat	9–11	fruit	spring/autumn	autumn
Citrus × paradisi	grapefruit	10–12	fruit	spring/autumn	summer
C. × paradisi 'Golden Special'	grapefruit	10–12	fruit	spring/autumn	summer
C. × paradisi 'Marsh'	grapefruit	10–12	fruit	spring/autumn	summer
C. × paradisi 'Morrison's Seedless'	grapefruit	10–12	fruit	spring/autumn	summer
C. × paradisi 'Ruby'	grapefruit	10–12	fruit	spring/autumn	summer
C. × paradisi 'Wheeny'	grapefruit	10–12	fruit	spring/autumn	summer
Citrus reticulata	mandarin, tangerine	9–11	fruit	spring/autumn	autumn–spring
Citrus sinensis	orange	9–11	fruit	spring/autumn	spring–summer
C. sinensis 'Joppa'	orange	9–11	fruit	spring/autumn	spring–summer
C. sinensis 'Ruby Blood'	blood orange	9–11	fruit	spring/autumn	spring–summer
C. sinensis 'Valencia'	orange	9–11	fruit	spring/autumn	spring–summer
C. sinensis 'Washington Navel'	navel orange	9–11	fruit	spring/autumn	spring–summer
Citrus × tangelo	tangelo	9–11	fruit	spring/autumn	summer
Corylus avellana	common hazel, cobnut, European filbert	4–9	nuts	spring	autumn
C. avellana 'Cob'	common hazel, cobnut, European filbert	4–9	nuts	spring	autumn
C. avellana 'Contorta'	common hazel, cobnut, European filbert	4–9	nuts	spring	autumn
C. avellana 'Cosford'	common hazel, cobnut, European filbert	4–9	nuts	spring	autumn
C. avellana 'Halls Giant'	common hazel, cobnut, European filbert	4–9	nuts	spring	autumn
Cucumis melo	melon	8–11	fruit	spring	summer
C. m., Cantalupensis Group	cantaloupe melon, rockmelon	8–11	fruit	spring	summer
C. melo, Inodorus Group	honeydew melon	8–11	fruit	spring	summer
C. melo, Reticulatus Group	netted melon	8–11	fruit	spring	summer
Cydonia oblonga	common quince	6–9	fruit	autumn–winter	autumn
Cyphomandra betacea	tamarillo, tree tomato	9–11	fruit	spring	summer

NAME	COMMON NAME	ZONES	EDIBLE PART	PLANTING TIME	HARVESTING TIME
Diospyros digyna	black sapote	11–12	fruit	autumn/winter	summer
Diospyros kaki	Japanese persimmon, kaki	8–10	fruit	autumn/winter	summer
Diospyros virginiana	American persimmon, possum wood	5–9	fruit	autumn/winter	summer
Durio zibethinus	durian	12	fruit	any	autumn
Eriobotrya japonica	loquat	8–10	fruit	summer	spring–autumn
Feijoa sellowiana	pineapple guava, feijoa	8–11	fruit	autumn/winter	autumn
Ficus carica	common fig	8–11	fruit	winter	summer–autumn
F. carica 'Black Mission'	common fig	8–11	fruit	winter	summer–autumn
F. carica 'Brown Turkey'	common fig	8–11	fruit	winter	summer–autumn
F. carica 'Genoa'	common fig	8–11	fruit	winter	summer–autumn
F. carica 'San Pedro'	common fig	8–11	fruit	winter	summer–autumn
Fortunella japonica	kumquat, round kumquat, marumi cumquat	9–11	fruit	spring/autumn	summer–autumn
Fragaria × ananassa	garden strawberry	4–10	fruit	spring/autumn	summer
F. × ananassa 'Aromel'	garden strawberry	4–10	fruit	spring/autumn	summer
F. × ananassa 'Honeoye'	garden strawberry	4–10	fruit	spring/autumn	summer
Fragaria vesca	strawberry, woodland strawberry	4–10	fruit	spring/autumn	summer–autumn
F. vesca 'Semperflorens'	strawberry, woodland strawberry	4–10	fruit	spring/autumn	summer–autumn
F. vesca 'Sweetheart'	strawberry, woodland strawberry	4–10	fruit	spring/autumn	summer–autumn
F. vesca 'Temptation'	strawberry, woodland strawberry	4–10	fruit	spring/autumn	summer–autumn
Garcinia mangostana	mangosteen	11–12	fruit	any	wet season
Juglans cinerea	butternut, white walnut	4–9	nuts	autumn–winter	autumn
Juglans regia	common walnut, Persian walnut, English walnut	4–10	nuts	autumn–winter	autumn
J. regia 'Wilson's Wonder'	walnut	4–10	nuts	autumn–winter	autumn
Litchi chinensis	lychee	10–11	fruit	spring–summer	summer
Macadamia integrifolia	smooth shell macadamia nut, Queensland nut	9–11	nuts	autumn	autumn
Macadamia tetraphylla	rough shell macadamia nut, bopple nut	10–11	nuts	autumn	autumn
Malus × domestica	common apple	3–9	fruit	spring/autumn	summer
M. × domestica	common apple	3–9	fruit	spring/autumn	summer
M. × domestica 'Adam's Pearman'	common apple	3–9	fruit	spring/autumn	summer
M. × domestica 'Ashmead's Kernel'	common apple	3–9	fruit	spring/autumn	summer
M. × domestica 'Blenheim Orange'	common apple	3–9	fruit	spring/autumn	summer

NAME	COMMON NAME	ZONES	EDIBLE PART	PLANTING TIME	HARVESTING TIME
M. × domestica 'Bramley's Seedling'	common apple	3–9	fruit	spring/autumn	summer
M. × domestica 'Cox's Orange Pippin'	common apple	3–9	fruit	spring/autumn	summer
M. × domestica 'Crofton'	common apple	3–9	fruit	spring/autumn	summer
M. × domestica 'Delicious'	common apple	3–9	fruit	spring/autumn	summer
M. × domestica 'Discovery'	common apple	3–9	fruit	spring/autumn	summer
M. × domestica 'Ellison's Orange'	common apple	3–9	fruit	spring/autumn	summer
M. × domestica 'Fuji'	common apple	3–9	fruit	spring/autumn	summer
M. × domestica 'Gala'	common apple	3–9	fruit	spring/autumn	summer
M. × domestica 'Golden Delicious'	common apple	3–9	fruit	spring/autumn	summer
M. × domestica 'Golden Harvest'	common apple	3–9	fruit	spring/autumn	summer
M. × domestica 'Granny Smith'	common apple	3–9	fruit	spring/autumn	summer
M. × domestica 'Gravenstein'	common apple	3–9	fruit	spring/autumn	summer
M. × domestica 'James Grieve'	common apple	3–9	fruit	spring/autumn	summer
M. × domestica 'Jonagold'	common apple	3–9	fruit	spring/autumn	summer
M. × domestica 'Jonamac'	common apple	3–9	fruit	spring/autumn	summer
M. × domestica 'Jonathan'	common apple	3–9	fruit	spring/autumn	summer
M. × domestica 'Liberty'	common apple	3–9	fruit	spring/autumn	summer
M. × domestica 'McIntosh Rogers'	common apple	3–9	fruit	spring/autumn	summer
M. × domestica 'Melrose'	common apple	3–9	fruit	spring/autumn	summer
M. × domestica 'Newtown Pippin'	common apple	3–9	fruit	spring/autumn	summer
M. × domestica 'Rome Beauty'	common apple	3–9	fruit	spring/autumn	summer
M. × domestica 'Starkspur Compact Mac'	common apple	3–9	fruit	spring/autumn	summer
M. × domestica 'Starkspur Supreme Red Delicious'	common apple	3–9	fruit	spring/autumn	summer
Malus pumila	crabapple	3–9	fruit	spring/autumn	summer
M. pumila 'Dartmouth'	crabapple	3–9	fruit	winter	any
Mangifera indica	mango	11–12	fruit	summer–autumn	summer
M. indica 'Alphonso'	mango	11–12	fruit	summer–autumn	summer
M. indica 'Kensington Pride'	mango	11–12	fruit	summer–autumn	summer

NAME	COMMON NAME	ZONES	EDIBLE PART	PLANTING TIME	HARVESTING TIME
M. indica 'Nam Doc Mai'	mango	11–12	fruit	summer–autumn	summer
M. indica 'Peach'	mango	11–12	fruit	summer–autumn	summer
M. indica 'R2E2'	mango	11–12	fruit	summer–autumn	summer
M. indica 'Strawberry'	mango	11–12	fruit	summer–autumn	summer
Morus alba	white mulberry	5–10	fruit	autumn–winter	summer
Morus nigra	black mulberry	6–10	fruit	autumn–winter	summer
Musa acuminata	banana	10–12	fruit	spring	summer
M. acuminata 'Dwarf Cavendish'	banana	10–12	fruit	spring	summer
Musa × paradisiaca	banana	10–12	fruit	spring	summer
M. × paradisiaca 'Lady Finger'	banana	10–12	fruit	spring	summer
Nephelium lappaceum	rambutan	12	fruit	spring	summer
Olea europaea	common olive	8–11	fruit	autumn/winter	summer
O. europaea subsp. *africana*	common olive	8–11	fruit	autumn/winter	summer
O. europaea 'Barouni'	common olive	8–11	fruit	autumn/winter	summer
O. europaea 'Manzanillo'	common olive	8–11	fruit	autumn/winter	summer
O. europaea 'Mission'	common olive	8–11	fruit	autumn/winter	summer
O. europaea 'Sevillano'	common olive	8–11	fruit	autumn/winter	summer
Pachira aquatica	Guiana chestnut, shaving brush tree, provision tree	10–12	fruit	summer	any
Passiflora edulis	passionfruit	10–12	fruit	spring/summer	autumn
P. edulis 'Lacey'	passionfruit	10–12	fruit	spring/summer	autumn
P. edulis 'Nellie Kelly'	passionfruit	10–12	fruit	spring/summer	autumn
P. edulis 'Panama Gold'	passionfruit	10–12	fruit	spring/summer	autumn
P. edulis 'Panama Red'	passionfruit	10–12	fruit	spring/summer	autumn
P. edulis 'Purple Gold'	passionfruit	10–12	fruit	spring/summer	autumn
Passiflora laurifolia	yellow granadilla, Jamaica honeysuckle	11–12	fruit	spring/summer	autumn
Passiflora quadrangularis	giant granadilla	10–12	fruit	spring/summer	autumn
Persea americana	avocado	10–11	fruit	spring	any
Phoenix dactylifera	date palm	10–12	fruit	spring	autumn–winter
Physalis peruviana	Cape gooseberry, ground cherry	8–11	fruit	spring	summer
Pinus edulis	pine nut, Rocky Mountain piñon	5–9	nuts	winter	autumn
Pinus pinea	Roman pine, stone pine, umbrella pine	7–8	nuts	winter	autumn
Pistacia vera	pistachio nut	8–10	nuts	autumn–winter	autumn
Prunus armeniaca	apricot	5–10	fruit	winter	summer
P. armeniaca 'Glengarry'	apricot	5–10	fruit	winter	summer

NAME	COMMON NAME	ZONES	EDIBLE PART	PLANTING TIME	HARVESTING TIME
P. armeniaca 'Morocco'	apricot	5—10	fruit	winter	summer
P. armeniaca 'Story'	apricot	5—10	fruit	winter	summer
P. armeniaca 'Trevatt'	apricot	5—10	fruit	winter	summer
Prunus avium	sweet cherry, gean, mazzard, wild cherry	3—9	fruit	winter	summer
P. avium 'Napoleon'	sweet cherry	3—9	fruit	winter	summer
P. avium 'Plena'	sweet cherry	3—9	fruit	winter	summer
P. avium 'Stella'	sweet cherry	3—9	fruit	winter	summer
P. avium 'Van'	sweet cherry	3—9	fruit	winter	summer
Prunus cerasus	morello cherry, sour cherry	3—9	fruit	winter	summer
P. cerasus var. austera	morello cherry	3—9	fruit	winter	summer
P. cerasus var. caproniana	amarelle cherry	3—9	fruit	winter	summer
P. cerasus var. marasca	maraschino cherry	3—9	fruit	winter	summer
Prunus × domestica	plum, European plum	5—9	fruit	winter	summer
P. × domestica 'Angelina Burdett'	plum, European plum	5—9	fruit	winter	summer
P. × domestica 'Coe's Golden Drop'	plum, European plum	5—9	fruit	winter	summer
P. × domestica 'Grand Duke'	plum, European plum	5—9	fruit	winter	summer
P. × domestica subsp. institia	damson plum, bullace	5—9	fruit	winter	summer
P. × domestica 'President'	plum, European plum	5—9	fruit	winter	summer
P. × domestica 'Stanley'	plum, European plum	5—9	fruit	winter	summer
Prunus dulcis	almond	6—9	nuts	winter	autumn
Prunus persica	peach, flowering peach, nectarine	5—10	fruit	winter	summer
P. persica 'Anzac'	peach, flowering peach	5—10	fruit	winter	summer
P. persica 'Dixired'	peach, flowering peach	5—10	fruit	winter	summer
P. persica 'Flordaprince'	peach, flowering peach	5—10	fruit	winter	summer
P. persica 'Golden Queen'	peach, flowering peach	5—10	fruit	winter	summer
P. persica 'Kernechter von Vorgebirge'	peach, flowering peach	5—10	fruit	winter	summer
P. persica 'Maravilha'	peach, flowering peach	5—10	fruit	winter	summer
P. persica var. nectarina	nectarine	5—10	fruit	winter	summer
P. persica 'Orion'	peach, flowering peach	5—10	fruit	winter	summer
P. persica 'Red Haven'	peach, flowering peach	5—10	fruit	winter	summer
P. persica 'Rekord aus Alfter'	peach, flowering peach	5—10	fruit	winter	summer
P. persica 'Robert Blum'	peach, flowering peach	5—10	fruit	winter	summer
P. persica 'Sherman's Early'	peach, flowering peach	5—10	fruit	winter	summer

NAME	COMMON NAME	ZONES	EDIBLE PART	PLANTING TIME	HARVESTING TIME
Prunus salicina	Japanese plum	5–10	fruit	winter	summer
P. salicina 'Friar'	Japanese plum	5–10	fruit	winter	summer
P. salicina 'Mariposa'	Japanese plum	5–10	fruit	winter	summer
P. salicina 'Narrabeen'	Japanese plum	5–10	fruit	winter	summer
P. salicina 'October Purple'	Japanese plum	5–10	fruit	winter	summer
P. salicina 'Queen Rosa'	Japanese plum	5–10	fruit	winter	summer
P. salicina 'Santa Rosa'	Japanese plum	5–10	fruit	winter	summer
P. salicina 'Satsuma'	Japanese plum	5–10	fruit	winter	summer
Psidium cattleianum	cherry guava	9–11	fruit	spring–summer	summer–autumn
P. cattleianum var. *littorale*	cherry guava	9–11	fruit	spring–summer	summer–autumn
P. cattleianum 'Lucidum'	cherry guava	9–11	fruit	spring–summer	summer–autumn
Psidium guajava	yellow guava	10–12	fruit	spring–summer	summer
Punica granatum	pomegranate	9–11	fruit	spring/summer	autumn
P. granatum 'Nana'	pomegranate	9–11	fruit	spring/summer	autumn
P. granatum 'Wonderful'	pomegranate	9–11	fruit	spring/summer	autumn
Pyrus communis	common pear	2–9	fruit	spring/autumn	summer
P. communis 'Beurre Bosc'	common pear	2–9	fruit	spring/autumn	summer
P. communis 'Bon Chrétien'	common pear	2–9	fruit	spring/autumn	summer
P. communis 'Conference'	common pear	2–9	fruit	spring/autumn	summer
P. communis 'Corella'	common pear	2–9	fruit	spring/autumn	summer
P. communis 'Josephine de Malines'	common pear	2–9	fruit	spring/autumn	summer
P. communis 'Packham's Triumph'	common pear	2–9	fruit	spring/autumn	summer
P. communis 'Red Bartlett'	Bartlett pear, Williams pear	2–9	fruit	spring/autumn	summer
P. communis 'Triumph von Vienne'	common pear	2–9	fruit	spring/autumn	summer
P. communis 'Winter Cole'	common pear	2–9	fruit	spring/autumn	summer
P. communis 'Winter Nelis'	common pear	2–9	fruit	spring/autumn	summer
Pyrus pyrifolia	nashi pear, Japanese pear, sand pear	4–9	fruit	spring/autumn	summer
P. pyrifolia var. *culta*	nashi pear, Japanese pear, sand pear	4–9	fruit	spring/autumn	summer
P. pyrifolia 'Kosui'	nashi pear, Japanese pear, sand pear	4–9	fruit	spring/autumn	summer
Ribes nigrum	blackcurrant	5–9	fruit	winter/spring	summer
R. nigrum 'Baldwin'	blackcurrant	5–9	fruit	winter/spring	summer
R. nigrum 'Ben Lomond'	blackcurrant	5–9	fruit	winter/spring	summer

NAME	COMMON NAME	ZONES	EDIBLE PART	PLANTING TIME	HARVESTING TIME
R. nigrum 'Jet'	blackcurrant	5–9	fruit	winter/spring	summer
Ribes silvestre	redcurrant, white currant	6–9	fruit	winter/spring	summer
R. silvestre 'Fay's Prolific'	redcurrant	6–9	fruit	winter/spring	summer
R. silvestre 'Jonkheer van Tets'	redcurrant	6–9	fruit	winter/spring	summer
R. silvestre 'Raby Castle'	redcurrant	6–9	fruit	winter/spring	summer
R. silvestre 'Red Dutch'	redcurrant	6–9	fruit	winter/spring	summer
R. silvestre 'Red Lake'	redcurrant	6–9	fruit	winter/spring	summer
R. silvestre 'Viking'	redcurrant	6–9	fruit	winter/spring	summer
R. silvestre 'White Grape'	white currant	6–9	fruit	winter/spring	summer
Ribes uva-crispa	gooseberry, European gooseberry	5–9	fruit	winter/spring	summer
R. uva-crispa 'Careless'	gooseberry, European gooseberry	5–9	fruit	winter/spring	summer
R. uva-crispa 'Crown Bob'	gooseberry, European gooseberry	5–9	fruit	winter/spring	summer
R. uva-crispa 'Invicta'	gooseberry, European gooseberry	5–9	fruit	winter/spring	summer
R. uva-crispa 'Leveller'	gooseberry, European gooseberry	5–9	fruit	winter/spring	summer
R. u.-c. var. *reclinatum*	gooseberry, European gooseberry	5–9	fruit	winter/spring	summer
R. uva-crispa 'Roaring Lion'	gooseberry, European gooseberry	5–9	fruit	winter/spring	summer
R. uva-crispa 'Whinham's Industry'	gooseberry, European gooseberry	5–9	fruit	winter/spring	summer
Rubus chamaemorus	cloudberry	2–8	fruit	winter	autumn
Rubus fruticosus	blackberry, bramble	5–10	fruit	winter	autumn
R. fruticosus 'Himalayan Giant'	blackberry, bramble	5–10	fruit	winter	autumn
R. fruticosus 'Loch Ness'	blackberry, bramble	5–10	fruit	winter	autumn
R. fruticosus 'Thornfree'	blackberry, bramble	5–10	fruit	winter	autumn
Rubus idaeus	raspberry, red raspberry	4–9	fruit	winter	summer–autumn
R. idaeus 'Autumn Bliss'	raspberry, red raspberry	4–9	fruit	winter	summer–autumn
R. idaeus 'Bicentennial'	raspberry, red raspberry	4–9	fruit	winter	summer–autumn
R. idaeus 'Canby'	raspberry, red raspberry	4–9	fruit	winter	summer–autumn
R. idaeus 'Chilcotin'	raspberry, red raspberry	4–9	fruit	winter	summer–autumn
R. idaeus 'Chilliwack'	raspberry, red raspberry	4–9	fruit	winter	summer–autumn
R. idaeus 'Everbearer'	raspberry, red raspberry	4–9	fruit	winter	summer–autumn
R. idaeus 'Glen May'	raspberry, red raspberry	4–9	fruit	winter	summer–autumn
R. idaeus 'Killarney'	raspberry, red raspberry	4–9	fruit	winter	summer–autumn
R. idaeus 'Nootka'	raspberry, red raspberry	4–9	fruit	winter	summer–autumn
R. idaeus 'Skeena'	raspberry, red raspberry	4–9	fruit	winter	summer–autumn
R. idaeus 'Taylor'	raspberry, red raspberry	4–9	fruit	winter	summer–autumn
R. idaeus 'Williamette'	raspberry, red raspberry	4–9	fruit	winter	summer–autumn
Rubus × *loganobaccus*	boysenberry, loganberry	5–10	fruit	winter	summer

NAME	COMMON NAME	ZONES	EDIBLE PART	PLANTING TIME	HARVESTING TIME
R. × loganobaccus 'Boysen'	boysenberry, loganberry	5–10	fruit	winter	summer
R. × loganobaccus 'Logan'	boysenberry, loganberry	5–10	fruit	winter	summer
Rubus 'Navajo'	blackberry, bramble	5–10	fruit	winter	autumn
Rubus parviflorus	thimbleberry	3–10	fruit	winter	summer
Vaccinium corymbosum	blueberry, highbush blueberry	2–9	fruit	autumn	summer
V. corymbosum 'Blue Crop'	blueberry, highbush blueberry	2–9	fruit	autumn	summer
V. corymbosum 'Blue Ray'	blueberry, highbush blueberry	2–9	fruit	autumn	summer
V. corymbosum 'Earliblue'	blueberry, highbush blueberry	2–9	fruit	autumn	summer
Vitis labrusca	fox grape	4–9	fruit	winter	summer–autumn
V. labrusca 'Carolina Black'	fox grape	4–9	fruit	winter	summer–autumn
V. labrusca 'Catawba'	fox grape	4–9	fruit	winter	summer–autumn
V. labrusca 'Concord'	fox grape	4–9	fruit	winter	summer–autumn
V. labrusca 'Isabella'	fox grape	4–9	fruit	winter	summer–autumn
V. labrusca 'Niagara'	fox grape	4–9	fruit	winter	summer–autumn
Vitis vinifera	grape	6–10	fruit	winter	summer
V. vinifera 'Albany Surprise'	grape	6–10	fruit	winter	summer
V. v. 'Cabernet Sauvignon'	grape	6–10	fruit	winter	summer
V. vinifera 'Chardonnay'	grape	6–10	fruit	winter	summer
V. vinifera 'Early Muscat'	grape	6–10	fruit	winter	summer
V. vinifera 'Festivee'	grape	6–10	fruit	winter	summer
V. vinifera 'Flame Seedless'	grape	6–10	fruit	winter	summer
V. vinifera 'Ganzin Glory'	grape	6–10	fruit	winter	summer
V. vinifera 'Golden Chasselas'	grape	6–10	fruit	winter	summer
V. vinifera 'Merlot'	grape	6–10	fruit	winter	summer
V. vinifera 'Müller Thurgau'	grape	6–10	fruit	winter	summer
V. vinifera 'Muscat Hamburg'	grape	6–10	fruit	winter	summer
V. vinifera 'Perlette'	grape	6–10	fruit	winter	summer
V. vinifera 'Pinot Noir'	grape	6–10	fruit	winter	summer
V. vinifera 'Purpurea'	grape	6–10	fruit	winter	summer
V. vinifera 'Riesling'	grape	6–10	fruit	winter	summer
V. vinifera 'Schiava Grossa'	grape	6–10	fruit	winter	summer
V. vinifera 'Semillon'	grape	6–10	fruit	winter	summer
V. vinifera 'Shiraz'	grape	6–10	fruit	winter	summer
V. vinifera 'Sultana'	grape	6–10	fruit	winter	summer
V. vinifera 'Waltham Cross'	grape	6–10	fruit	winter	summer
Ziziphus jujuba	Chinese date, jujube	7–10	fruit	winter	autumn–winter

INDEX